Voyager from Xanadu

Voyager from Xanadu

RABBAN SAUMA AND THE FIRST JOURNEY FROM CHINA TO THE WEST

MORRIS ROSSABI

KODANSHA INTERNATIONAL
Tokyo • New York • London

Distributed in the United States by Kodansha America, Inc.,
114 Fifth Avenue, New York, New York, 10011.
Published by Kodansha International Ltd.,
17–14 Otowa 1-chome, Bunkyo-ku, Tokyo 112,
and Kodansha America, Inc.

Printed in the United States of America

First edition, 1992

92 93 94 95 7 6 5 4 3 2 1

Library of Congress Cataloging-in-Publication Data
Rossabi, Morris.
Voyager from Xanadu: Rabban Sauma and the first journey from
China to the West / Morris Rossabi.—1st ed.
p.   cm.
Includes bibliographical references (p.   ) and index.
ISBN 4–7700–1650–6 (hc)
1. Sâuma, Rabban, d. 1293?—Journeys. 2. Voyages and travels.
3. Diplomats—China—Travel. I. Title.
DS752.6.S28R67 1992
909'.2'092—dc20
[B]   91–46286
                                                                                          CIP

Grateful acknowledgment is given to AMS Press, Inc. for permission
to reprint excerpts from *The Monks of Kublai Khan, Emperor of China,*
translated by E. A. Wallis Budge.
Published by Religious Tract Society, 1928.
Used by permission of AMS Press, Inc.

❧   ❧   ❧

Book design by Louise B. Young

The text of this book was set in Baskerville.
Composed by Graphic Composition, Inc.
Athens, Georgia.

The jacket was printed by
Phoenix Color Corporation
Long Island City, New York

Printed and bound by
R. R. Donnelley & Sons Company
Harrisonburg, Virginia

CONTENTS

Illustrations
vii

Preface
ix

A Note on Transliteration
xiv

Principal Figures
xv

1. *Setting the Stage*
1

2. *A Pilgrimage to the West*
37

3. *The Mongols, the Muslims, and the Europeans*
83

4. *An Embassy to the West*
99

5. *Paris, Bordeaux, Rome, and Return*
139

Notes
181

Selected Bibliography
197

Index
211

ILLUSTRATIONS

Divisions of the Mongol Empire in 1279, with Rabban Sauma's route from China through Central Asia

Map of China (Chataio), showing Tai-tu (Chambalech), based on Marco Polo's account

A Nestorian worshipper

Chinggis Khan and his four sons

Khubilai Khan on a Hunt

Plan of Tai-tu during the Yüan Dynasty

Portrait of Khubilai Khan

Khubilai Khan presenting the letter patent to the Polo brothers

Ilkhanate Persia at the time of Rabban Sauma's arrival

Arghun Khan in his garden

Charles of Anjou

A King, very probably Edward I

Modern reconstructed plan of Acre

The Holy Land and its environs, ca. 1280

Rabban Sauma's travels in the West

Dome, Hagia Sophia

Mosaic of the Virgin, Hagia Sophia

Tomb of St. Peter

Tabernacle, Basilica of San Paolo Fuori le Mura

Chains of St. Peter

A portal of the Church of Saint-Denis

Stained-glass medallion depicting Judith with the head of Holofernes, Sainte-Chapelle

Mar Yaballaha's seal

PREFACE

Rabban Sauma is far from a household name in the West. Nor is he particularly renowned in his native land of China. The mission that brought him to Europe in the late 1200s, an embassy on behalf of the Mongol ruler of Persia, was potentially one of the most dramatic and significant in history; but he remains virtually unknown save to a small group of scholars specializing in the Mongol era.

No doubt this is true largely because of the curious fate of Rabban Sauma's own writings about his life and travels. Shortly after he died in Persia, they were translated into Syriac. In addition to adding some remarks of his own, the translator also made a number of cuts. In the middle of the fourteenth century, toward the end of Mongol rule in Persia, both Rabban Sauma's original text and the Syriac text disappeared. Knowledge of this invaluable source was lost for more than five hundred years. The only known references to Rabban Sauma's mission were limited to perfunctory accounts—in the Vatican, English, and French archives—of his meetings with the Pope and the Kings of France and England and to brief notices in a couple of Syriac and Arabic sources. Since these sources yielded few details, they received scant attention. No Chinese source that I am aware of describes his mission or even mentions him. The traditional Chinese his-

tories, ordinarily a treasure trove for historians, slight men of
nonofficial background and men involved with foreigners
and foreign travel, as well as women of any background. The
omission of Rabban Sauma from the Chinese sources is
therefore not unusual, although it is lamentable.

Rabban Sauma was thus virtually unknown for centuries,
and he would have remained so if it had not been for a for-
tuitous incident in March of 1887. A certain Mr. Salomon,
who lived in northwest Persia, came across a young Turk who
belonged to the same Christian sect as Sauma and the Syriac
translator and had in his possession a Syriac manuscript. Invited to inspect this manuscript, which was in fact the translated and edited account of Rabban Sauma's life and travels,
Salomon recognized its value, quickly had it copied, and sent
it to a well-known specialist on Syriac writings, Father Bedjan.
This find and the attendant publicity in Persia led to the discovery of another manuscript of the work, which the British
Museum purchased in 1888. These fortunate circumstances
rescued Rabban Sauma from oblivion and made it feasible
to write about his life and his unique embassy to medieval
Europe.

I should add that several translations of the Syriac text of
the narrative of Rabban Sauma's life and travels have appeared, all of which include notes and introductions by the
translators. One, in French, was published in the last decade
of the nineteenth century, and two in English, one complete
and the other partial, were produced in the 1920s. A Russian
translation was printed in the USSR in 1958. The explana-
tory material in all except the Russian version focuses on Rabban Sauma's religious views and the theological issues and
controversies portrayed in the work. Rabban Sauma's presentation of his version of Christianity, in contrast to Western
Christianity, captivated these writers, and they slighted the
significant political dimensions of Sauma's embassy. Although the Russian translator began to address the diplo-

matic objectives of the mission, she was somewhat hampered by ideological considerations and showed more concern for its socioeconomic significance. Nonetheless, her notes on the text and its author are invaluable.

My own method has been to use Rabban Sauma's account along with the Syriac translator's additions as a starting point. My aims have been to expand upon and explicate the text, to give sufficient background information to place Rabban Sauma's travels and observations in context, and to show the larger significance of his work. I have not attempted to write a complete social history of the regions through which he traveled. The diplomatic and religious ramifications of Rabban Sauma's travels in Europe and the Middle East have been my primary concern, although I have not neglected his cultural observations. My main interest has been to retrieve Rabban Sauma from an obscure corner of the historical record and to bring him to the attention of a wider public. His life and adventures have a touch of the fantastic about them and deserve to be better known.

Rabban Sauma's account of his journeys is of more than routine interest for another reason: His narrative remains the only one of its era to provide an East Asian perspective on European ways and rites. It would have been even more valuable had it been more detailed, but some sections are tantalizingly brief, at least partly because of the Syriac translator's deletions.

How fascinating it would have been if what survived of the account told us more about politics, customs, material culture, and daily life in the places Rabban Sauma traveled to—precisely the sort of information the Syriac translator seems to have found not worth recording. It would have been interesting, too, to know more about European reactions to Sauma's visit. The Europeans, in particular the Pope and the Kings of France and England, must have been amazed by the arrival of this Asian cleric and the audacious proposal he made. The extant text, however, supplies only glimpses of how they felt about him. In addition, it reveals little about Rabban Sauma himself. It seems a pity that more of his personality does not shine through. Nonetheless, the available text conveys a sense of the drama of his life and his remarkable journeys.

I decided to write a book about Rabban Sauma just as I was completing a biography of Khubilai Khan, a ruler who played a significant role in his career. A study of Sauma's mission struck me as a unique means of understanding a critical period in Eurasian history as well as of learning about an early Asian view of Europe. Besides, in these days when multiculturalism is in the air, it seemed fitting to write about a man who flourished in a variety of cultures and who worked to build bridges between them.

I should like to thank the Lucius Littauer Foundation for supporting a trip to Europe to examine at first hand some of the sites described by Rabban Sauma. I am also grateful to Dr. Hans-Ulrich Vogel and Professor Rudolf Wagner of the University of Heidelberg for inviting me to address their sinological seminar, and I want to thank the audience of faculty and students for some of the most useful comments and questions I have ever received at any lecture. I was honored to be invited to present a portion of the book as the first Joseph F. Fletcher, Jr., Memorial Lecture at the Arthur Sackler Gallery of the Smithsonian Institution. I also presented lectures on Rabban Sauma at the University of Toronto and El Colegio de México. I am grateful to Ms. Ingrid Mei for typing the manuscript and to Mr. Karl Ryavec for drawing the maps.

I have profited from the comments, views, and assistance of the following friends and colleagues: Professor Pei-yi Wu of Queens College, Ms. Mary Jo Robertiello, Professor Barbara Miller of Barnard College, Mr. Max Greenwood, Ms. Gayle Feldman and Mr. David Reid, Professor Caroline Bynum of Columbia University, Professor Michael Altschul of Case Western Reserve University, Professor Charles Wood of Dartmouth College, Professor Cynthia Macdonald of the University of Houston, William and Susan Frost, Professor Herbert Franke of the University of Munich, Dr. Rolly Phillips of the Fieldston School (who translated a valuable Latin source), Drs. Patrizia and Roberto Levi, Madame Paulette Decraene, Tom and Harriet Burnett, Professor Michael Davis of Mount Holyoke College, Gail and Gordon Derzon, Ruth and Stephen Helman, Debora Kramer, Ms. Joanna Jellinek, Dr. David Morgan of the School of Oriental and African Studies, University of London, Professor Paul Avrich of Queens College, Professors Frederick Mote and Arthur Waldron of Princeton University, and Professor Myron Cohen of Columbia University. My editor, Helena Franklin, deserves enormous credit for suggesting revisions that have improved the text immeasurably. Susan M. S. Brown, who copyedited the manuscript, and Louise B. Young guided the book splendidly through the process of publication.

I am also indebted to the Columbia University Libraries, the Vatican Library, the Harvard Yenching Library at Harvard University, the Princeton University Library, the Library of Congress, and the Library of the School of Oriental and African Studies of the University of London for providing me with books and articles essential to the completion of this book.

My wife deserves a special paragraph for all the help she provided in the preparation of this book. She assisted me with Russian translations, traveled with me in Italy and France, and took many of the photographs included here. She also read and reread the text, making numerous suggestions for its improvement.

A NOTE ON TRANSLITERATION

I have adopted the Wade-Giles system to transliterate Chinese, although I have used certain names and terms that have become commonly accepted in English (Kashgar, Khotan, and so on). In the text I have used the contemporary Chinese designation *Tai-tu* for what is now the city of Peking. I have given the Italian and French names for sites in Italy and France rather than the English versions or translations.

I have used Antoine Mostaert's scheme for the transliteration of Mongolian, as modified by Francis W. Cleaves, except for these deviations:

č is rendered as *ch*
š as *sh*
ɣ as *gh*
q as *kh*

Principal Figures

From East Asia

Chinggis Khan (r. 1206–1227), founder of the Mongol Empire, conqueror of Central Asia, the Tangut Empire in Northwest China and part of the territory of the Chin Dynasty of North China.

Güyüg Khan (r. 1246–1248), Great Khan of the Mongols, Chinggis's grandson and Khubilai's cousin.

Khubilai Khan (r. 1260–1294), Great Khan of the Mongols, founder of the Yüan dynasty of China, Chinggis's grandson.

Markos (Mar Yaballaha) (1245–1317), Nestorian monk, traveling companion of Rabban Sauma and Patriarch of the Nestorian Church (1281–1317).

Möngke Khan (r. 1251–1259), Great Khan of the Mongols, Khubilai's brother.

Ögödei Khan (r. 1229–1241), Great Khan of the Mongols at the time of their conquest of much of Russia and their final destruction of the Chin Dynasty of North China, Chinggis's son.

Rabban Sauma (Bar Sauma) (ca. 1225–1294), Nestorian monk, first voyager from China to the West.

From Central Asia and the Middle East

Abakha Khan (r. 1265–1282), Mongol Ilkhan of Persia at the time of Rabban Sauma's arrival in the Middle East.

Andronicus II (r. 1282–1328), Byzantine Emperor at the time of Rabban Sauma's arrival in Constantinople.

Aḥmad (Tegüder Khan) (r. 1282–1284), Mongol Ilkhan of Persia, convert to Islam.

Arghun Khan (r. 1284–1291), Mongol Ilkhan of Persia, who chose Sauma as ambassador to Western Europe.

Berke Khan (r. 1257–1267), Mongol ruler of the Golden Horde of Russia, convert to Islam, Chinggis's grandson.

Geikhatu Khan (r. 1292–1295), Mongol Ilkhan of Persia, Arghun's brother.

Ghazan Khan (r. 1295–1304), Mongol Ilkhan of Persia, convert to Islam, Arghun's son.

Hülegü Khan (r. 1258–1265), founder of the Ilkhanate of Persia, Khubilai's brother.

Mar Denha (d. 1281), Patriarch of the Nestorian Church.

Michael VIII (Michael Palaeologus) (r. 1261–1282), Byzantine Emperor who recaptured Constantinople from the Venetians, supporter of union with the Catholic Church.

From Europe

Charles of Anjou (r. 1266–1285), King of Naples and Sicily at the time of the Sicilian Vespers revolt (1282), St. Louis's brother.

Edward I (r. 1272–1307), King of England who met Rabban Sauma in Bordeaux.

Innocent IV (Pope, 1243–1254), Pope who convened the Ecumenical Council in Lyons (1245).

John of Plano Carpini, Papal emissary to the Mongols, 1245–1247.

Julian, Dominican ambassador to the Mongols, 1236.

Louis IX (St. Louis) (r. 1226–1270), King of France, leader of Crusades (1248–1250 and 1270).

Nicholas IV (Jerome of Ascoli) (Pope, 1288–1292), Pope at the time of Rabban Sauma's second visit to Rome.

Philip III (Philip the Bold) (r. 1270–1285), King of France who added territory to the nation, son of Saint Louis.

Philip IV (Philip the Fair) (r. 1285–1314), King of France at the time of Rabban Sauma's arrival in Paris, grandson of St. Louis.

William of Rubruck, Emissary to the Mongols, 1253–1255.

Voyager from Xanadu

1

SETTING THE STAGE

On June 23, 1287, the citizens of Naples were startled by the arrival of a ship carrying an Asian cleric who had traveled all the way from Tai-tu, the fabulous capital of the Mongol ruler Khubilai Khan, now the city of Peking. He was not the first voyager from the Mongol world to enter Europe, but all his predecessors had come from the Middle East; he was the first ever to arrive from as far away as China. Indeed, he is known as "the first identified Chinese to reach Europe."[1] This adventurous cleric, who was called Rabban Sauma, had traveled from Tai-tu to Persia and lived there for several eventful years before setting forth for Europe.

Rabban Sauma's own account of his life and travels has survived, although in truncated form, offering an explanation of his journeys' objectives and descriptions of his encounters and observations along the way.[2] On his death, he left a diary of his hazardous trip from China to Persia and both a diary of and a report on his momentous voyage from Persia to Europe in pursuit of a remarkable ambassadorial mission. He also left his own account of his early life in China, including his induction into a Christian monastic order, and of the time he spent in Persia both before and after his journey to Europe. The original text of all these writings, which were mostly in Persian, was lost. However, a Syriac translation by a near contemporary of Rabban Sauma has come down to us. It contains additional remarks by the translator, supplementing the author's words and carrying the story through to his death and the death of the close friend who had accompanied him to Persia from China. Unfortunately, the Syriac translator, a fellow Christian and cleric, also deleted substantial portions of Rabban Sauma's narrative of his life and travels, retaining the sections on religion but removing some of the observations on secular matters. Nonetheless, what is left provides enough details of Rabban Sauma's experiences and views to offer a fascinating glimpse of the thirteenth century in East Asia, the Middle East, and Europe, as well as of an extraordinary man and his journeys.

Like his contemporary Marco Polo, Rabban Sauma met principally with the rulers of the regions he visited. Polo, however, spent almost two decades in the foreign lands to which he voyaged, whereas Sauma stayed in Europe for less than a year (though he had been away from home for much longer, having left China around ten years earlier and lived in Persia for about eight). It is perhaps not surprising, then, that his account of his trip to Europe is not as long or as detailed as Polo's famous chronicle, and clearly would not have been even in uncut form. Indeed, the entire extant text of the monk's account of his life and travels, most of which deals with his sojourn in Europe, runs to only about one hundred pages in English translation. Still, it is "the only known Asian equivalent to the narratives of Carpini, Rubruck, and Marco Polo,"[3] the three most renowned contemporary European travelers to the Mongol lands and China. Moreover, because Rabban Sauma came to Europe as an official emissary, his mission had greater diplomatic and political significance than Polo's.

Why did Rabban Sauma leave his native land of China? Why did the Ilkhan, the Mongol ruler of Persia, send an embassy to Europe, attempting to form an alliance which could have changed the history of Eurasia? Why did he select Rabban Sauma for this delicate mission, one that would bring the monk face to face with European kings, an emperor, and the Pope? Why would the Ilkhan—who was not a Christian—ask Sauma to promote a Crusade? How successful was Sauma's embassy? Why indeed were there so many missions between East and West during the Mongol era? The answers to these questions illuminate a remarkable period in world history.

The Mongol age marked a major step in the direction of truly global history. Europeans reached Asia for the first time, and economic and cultural developments on one continent had reverberations on the other. The so-called Pax Mongolica extended across Eurasia, and, although it was not as peaceful as its name implies, it enabled craftsmen, merchants, and missionaries to travel from Italy and France to China. It also enabled Rabban Sauma to make the same journey for the first time in the opposite direction.

EAST AND WEST IN MONGOL TIMES

East Asia and Europe had had indirect contacts since the first century B.C. Trade between the Roman Empire and China had been conducted as early as that time, and the so-called Silk Road had been developed as the main East-West thoroughfare. Yet intermediaries transported the goods; neither the Chinese nor the Romans traded directly with each other. With the fall of China's Han dynasty in the third century A.D. and the ensuing chaos in the Middle Kingdom, this long-distance commerce was interrupted until the T'ang dynasty (618–907), when trade between the Middle East and China revived. Europeans and Chinese still had not come face to face, but caravans laden with goods traveled from modern Syria, Arabia, and Iran to China and back, and vessels from the Red Sea or the Persian Gulf wound their way via India and Southeast Asia to the harbors of Southeast China. T'ang and Sung (960–1279) silks and porcelains were renowned in the Arab world and were prized as far away as the Fatimid Egyptian capital of Fusṭāṭ.[4] Similarly, aromatics such as frankincense, myrrh, and jasmine oil, medicines such as asafetida and aloeswood, and animals such as horses and camels arrived in China from the Middle East.[5] However, this long-distance trade was irregular, particularly when the Chinese dynasties and the Islamic caliphates or dynasties were in decline and could not prevent brigandage, piracy, high tariffs, and protection costs.[6]

Even when this trade was carried on, it was limited to West Asia and East Asia. Europe played no role in it because its own political fragmentation and development of a manorial economy destroyed both opportunities for participation in this commerce and demand for its products. Although historians of Europe no longer necessarily refer to the period after the fall of the Roman Empire as "the Dark Ages," this era certainly witnessed a decline in trade and relations between the civilizations of Europe and the Middle East. However, the Crusades in the late eleventh and twelfth centuries, motivated in part by religious zeal and in part, increasingly, by a simple desire to plunder Islamic territories, renewed contacts between the Christian and Islamic worlds. The Crusaders' establishment of European bases in Acre and other sites near the Holy Land (collectively known as the Outremer) and their seizure of Jerusalem from the Muslims contributed to this change. Trade between the West and the Middle East began to develop via the Mediterranean.

Mongol conquests in the thirteenth century, in turn, not only increased contacts between China and the Middle East but also led to the first direct relations between Chinese and Europeans.[7] Starting with probes, raids, and attacks, the Mongols, within the first four decades of the century, had conquered the largest domain in world history; their territory encompassed North China, Central Asia, much of Russia, and parts of Persia. By the end of the 1270s, Mongol armies had destroyed the Southern Sung dynasty of China and the 'Abbāsid caliphate, which had ruled a large portion of the Middle East, including the rest of Persia, and had compelled the Koreans to submit. Although these conquests did not entirely secure the way from East to West, the relative stability along the principal trade routes promoted the greatest movements of peoples, goods, and ideas in the history of Eurasia.

Westerners were the first to initiate direct contact with China. As early as the twelfth century, mythical stories about a benevolent Christian ruler named Prester John, who was said to live among the nomads of Central Asia, were circulating in Europe. The Christian world believed that this magnanimous monarch could be persuaded to join a Crusade against the Muslims. According to the contemporary Western annalists, he had defeated the Saracens and appeared willing to help the Crusaders. A curious and undoubtedly forged letter from Prester John, affirming his devotion to Christianity, reached the Byzantine Emperor around 1165.

Christian communities in the Middle East that had learned of the existence of coreligionists in East and Central Asia perhaps initiated the myth of Prester John. Evidently, he was modeled on Yeh-lü Ta-shih, the midtwelfth-century ruler of the Khara Khitay state in Central Asia who had routed the Central Asian and Persian Muslims. However, the Khara Khitay ruler was not a Christian. Nor did he have any intention of collaborating with the West.[8]

More accurate accounts began to appear as the Mongols reached westward in the 1230s. Seeking to find out about the interlopers from the East, King Béla IV of Hungary dispatched the Dominican friar Julian as an emissary to the Mongols. Departing in the spring of 1236, Julian never reached the Mongols' camp, but he met two envoys, who delivered an ultimatum from Batu, the leader of the Mongol forces in the West.[9] Batu demanded that the Hungarians submit to the Mongols and turn over enemies of his who had sought and received sanctuary in Hungary. Julian returned to his homeland not only with the ultimatum but also with a written account for Béla about the intruders from the East.

Julian began by reporting incorrectly that the Mongols' conquests and movements to the West had been precipitated by the widening of a war between one Mongol chieftain and the sister of another, but his other observations were considerably more accurate. He revealed that the Mongols intended to expand across Europe to Rome and that their cavalry and resulting mobility offered remarkable advantages in their military campaigns. He also provided a sketch, based on hearsay, of the Mongol court's sumptuous palaces, with their pillars and gates of gold, and he alluded to the vast wealth commanded by the Mongols as a result of their conquests.

The Mongol invasions of Poland and Hungary in 1240–1241 made Western Europe aware of the threat from the descendants of Chinggis (better known in the West as Genghis) Khan, who had ruled from 1206 to 1227 and was responsible for much of the expansion of the Mongol territories from 1209 through the 1220s. Yet the Europeans could not unite to confront the Mongols. Europe's spiritual leader, the Pope, and one of its most important monarchs, the Holy Roman Emperor Frederick II (r. 1220–1250), were hostile to each other because Frederick challenged the Church's claim to political supremacy over secular rulers. The conflict between the Holy Roman Emperors and the Popes had been simmering since the middle of the eleventh century and had weakened the European forces during the Crusades.[10] Innocent IV (Pope, 1243–1254) arranged a rapprochement with Frederick II in 1244, but it hardly lasted for the year. Political unrest within Rome also plagued the Pope. Compelled to flee to Lyons because of this turbulence, Innocent IV convoked the Thirteenth Ecumenical Council in 1245 to discuss the problems facing Christian Europe. He widened the breach with the Holy Roman Empire by excommunicating Frederick II. The launching of another Crusade to recover Jerusalem, which had once again fallen to the Muslims, was another important item on the Council's agenda. The rulers of the Ayyubid dynasty, which had been founded by the great Salāḥ al-Dīn (Saladin, r. 1169–1193) and controlled Egypt and Syria, and their Turkish military mercenaries, the Mamlūks, had defeated the Europeans in a major battle near Gaza in October of 1244 and had subsequently occupied Jerusalem. King Louis IX (St. Louis) of France (r. 1226–1270), a devoted Christian, was designated the leader of a Crusade to recapture the Holy Land. The Council's other principal concern was securing an evaluation of the Mongol threat. The Pope sent three missions, one in 1245 and two in 1246, to elicit information about the Mongols and to seek to convert them or at least to establish friendly relations with them.[11]

John of Plano Carpini led the most renowned of these missions; he was the only one of the three emissaries to reach Khara Khorum, the capital of the Mongols, and to return with a detailed report on his travels, which he entitled *History of the Mongols* (or *Ystoria Mongolarum*).[12] He carried with him two Papal letters, one urging the Mongols to convert to Christianity and the other demanding that they abandon their military campaigns in the West.[13] Reaching the Mongol homeland in August of 1246, after a year's travel, John witnessed the enthronement of Chinggis's grandson, the Great Khan (or Khan of Khans) Güyüg (r. 1246–1248).

The political structure of the Mongol Empire at the time John encountered it differed considerably from the tribal organization of pre-Chinggisid times. The Mongols' traditional pastoral nomadic life-style had not lent itself to the formation of groups larger than tribes of a few thousand people, and "any would-be supratribal ruler had to bring to heel a highly mobile population, who could simply decamp and ignore his claims to authority."[14] Before Chinggis's era, the members of each tribe, who often shared a common ancestor, had traveled together in search of water and grass for their flocks and herds. Their peripatetic way of life prevented the development of a complex government or administration. Instead a tribal leader, often with the assistance of a shaman, who performed religious and ritual ceremonies and "cured" the ailing, personally ruled over a small group.

The Mongols' expansion beyond their native steppelands has prompted much speculation about their motivations and the causes for their sudden eruption into the neighboring territories. Scholars have suggested disputes with sedentary states such as China over trade or land, the gradual desiccation of Mongolia, a decline in the mean annual temperature in the steppelands, a desire for booty, a mission of world conquest entrusted to the Mongols by their supreme deity, the Sky God, and Chinggis's own drive for fame and power as reasons for the conquests. In any case, while individual Mongol tribes could and often did engage in hit-and-run raids against their more settled neighbors, they had to forge alliances of many tribes before they could make permanent and substantial gains.

Chinggis Khan succeeded in overcoming parochial loyalties to establish a simple supratribal structure and a powerful, well-disciplined army to assist in his expansionism. However, although tribal chiefs developed a personal allegiance to him, they were not necessarily loyal to the office of Khan (or ruler of many tribes), which he assumed. If a succeeding Khan was ineffective, did not provide booty for the tribal chiefs, or was considered to have betrayed them, they had no compunction about severing their relationship with and ending their support for him. Each succeeding Khan was thus under great pressure to continue military conquests and expansion. Moreover, once one died, since the tribal leaders had no loyalty to such abstract concepts as a permanent office of Khan or to a Mongol state or nation, they did not feel obligated to remain in the confederation. This lack of cohesion, together with a relatively weak identification as a distinct group, repeatedly hampered the Mongols. The fragmentation of the Mongol domains after the death, in 1241, of Chinggis's son and successor, Ögödei, was therefore not unexpected. Indeed, following succession struggles and civil wars in the 1240s and 1260s, there would be four virtually autonomous Mongol domains within the so-called Mongol Empire. By the time of John of Plano Carpini's visit, two already existed: The Golden Horde dominated Russia and the Chaghadai Khanate controlled Central Asia. Later, the Ilkhanate, established around 1258, would hold sway in Persia, while the Yüan dynasty, founded in 1271, would rule North China and the traditional homeland of the Mongols and, by 1279, South China as well. The Great Khan, who administered Mongolia, was in theory the supreme ruler of the entire Mongol Empire, but as early as the accession of Chinggis's grandson Khubilai (also known as Kublai) to the Great Khanate in 1260, other Khanates, particularly the Golden Horde and the Chaghadai, would challenge his authority.

The Mongol Khans attempted to use religions to foster unity and help them rule. Shamanism, a worldview ideally suited to the tribal stage of Mongol development, was inadequate when the Mongols tried to govern the sedentary civilizations they had subjugated; they needed a more highly structured and sophisticated religion to legitimize themselves and win over subjects. Some of the Mongol rulers sought to achieve this grander vision by converting to the religions of their conquered subjects. Others, Khubilai Khan in particular, attempted to win over non-Mongols in their domains by patronizing the native religions. Even if they did not cultivate these religions, most of the Khans adopted a policy of toleration or benign neglect. As a result, various religions flourished in the Mongol domains. Buddhism attracted the early Yüan rulers of China and some of the early Ilkhans of Persia;

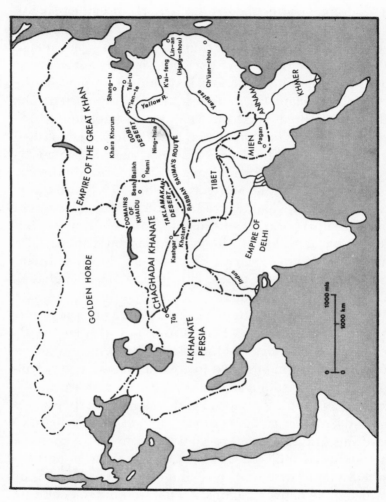

Divisions of the Mongol Empire in 1279, with Rabban Sauma's route from China through Central Asia. (Copyright © 1992 by Morris Rossabi.)

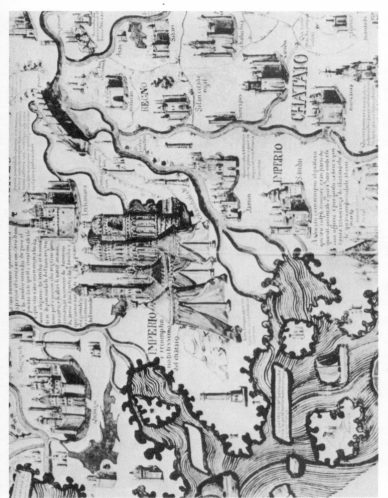

Map of China (Chataio), showing Tai-tu (Chambalech), based on Marco Polo's account. From a Marco Polo manuscript, Italian, 1459.

a few Khans of the Golden Horde favored Islam; some of the women in the Mongol elite were—like Rabban Sauma and the Syriac editor-translator—ardent believers in Nestorianism, a form of Christianity whose adherents subscribed to unorthodox views of the Trinity. However, despite their religious flexibility, the Mongol rulers certainly would not accept challenges to their authority or humiliating demands from other states or individuals.

Thus Pope Innocent's letter, as transmitted by John of Plano Carpini, enraged the Great Khan Güyüg, and John's relations with the Khan proved tumultuous. Güyüg did not appreciate receiving a lecture on religious conversion or a demand to discontinue his military campaigns. He responded with a haughty letter commanding the Pope and the European monarchs to submit to the Mongols. If they refused, Güyüg warned that "we shall know for certain that you wish to have war. After that we do not know what will happen, God alone knows."[15]

John's mission appeared a dismal failure. Not only had he been unable to proselytize among the Mongols but he had also been unable to interest Güyüg in an alliance against their common enemy, the Muslim states in the Middle East. A collision between Europe and the Mongols seemed unavoidable, and John conveyed this message to Innocent IV as soon as he reached Lyons on November 18, 1247.

Although his diplomatic mission had failed, John's trip produced something of great value in his *History of the Mongols*. In the words of a distinguished historian:

> . . . with his report he lifted the veil of mystery that had divided the Western world from the interior of Asia from time immemorial. This is an extraordinary achievement in itself. But its symptomatic value and its importance in the history of culture and literature are increased by the fact that this report is the first document of a systematic and objective representation of life and events sketched from

direct experience and with a keen sense of pertinent and
essential details.[16]

John's report offers among the first European portraits of
the *ger*, the Mongol tent, which "at the top in the middle [has]
a round opening which lets in the light, and is also to enable
the smoke to escape, for they always make their fire in the
middle." [17] John also provided an astute and detailed though
frequently biased account of Mongol rituals, beliefs, and customs, some bizarre and extraordinary by our standards, some
merely intriguing. He described the Mongols' intense attachment to their animals, their military tactics and strategy, and
their religious practices. He showed a particular interest in
social customs that would have struck him as unusual, such as
that of having a younger brother marry his elder brother's
widow—a practice that, surprisingly, he did not disparage. In
addition, he mentioned that "each man has as many wives as
he can keep, one a hundred, another fifty, another ten . . . ,"
numbers which perhaps applied to the chiefs but not the ordinary Mongol. He noted that the Mongols executed any un-
authorized person who crossed the threshold of a chieftain's
residence or anyone who urinated within a *ger* or other dwell-
ing. Their drinking and eating habits fascinated him, and he
described them graphically and with obvious distaste:

> Drunkenness is considered an honourable thing by them
> and when anyone drinks too much, he is sick there and
> then, nor does this prevent him from drinking again. . . .
> If anyone takes a morsel and, unable to swallow it, spits it
> out of his mouth, a hole is made under the dwelling and he
> is dragged out by that hole and without any mercy put to
> death.[18]

The two other Papal missions dispatched as a result of the
Ecumenical Council, both in 1246, made no more diplomatic
headway than John's. The Dominican Andrew of Longjumeau reached Tabrīz in Persia, where he met with a low-

ranking Nestorian retainer of the Mongols but not with their commander in the Middle East.[19] Friar Ascelinus had an audience with the commander, but neither emissary bowed down nor offered gifts or tribute, ensuring their decidedly cool receptions. An envoy from the Great Khan Güyüg, sent in response to John of Plano Carpini's mission, suddenly appeared and presented Ascelinus with a letter demanding European submission.[20]

Despite these unpromising overtures, there was still hope that the Europeans and Mongols could come to an agreement and unite against their common enemy, the Muslims of the Middle East. Even as the Muslims' occupation of the Holy Land incensed Christian Europe, their resistance to the Mongols' westward expansion antagonized the Khans.[21] Ayyubid commanders in Syria seemed intent on rejecting Mongol "orders of submission" and fending off Mongol influence in the Middle East. Confronted with this resistance, late in 1248 a Mongol commander in the Middle East dispatched two Nestorian envoys to Cyprus, where St. Louis was preparing for an attack against the Ayyubids, having set off on the Seventh Crusade, mostly with his own troops. These envoys bore a letter with a plan for a joint campaign against the Muslims.[22] They proposed that St. Louis unleash an assault on Egypt the following spring to divert the rulers there while the Mongols attacked the 'Abbāsid caliphate in its capital city of Baghdad. The two Nestorians pointed out that such coordinated invasions would hinder cooperation between the Ayyubid Sultan in Egypt and the 'Abbāsid Caliph. To make their offer of collaboration more palatable to the French monarch, they also claimed that Güyüg's mother was the daughter of Prester John and that Güyüg had converted to Christianity, intended to protect Christian property in the Middle East, and planned to help St. Louis recover the Holy Land from the Muslims.[23] These incredible, completely false assertions were clearly designed to make St. Louis more receptive to the Mongol proposal.

Impressed by this embassy, St. Louis had an elaborate portable chapel built and offered it as a gift to Güyüg. He also sent two embassies of his own to the Mongol court, both of them ill-fated.

The first, led once again by the unfortunate Andrew of Longjumeau, carried a letter from St. Louis praising the Mongol rulers for their support of Christianity and perhaps suggesting that they join with him in an alliance against the Muslims. Andrew arrived in the Mongol domains during the struggle for succession that followed the death of the Great Khan in 1248. The mother of one contender for the throne greeted Andrew and portrayed him as a tribute bearer whose monarch was willing to capitulate, thus bolstering her son's claim. Seizing this opportunity, she composed a haughty letter to St. Louis, admonishing him to accept Mongol overlordship in the West and to offer annual tribute of gold and silver.[24] Dejected by his reception at the Mongol court, Andrew headed west and caught up with the dispirited St. Louis in Palestine in the spring of 1251. The French King's Crusade had ended disastrously, and he himself had been captured by the Muslims in April of 1250 and endured the humiliation of paying a ransom to gain his freedom. The treatment of his embassy to the Mongols added insult to injury.

He was not discouraged, however. In 1253 he sent still another mission, led by William of Rubruck, a Franciscan friar in his entourage. Determined not to be rebuffed again, he insisted that William not represent himself as an official emissary but instructed the friar to broach the possibility of cooperation. William's interviews with the new Great Khan, Möngke, Güyüg's first cousin and Khubilai Khan's older brother, turned out to be frustrating, for they talked at cross-purposes.[25] Möngke apparently found the Franciscan dogmatic and overly intent on proselytizing for his religion. In turn, William was appalled by some of the religious dignitaries in Möngke's court. He described the Buddhists as deceptive and dogmatic, the Muslims as mean-spirited, and the

Nestorian Christians as ignorant, superstitious, and corrupt. He complained that the Nestorian "priests are ignorant of Syriac, the language of their liturgy; they are guilty of usury; their practices are contaminated by borrowing from Islam; they marry, and take a second wife on the death of the first, while some are polygamous."[26]

Möngke's and Rubruck's mutual antagonism made a rapprochement virtually impossible. Möngke dispatched a letter, via Rubruck, to St. Louis; in it he set forth the Mongol claim to universal rule and demanded that the French monarch send official envoys to indicate his acceptance of subordinate status. This uncompromising message did not augur well for cooperation between the Great Khan and Christian Europe. The only positive contribution of William's mission was his firsthand written report on the Mongols' customs and economy.

William's account repeats some of John of Plano Carpini's observations but supplements them with additional details gained from his stay in the Mongol domains. Like John, William wrote about the *ger* and Mongol religious practices, diet and drinking habits, and clothing. He also briefly sketched the Mongol techniques of making *koumiss* (fermented mare's milk) and of hunting, and he devoted considerable space to women's tasks, which included driving wagons, sewing clothes, tending and sometimes milking goats and sheep, and making felt. Surprisingly, he did not mention that women also took part in combat. He was fascinated by the splendor of the Mongol court and by the unusual and beautiful objects to be found there. A French craftsman named Guillaume Boucher, whom the Mongols had captured during their military campaigns in Eastern Europe and who now lived in the Mongol capital, Khara Khorum, fashioned for his overlords a silver tree decorated with four silver lions and a gilded serpent, each of which dispensed wine, *koumiss*, and other liquors; this contraption particularly intrigued William.

William's other observations—including descriptions of paper money, not then found in Europe, Chinese writing, and Buddhism—have inspired some scholars to rank him with Marco Polo as a travel writer. Yet his disdain for some Mongol practices certainly did not endear him to his hosts. Their taboo on bathing (which they believed would provoke the gods into unleashing devastating thunderstorms), their unattractive habit of defecating in public,[27] and their prolonged drinking bouts repelled him, and he could not totally hide his disgust from the Mongols.

Renewed hope for closer collaboration arose as a result of the campaigns of Möngke's younger brother Hülegü. Intent on enlarging their domains in the West and on defeating the hostile Islamic dynasties, the Mongols dispatched Hülegü in 1256 to pacify the Middle East. The well-known fervent Nestorianism of Hülegü's wife assured support from Middle Eastern Christians, including those in the Christian kingdom of Lesser Armenia, also known as Cilicia.[28] Two years later, Hülegü's forces entered Baghdad, overthrew the 'Abbāsid dynasty, and executed the last Caliph, probably by the traditional Mongol technique designed to show respect for royal blood: rolling him up in a carpet and having horses trample him to death to avoid shedding his blood.[29] Hülegü thus became the ruler of Persia and some adjacent areas of the Middle East, although he did not assume the title of Ilkhan till 1261.

After the capture of Baghdad, Hülegü and his forces continued to approach the Mediterranean, even seizing land in Syria, until his campaigns came to an abrupt halt in 1260. In that year he learned of the death of the Great Khan Möngke and decided to return to the Mongol homeland to participate in choosing his brother's successor.[30] He assigned his second in command, Ked Bukha, to conquer Damascus and then to occupy the rest of Syria, which was in the hands of Egypt's Muslim rulers. Mongol armies seemed to be irresistible, and it appeared that Hülegü's troops could do without him. Because of the changed political situation in Egypt, this proved to be a miscalculation. In 1249 the Turkish mercenaries of the Ayyubid dynasty had overthrown their masters and established the Mamlūk dynasty, which commanded a much more effective and powerful army. Hülegü's departure therefore left Ked Bukha facing a more formidable foe than had been anticipated.

Both sides had sizable forces under their command. The Mongols met with some success, occupying Damascus, but on September 3, 1260, Mamlūk forces clashed with Ked Bukha's troops in a historic battle at 'Ayn Jālūt ("Spring of Goliath") in Syria. By the end of the day, the Mongols had been defeated, and Ked Bukha had either been killed in battle or, as the great Persian historian Rashīd al-Dīn wrote, captured and beheaded.[31] Mamlūk troops then overwhelmed the Mongols in Damascus, and within a few months they had liberated all of Syria and averted a last-ditch effort by the Mongols to retrieve Aleppo. This defeat was a devastating blow to Mongol ambitions.[32]

On learning of the fiasco at 'Ayn Jālūt, Hülegü, without ever having reached the Mongol homeland, returned late in 1260 to try to contain the damage. He rallied the battered detachments who had survived the battle and organized his own troops for a renewal of hostilities with the Mamlūks. Not only did he wish to avenge the defeat at 'Ayn Jālūt but he also feared that the Mamlūks would stir up their fellow Muslims in Persia, who constituted the vast majority of the population in his domain, to overthrow Mongol rule.

Fissures in the Mongol world, however, stymied efforts at avenging the defeat. Berke, the ruler of the Golden Horde in Russia and Hülegü's cousin, had converted to Islam; he was thus distressed by Hülegü's suppression of the 'Abbāsid caliphate and the current hostilities with the Mamlūks. In addition, both Hülegü and the Golden Horde laid claim to

Āzarbāyjān, a major thoroughfare for East-West trade and thus a lucrative source of revenue in the form of transit and commercial taxes. Both of them wanted to possess the abundant pasturelands of Āzarbāyjān, which they required for their cavalry horses and flocks.[33] Such religious discord and territorial disputes created a wide gulf between the two segments of the Mongol Empire and led inevitably to warfare. Perhaps seeking to capitalize on his adversaries' defeat at 'Ayn Jālūt, Berke immediately allied himself with the Mamlūks. By 1262 he was battling with his cousin Hülegü for control of Āzarbāyjān. Through the remaining three years of Hülegü's reign, the warfare between the two Mongol realms persisted.

Hülegü thus faced the hostile Golden Horde in the north and the Mamlūks in the west. The Ilkhanate also found itself at odds with its eastern neighbors, the Mongols of Central Asia's Chaghadai Khanate. Disputes over territory provoked most of the animosity, although religious conflicts may have contributed as well.[34] Muslims constituted the majority of the population in the Chaghadai domains, and they resented what they perceived as the early Ilkhans' favoritism toward Nestorian Christianity and—particularly after Hülegü's time—Buddhism as well.

Surrounded by such hostile neighbors, Hülegü naturally sought allies in order to survive and perhaps expand. His need for them was all the greater because the Mongols' greatest strengths in warfare, their mobility and their cavalry, were somewhat neutralized by the insufficiency of pastureland in the Middle East and North Africa. Thus, if he wanted to defeat his Mamlūk enemies and resist the Golden Horde and Chaghadai Khanate, Hülegü required assistance. One possible source of support remained Christian Lesser Armenia, which the Mongols had occupied briefly from 1236 through the 1240s and whose leaders, even more fearful than the Ilkhans of the Islamic Middle East, supported the Mongols who opposed the Muslims. The ruler of Lesser Armenia, Het'um (r. 1226–1269), had demonstrated his links with the Mongols by undertaking, in 1254, a personal embassy as far away as Khara Khorum and by sending his troops to assist Hülegü during his campaigns in Syria in 1260. Lesser Armenia continued thereafter to side with Hülegü and his immediate successors. However, its resources, both manpower and supplies, were too limited to be of much help to the Ilkhans.

Another reliable potential ally was the Great Khanate based in Mongolia and China. Hülegü was on good terms with his brother Khubilai because the Ilkhan had supported Khubilai in his struggle against their brother Arigh Böke for the leadership of the Mongol world. Yet Hülegü had been unable to provide more than verbal support to Khubilai; his base of power was simply too distant to enable him to offer tangible assistance. Similarly, after Khubilai defeated Arigh Böke and assumed the title of Great Khan, he could not supply much aid from the easternmost section of the Mongol domains, in China, to his beleaguered relative in Persia. Khubilai was also preoccupied with the subjugation and pacification of Southern China and the establishment of an effective government in North China, tasks that required considerable resources and would not be completed until 1279.[35]

Because Hülegü was thus limited in his choice of allies, Christian Europe emerged as the likeliest possibility. If he hoped to overcome the Mamlūks and to gain land in Syria, he needed to join with the Europeans. The Crusader states along the eastern Mediterranean were possible partners, as were the Western European kingdoms and the Papacy. Clearly, neither haughty letters nor orders of submission such as the Mongols had resorted to in past dealings with the West would serve Hülegü's purposes. He had to approach the Europeans as equals.

The fact that the Ilkhan and the Europeans shared an

enemy in the Islamic dynasties of the Middle East gave Hülegü some cause for optimism. However, other factors stood
in the way of a successful alliance. Divisions within Europe,
among states and even cities, jeopardized prospects for collaboration. A disunited, frequently warring Europe could
not join the Ilkhanate in effective military campaigns against
the Muslims. Hülegü, however, appears to have been unaware of the rifts dividing the Christian West.

Another obstacle was the fact that many Europeans would
rebuff overtures for an alliance from the Ilkhans because
they perceived the Mongols as barbaric. The Crusader states,
or the Outremer communities, were particularly suspicious
about Mongol motives. As late as the 1260s they remembered
the devastation wrought by Mongol armies during the invasions of Poland and Hungary in 1241. Some may have concluded that the Mongols were a greater threat than the Mamlūks.[36] Yet they would not join with the Mamlūks, who were
dreaded Muslims from their viewpoint, against the Mongols.
Thus, the Crusader States generally adopted a policy of neu-
trality, which they would have cause to regret when confronted with Mamlūk attacks on their own communities in
the late thirteenth century.

In spite of all these stumbling blocks, Hülegü revived the
idea of collaboration with Christian Europe. Facing a period
of protracted conflict with the Golden Horde, the Chaghadai
Khanate, and the Mamlūks, he turned to the West for assistance, and from this time on it was the Ilkhans who generally
took the initiative in seeking a cooperative relationship.

In 1260 Hülegü had received a Dominican envoy named
David of Ashby, who had been sent by the European monarchs and the Pope to ascertain the Mongol ruler's intentions
and to seek guarantees for the safety of the Outremer communities. Because they had not authorized David of Ashby to
negotiate or even to discuss a possible alliance with the Mongols, his arrival at Hülegü's camp did not signal a Western

Christian desire for formal collaboration with the Ilkhans.[37]
Nonetheless, in 1263 Hülegü capitalized on David's embassy
by sending one of his own.

In the following year one of his envoys reached the Vatican.
Urban IV (Pope, 1261–1264) welcomed him but did not commit himself to an alliance. The Vatican, which had more
pressing concerns in European politics, including the conflict
with the Holy Roman Emperors, could not consider additional entanglements. The Pope could not resist making an
attempt to proselytize, however. He urged Hülegü to be baptized and, in effect, to convert to Christianity (a message that
reached the Ilkhanate only after Hülegü's death in 1265).[38]
The thirteenth-century Christian world was engaged in its
first serious proselytizing campaign. Within Europe missionaries were seeking, for example, to convert the Jews in order
to achieve a more homogeneous society. According to one
historian of the Jews, "vigorous self-confidence combined
with uncertainty and insecurity moved the leadership of western Christendom to press for enhanced homogeneity within
and for expansion of the borders of Christian domination
without."[39] The Christian hierarchy in the West therefore
welcomed religious contacts with the Ilkhans as a possible
means of expanding the world of Christianity in the East but
it was not as receptive to a political alliance. This did not deter
the Ilkhanate from trying again—indeed, from send-
ing, some twenty years later, its most remarkable embassy to
Europe.

EARLY LIFE OF A NESTORIAN MONK

Within the context of such increases in East-West interchanges and of attempts by the Mongols to foster an alliance
with the Europeans, the travels of Rabban Sauma may seem
less extraordinary. After all, the Pax Mongolica permitted
many Venetians, Genoese, and other European merchants to
travel to Persia and a few to reach all the way to China. Yet

Rabban Sauma's journey was exceptional because the vast majority of travelers and traders set forth from West to East. The number of envoys and merchants dispatched from China to Central Asia and Persia was paltry, and no one at all had ever before gone from East Asia to Europe. Even more remarkable than Rabban Sauma's journey to Europe is his account of it. To be sure, a few of the diaries written by some of the handful of travelers who went from China to Central Asia at this time have survived, but no other medieval voyager from China—or, for that matter, Asia—wrote about the distant lands of the Christian West.[40] The contrast to the number of contemporary European and Persian descriptions of the Mongols that have come down to us is striking. Rabban Sauma was exceptional in yet another way: He started westward for personal spiritual fulfillment; the vast majority of travelers departing from China went on official diplomatic missions. Only after his arrival in Persia was he entrusted with ambassadorial responsibilities.

His father, Shiban, was descended from a prominent Önggüd family that lived in the area where Khubilai Khan would build his capital of Tai-tu. Based principally in the Ordos region, north of the Great Wall along the bend of the Yellow River, the Önggüd were among the first of the Turkic peoples to throw in their lot with Chinggis Khan and the early Mongols.[41] In 1204, two years before Chinggis took the title of Khan, the Önggüd ruler had accepted Chinggis's supremacy and shortly thereafter confirmed his loyalty by giving his son in marriage to one of Chinggis's daughters.

Although many among the Önggüd remained pastoral nomads, some had developed a more complex economy and culture, settling in towns and becoming farmers, craftsmen, merchants, and miners. Foreign merchants sought objects, including silk robes, produced by their artisans. In addition, several generations earlier, missionaries from Central Asia had converted many of the Önggüd to Nestorian Christianity. The transformation from shamanism, which necessitated no written texts, to Christianity, with its emphasis on knowledge of the Bible, entailed the development of a literate clergy. Together with the more numerous Uyghur Turks of Northwest China, many of whom also converted to Nestorianism, the Önggüd thus had skills required by the Mongols, among whom literacy was scarce. They proved invaluable to the Mongols in helping to devise an administration for the domains Chinggis and his successors had subjugated, and they often served as translators, scribes, and officials.[42] It may seem surprising that, as foreigners, they were not discriminated against, but they benefited from the Mongols' policy of toleration and recruitment of non-Mongols. Their renown had spread to the West, in part because of their Christian faith. Marco Polo, for example, erroneously referred to Prester John as an Önggüd.

Shiban was well connected and highly respected in this sophisticated and prosperous community. He married a woman of similar background, but they could not conceive a child. They prayed continually to God, and He finally blessed them with a baby boy, whom they named Bar Sauma, "the son of the fast" (*Rabban* was an honorific title, which would be granted him later in life). The quasi-devotional sketch of Bar Sauma's birth, which the Syriac editor-translator of Rabban Sauma's account appended to it, does not give a precise date, only noting that it occurred "circa 1225," about ten years after Chinggis Khan had taken over the region where the future traveler was born. A touch of exaggeration has perhaps filtered into the editor-translator's description of Sauma's ardent devotion to the Nestorian faith from his earliest days. Yet his piety, even as a young boy, cannot be doubted.

His faith, Nestorianism, had diverged from the orthodox form of Christianity in the fifth century and had been condemned as heretical shortly after the Council of Ephesus (431). Nestorianism distinguished between the human Christ and the divine Christ. In effect, it viewed them as two distinct entities, rather than as fused in one person as in the Catholic conception of Jesus. According to the Nestorians, in his divine nature Jesus was the Son of God the Father. In his human nature, by contrast, Jesus was born of Mary. The Virgin was the mother of this human Christ (*christotokos* or "bearer of Christ") but not of God (*theotokos* or "God bearer") because God had always existed and by definition a human could not be his mother. Nor could God die, as Jesus had. In short, Nestorians drew a line between the human Christ and the Son of God and maintained, in the words of one summary, that Jesus's "Godhead is not from the substance of His Mother, neither His Manhood from the substance of His Father." [43] In the process, they challenged the central role of Mary, for in their view she was simply the mother of the remarkable man Jesus, and they believed she had been too lavishly extolled and highly elevated in the Catholic Church's teachings.

Their concept of the Trinity diverged from the Catholic version as well, for they perceived the Father as the progenitor, the Son (Jesus in his divine nature) as the one produced, and the Holy Spirit as proceeding from both. The fact that the three were not presented as coequals, that the Father was given primacy, subverted the idea of the Trinity. However, there were many similarities between Western Christianity and Nestorianism, including the Nestorians' retention of the sacraments, though in a slightly different form than in the West.

After their faith was declared heretical, Nestorians had been compelled to depart from the Roman and Byzantine empires and had sought and obtained sanctuary in the Middle East, Central Asia, and ultimately as far east as China. [44] Other heretical Christian sects, such as the Jacobites, also received a warm reception and succeeded in attracting converts in the Middle East, but none approached Nestorianism in geographic distribution throughout Asia. By the late fifth century, Nestorians had founded bishoprics in Marv and Nishapur (in Persia) and Harāt (in modern Afghanistan). From the sixth through the ninth century, Nestorian missionaries began to proselytize and converted many Turkic Central Asian peoples to Christianity. Early in the T'ang dynasty (618–907), Nestorians reached China and built churches and other monuments. They continued their missionary activity throughout this era, although their efforts dissipated as the dynasty declined. An inscription on a stele erected in 781 in Hsi-an listed the names of seventy Nestorian missionaries in China, an indication of the growth of the sect. By the late eleventh or early twelfth century, they were proselytizing among the Mongols; eventually they even converted some of the Mongol elite, particularly the women. The Mongol capital at Khara Khorum had at least one Nestorian church.[45]

During the thirteenth century, Nestorians were particularly pervasive in the Middle East and Central Asia, a fact which may seem surprising as the area is now almost entirely Muslim. However, it was only after the decline of the Mongols in Central Asia and Persia in the late fourteenth century and the concomitant growth of Islam that Nestorians there gradually abandoned their faith because of voluntary conversion or coercion. At about the same time Nestorianism gradually died out in China, where it had been less widespread to begin with. Thereafter, the sect survived principally in the Middle East, though more and more tenuously.

The remarkable spread of Nestorianism may be attributed to the zeal and astuteness of its missionaries and leaders. The early missionaries had the selfless dedication and motivation associated with true believers. Although the Catholic envoy William of Rubruck rebuked the Nestorian clergy he encountered in thirteenth-century Central Asia and Mongolia for their corruption, ignorance, and misinterpretation of Christian doctrine, he probably overstated the excesses of some of their extremely successful religious leaders. Nestorian links with trade also contributed to the spread of the religion. The Nestorians were in general said to be "keen men of business,"[46] and the Nestorian Church flourished all along the Old Silk Roads because many Nestorians were merchants, and traders played vital roles in proselytizing for the religion. Nestorianism was thus particularly prominent in towns.

The flexibility of the Nestorian clergy also promoted the rapid growth of the sect. They accommodated the cultures of the people they sought to convert. Their refusal to forbid polygamy is a case in point, and they had no objections when some secondary wives of Khans or nobles were permitted to convert to Nestorianism. This lack of rigidity encouraged good relations with other religions in the Mongol domains, and as long as the Mongols remained in power, their policy of religious toleration largely protected Nestorians against persecution and discrimination.

These accommodations with other religions and cultures resulted in deviations from the rituals and structure of the Catholic and Orthodox churches. Moreover, because of this practice of borrowing from and accommodating indigenous beliefs and practices, Nestorians in various regions in Asia differed in their performance of rituals, most often only slightly, but on occasion considerably.

The looseness of the Church's organization certainly contributed to its flexibility and hence its spread and popularity. The Patriarch, or Catholicus, was the leader of the Church and from about the fifth century resided in Seleucia-Ctesiphon, on the outskirts of Baghdad. He appointed Metropolitans to handle the Church's affairs in the principal territories where the religion had taken hold and to supervise the bishops within their lands. Transport and communication difficulties prevented centralization and made many Metropolitans virtually autonomous, a fact they took advantage of to make doctrine and rituals even more flexible.

A number of features of Nestorianism had particular ap-

A Nestorian worshipper. Wall painting from a temple in
Qočo, ninth century.

peal for ordinary people. The Nestorians emphasized festivals, incorporating features of the native cults. Some monks and priests blessed objects brought to them by simple folk, and they sometimes turned the graves of martyrs and "miracle workers" into pilgrimage sites. The bones and relics of these figures became objects of veneration. Visits to sacred sites and possession of sacred relics became significant values for Nestorians. Finally, the Nestorian clergy's knowledge of medicine, "their practical treatment of the diseases of the body, and the healings they effected,"[47] attracted converts.

According to the account of Rabban Sauma's youth found in the narrative of his life and travels, his interest in sacred relics and his religious ardor surprised his parents. They provided him with a religious education, and he proved to be an extraordinarily diligent student. At an early age he developed close ties to a Nestorian church in his birthplace, becoming a "Keeper," a position about which no additional details are found in the sources. Perhaps somewhat hyperbolically, the Syriac editor-translator portrayed him as utterly and unshakably devoted to a life of the spirit and to a religious vocation. He states that Sauma "led a life of strict chastity and humility."[48] Bar Sauma wished to divorce himself from this world to concentrate on serving the Lord. At twenty years of age, he renounced meat and alcohol, acts that caused his parents great anguish, for they now recognized his desire to abandon the secular world to become a monk.

Nestorian monks, like the Patriarch, Metropolitans, and bishops, were required to be celibate, although the priests and deacons who constituted the secular clergy were encouraged, if not required, to marry. Having arranged a marriage for him, Sauma's parents were concerned about his decision and pleaded with him to delay making such a commitment. The fact that their argument centered on the continuation of the family line reflects the influence of Chinese civilization on them.[49] They asserted that the fate of future generations was their principal concern. Who would inherit their property and wealth? They asked plaintively, "how can it possibly be pleasing to thee for our seed and name to be blotted out?"[50] Families assimilating to Chinese culture and thus eager for heirs would find this argument persuasive, and Bar Sauma responded by postponing his plan to become a monk for a time, which proved to be three years.

During that period he continued his studies with the teacher his parents had selected years earlier, and he prepared for a religious vocation. His persistence and obvious commitment finally convinced his parents that they ought not interfere, and they reluctantly canceled the arranged marriage. The nuptials had already been partially completed according to Nestorian rite before he reached the age of twenty; Sauma and his espoused had announced their intention to marry in front of a cross and in the presence of a priest. The actual, final marital ritual had not taken place, however, and the marriage had not been consummated, for Sauma's narrative unequivocally states that he had remained chaste.[51] It does not reveal whether an annulment took place, but such proceedings generally had to be formal and public so that the "abandoned" spouse could remarry. Nestorians permitted annulments of marriages for those who renounced the secular life.

Shortly after Sauma's parents withdrew their objections to his stated goals, he gave all his worldly possessions to the poor. Because of his strenuous efforts and diligence, he had already been informally accepted as a part of the secular clergy of the Nestorians. His hard work and careful study of the Bible persuaded the religious leaders that he was prepared to become part of the regular clergy. In 1248 Mar Giwargis, the Metropolitan of what eventually became the Mongol capital of Tai-tu, formally inducted Sauma into the Nestorian clergy. By the age of twenty-five, Sauma had taken his monastic vows and attained his ambition of pursuing a religious vocation.

That same year momentous changes were taking place in the Mongol domains in the East. These derived from the fact that the Mongols lacked a regular, orderly system of succession. When a Great Khan died, an assemblage of Mongol nobles (known as a *khuriltai*) would meet to select a new ruler, but they had too many potential candidates to choose from. They could select the dead Khan's younger brother or his youngest son (a system known as ultimogeniture) or a member of the royal family whom they considered the most meritorious. This loose system provoked repeated struggles. After Chinggis Khan's death, his son Ögödei had succeeded him as Great Khan in 1229, but other descendants of Chinggis had not approved of Ögödei's election. Ögödei's brother Tolui and his family, particularly his wife, never fully accepted his succession, and they bided their time to challenge the house of Ögödei. Ögödei died in 1241 and was eventually succeeded by his son Güyüg, by most accounts a ruthless and hotheaded young man. Güyüg reigned for only two years, however, before he died in 1248, precipitating a contest for the throne and a bloody purge that would alter the course of Mongol history and would also have an impact on Bar Sauma.[52]

The house of Tolui, under the leadership of his eldest son, Möngke, and with the ardent and ingenious support of Möngke's mother, Sorghaghtani Beki, emerged victorious after three years of jockeying for power with the house of Ögödei.[53] A bloody conflict then ensued. This struggle for the Great Khanate was the first that entailed violence, and it eventually fostered a rift within the Chinggisid line. During its course numerous members of the Mongol imperial family were captured and executed. Cousins turned against one another. Ögödei's grandson, a contender for the throne, was executed, as was the widow of the previous Great Khan, Güyüg. Two prominent Nestorian Christian government ministers and seventy-seven military commanders were killed, and several of them had their mouths "stuffed with stone until

Chinggis Khan and his four sons. From a manuscript of Rashīd al-Dīn's fourteenth-century history of the world, *Jami 'al-Tawanikh*, in the Bibliothéque Nationale, Paris.

they died."[54] The new Great Khan, Möngke, ultimately prevailed. Remnants of the house of Ögödei, however, survived. Some fled to Central Asia, where they joined with the ruling house of Chaghadai, descendants of another of Chinggis's sons, who also opposed the line of Tolui. Möngke thus encountered resistance in attempting to gain the allegiance of the Mongol governors of the diverse territories that had earlier been subjugated. Mongol unity, always somewhat tenuous, was undermined still further.

Having committed himself to a spiritual life, Bar Sauma was scarcely aware of the changes wracking the Mongol world, changes which would eventually have a profound influence on his life and career. As soon as he had been accepted into the community of monks, he built a cell and isolated himself. Most monks lived not in monasteries but in communities, self-supporting in some regions but provided with supplies by the devout in other areas. Nonetheless, they ate, worked, prayed, and studied together. Sauma's choice of a reclusive life therefore distinguished him from his fellows, and his self-imposed isolation contributed to his image as an atypical and extremely studious and pious monk. Some members of the monastic communities cared for the ill and afflicted, and the fact that he did not set Sauma further apart from other monks. During this time he devoted himself to his faith and to the adoration of Jesus. The account of this significant period in his religious life yields almost no details about his activities. How did he spend his time? Did he read works about and enrich his knowledge of Christianity? Did he study the books on Nestorian services and rituals? Since he could read Syriac and Turkic texts and may have been proficient in written Chinese, he certainly had access to a wide variety of sources. Did he meditate or seek a mystical communion with the Divine? How did he support himself or obtain support from others? All these tantalizing questions must remain unanswered.

Yet some inferences may be drawn from Sauma's later behavior. In 1255, after seven years of seclusion, he chose to
isolate himself even further from the community of men.
Leaving his cell in Tai-tu, he moved about thirty miles southwest to Shih-tzu ssu (or "Temple of the Cross") in the Fang
Mountains. When he reached the mountains, his piety and
fervent attachment to the Christian God became well known,
and, as his fame spread, many students were attracted by his
remarkable example. Quite a few would-be disciples arrived
at his retreat and sought instruction. They wanted to be
uplifted by his words, his teachings, and his life-style. These
zealous pilgrims may have supplied him with food, drink, and
the other necessities of life, although he did not encourage
them to come or to help him. He tolerated their interruptions
but still dedicated himself to his own vision and practices.
Without some outside stimulus, Sauma would no doubt have
continued such a life for the rest of his days, remaining a religious hermit with a regional reputation as a sage and pious
Christian.

Sauma's story took a different turn, however, when a dynamic young man, also of Önggüd Turkic extraction, arrived
to study with him in 1260. Born in 1245, Markos, a talented
and devout Nestorian, came from one of the centers of the
Önggüd peoples, which is often described as their northern
capital. His birthplace, now known as Yisun Sümeyin Tor (or
"Ruins of Nine Temples") but called Kosheng in Rabban Sauma's account, Tenduc by Marco Polo, and T'ien-te by the Chinese, was about one hundred miles northwest of the present
town of Kuei-hua in Inner Mongolia. Ruins discovered in the
1930s showed that there had once been a walled town with
wooden houses and royal palaces surrounded by beautiful
gardens on the site.[55] Excavators found fragments of Chinese
tiles, testifying to a lively commerce with China during the
Mongol period. Numerous crosses and inscriptions bear witness to the strong religious milieu in which Markos was
reared.

The youngest of four sons of an archdeacon, Markos was the most eager, precocious, and studious of the brothers, and he was particularly avid for religious instruction. He apparently outstripped the teachers in his region and determined to look elsewhere. Bar Sauma's reputation had spread to many of the Önggüd Nestorian communities of North China, and Markos, as a young boy, heard about him. He decided to meet with and perhaps live near the highly respected Nestorian who had settled in the Fang Mountains. Yet realizing such a plan would entail a two-weeks' voyage, long for a young man who had apparently never traveled alone except in the immediate vicinity of his home. Members of his community, not to mention his relatives and family, tried to dissuade him from departing. Markos either ignored or overrode these objections and at the age of about fifteen journeyed for fifteen days to reach what in the twentieth century would be termed his "guru."

Markos's arrival astounded Bar Sauma, who was impressed by the young man's tenacity and resoluteness. When Markos revealed that he wished to remain with his "master" and become a monk, Bar Sauma said that his visitor was too young to understand the difficulties and deprivations of the monastic life. Like the members of Markos's own community, Bar Sauma sought to convince him that his place was at home, pointing out that even mature monks found the life arduous. How could Bar Sauma permit such a naive young Christian to make a commitment to this life of discipline and deprivation? In spite of such attempts to dissuade him, the youthful visitor remained adamant. He brushed aside all of Bar Sauma's arguments and began his religious studies and meditations with the older man. Sauma's narrative fails to describe these studies in any detail. The two men probably focused on preparing Markos to take his monastic vows. He lived with Sauma, pursuing the same ascetic existence, fasting, praying, and dressing and eating simply. Within three years Markos had so impressed the Nestorian clergy that they accepted him into the monastic community. With Bar Sauma and the other monks, he worked to cultivate "purity and holiness, and they were comforted by God unto Whom they had committed their souls."[56]

The two men whom fate had linked and whose careers would be inextricably intertwined lived together for more than a decade in their mountain retreat. They appeared to be fulfilling their religious vocation. Yet the centers of the Christian religion were remote, and Markos at least yearned to visit the ancient sites associated with Christianity and to mingle with and meet coreligionists from other parts of Asia. Markos was much more of an activist than the comparatively reclusive Sauma and dreamt of an adventurous undertaking. Events unfolding in the Mongol, Muslim, and Christian worlds after 1260 would help him to achieve his desire—indeed, to go beyond his and Bar Sauma's wildest expectations.

2

A PILGRIMAGE TO THE WEST

CRISIS IN THE MONGOL WORLD

The year 1260 was pivotal for the Mongol domains, marking significant rifts within the Mongol khanates and among the Mongol commanders. As indicated earlier, the Golden Horde was on the brink of forging an alliance with the Mamlūks in opposition to the Mongol rulers of Persia.[1] Faced with such powerful united enemies, the Ilkhans needed outside support. However, they could not count on such assistance from the traditional center of the Mongol world, for the year 1260 was also a turning point for the Mongols' eastern domains. In August of the previous year, the Great Khan Möngke had died, probably of dysentery, while campaigning against Southern Sung China. His two younger brothers, Khubilai Khan and Arigh Böke, then competed for the Great Khanate. In 1260 two *khuriltai* elected two Great Khans, setting the stage for a civil war between Khubilai, whose strength lay in North China, and Arigh Böke, whose troops were based in Mongolia. Having access to the abundant resources of North China, Khubilai appeared to be in the stronger position, although the Ilkhan Hülegü, his principal ally among the Mongol Khans, was preoccupied elsewhere after the defeat of his forces at 'Ayn Jālūt and could not assist him. Arigh Böke counted on securing the support of the

Khubilai Khan on a Hunt, by Liu Kuan-tao. Hanging scroll, ink and colors on silk, signed and dated 1280. From the National Palace Museum, Taipei.

Chaghadai Khanate of Central Asia, which would create greater balance between the two sides. The Chaghadai Khan at first listened to Arigh Böke's entreaties but eventually betrayed his erstwhile ally. Without external assistance, Arigh Böke was vulnerable, and Khubilai defeated him by 1264. He faced no powerful rivals for the remaining thirty years of his reign.[2]

Nonetheless, Khubilai's position remained somewhat insecure, a fact that influenced not only the rest of his reign but also the careers of Bar Sauma and Markos. Southern China refused to accept his orders of submission. Southern Sung troops fought against Mongol armies for more than a decade before they were finally defeated in 1279. Khubilai also encountered opposition from descendants of Ögödei who had fled to Central Asia after Khubilai's brother Möngke defeated them in the struggle for the Great Khanate in 1251. One of Khubilai's cousins, Ögödei's grandson Khaidu, not only re-

sented the transfer of the Great Khanate from his grandfather's line to that of Khubilai's father, Tolui, but also feared
the growing influence of non-Mongol, nonnomadic groups
in Khubilai's domain in China. By 1269 he had built up a
powerful army and persuaded the Chaghadai Khan, who became simply a puppet, to recognize his supremacy in the region. Khaidu became embroiled in border disputes with
Khubilai, which led to repeated raids and wars. Moreover,
along China's northeastern frontiers, Korean dissidents challenged the Korean monarch supported by Khubilai, who ultimately had to send troops to ensure the success of his candidate for the throne. Partly to prevent trade between Japan
and his enemies in South China, he dispatched embassies to
the Land of the Rising Sun to demand that the rulers of Japan accede to Mongol superiority, but the Japanese refused,
prompting an abortive Mongol invasion in 1274.

Khubilai's concerns in foreign relations were matched and
actually dwarfed by his effort to establish a government in
China. He had to do whatever he could to ensure his acceptance both as Khan of the Mongols and as the first Mongol
Emperor of China and to facilitate the rule of a tiny Mongol
minority over the much more numerous Chinese population.
Chinggis and his successors as Great Khan, in particular
Khubilai's brother Möngke, had begun to set up an administration, but Khubilai still needed to establish government offices, recruit officials, develop court ceremonies and rituals,
integrate Mongol and Chinese military forces, and promote
the Chinese economy, among other tasks. In 1256 he had
built a summer capital in K'ai-p'ing, which was later renamed
Shang-tu (and eventually became known to Europeans as
Xanadu). A few years later he would be preoccupied with
constructing a grand and meticulously planned capital in
Tai-tu.

Such was the realm in which Bar Sauma and Markos took
their first steps toward their great adventure, and such was

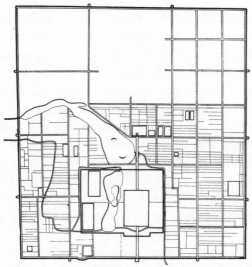

Plan of Tai-tu during the Yüan dynasty. From *K'ao'ku* 1 (1972). A notable feature is the innovative grid layout with gates all around permitting entrance into the city. In the center is the Imperial Capital, surrounded by ponds, temples, and government offices.

the situation that would help to force Hülegü's successors, as it had him, to look not to Khubilai but to the Christian West for support against their fellow Mongols of the Golden Horde and the Muslim Mamlūks of Egypt.

BAR SAUMA AND MARKOS BEGIN THEIR JOURNEY

Bar Sauma and Markos would eventually play critical roles in this proposed alliance. Their involvement started innocently enough, with a desire to visit and venerate the tombs of the saintly martyrs and the Fathers of the Nestorian Church, a project that required a trip to the Middle East. Markos, in particular, was also eager to go to the holy city of Jerusalem to receive indulgences or, in his words, "complete pardon" for his offenses and absolution for his sins. Neither of the Nestorian clerics intended or even expressed a wish to travel on to Rome. Their seclusion from the secular world may have kept them ignorant of that center of the Western Christian world. The Mongol court, having received Papal emissaries, was much better informed about Rome and the religious hierarchy based in the Vatican.

It was Markos who first proposed the journey west. Bar Sauma initially objected and tried to frighten Markos by emphasizing the arduousness of the voyage, the fatigue traveling such a long distance would entail, and the perils (inhospitable terrain, bandits, and sudden catastrophes such as avalanches, ice storms, and flash floods) that faced travelers heading across Central Asia to the Middle East.[3] Markos was undeterred, however. He had become convinced that his spiritual fulfillment lay in the Holy Land and that spiritual treasures awaited him en route and at his destination. His faith overrode fear of the unknown and concern about the hurdles to be faced, and he continued to try to persuade Bar Sauma of the religious value of such a trek. Sometime around 1275, reputedly the year of Marco Polo's arrival in China, Markos's unrelenting lobbying persuaded his fellow monk to change his mind. Bar Sauma decided to accompany his younger friend, and they pledged always to travel jointly, whatever the hardships or difficulties they encountered. It was to prove a pledge they would not be able to keep.

The two Nestorian clerics had much to do before they could set forth. First, they donated their remaining belongings, pitiful as they were, to the poor, left their mountainside home, and traveled to Tai-tu to recruit escorts and obtain provisions. Because they had taken vows of poverty, they needed to raise funds from the local Nestorian community and from the Mongol court. Here they confronted impediments to their plan, for the Nestorians in Tai-tu were not sanguine about the monks' expedition. They warned the two clerics of the arduousness and hazards of the trip and went so far as to predict that the monks would never reach their destination. In addition, they argued that because the Bible had indicated that "the kingdom of God is within you,"[4] the

two monks had no reason to go anywhere. Waving these objections aside, Bar Sauma and Markos asserted that they were
accustomed to hardships. They would not be intimidated by
the risks they faced. Both considered themselves, in the con-
ventional sense, dead already, since they had divorced themselves from secular life. They did not fear physical death if it
overtook them on their way to fulfilling their dream of visiting the holy sites of the Christian Church. Asking that their
fellow Nestorians pray for them, they finally won the community over.

However, they still needed financial support. Such a long
trip was costly. Bar Sauma and Markos would require escorts,
baggage handlers, and camel and horse grooms among other
assistants. A fourteenth-century European commercial
handbook, which describes the route from the West to China,
mentions merchant caravans consisting of approximately
sixty men.[5] Because the two clerics would not have been
transporting large quantities of commodities for trade, they
would not have required such a sizable contingent. Joining a
merchant caravan would have enabled them to cut expenses.
However, they wished to linger in various locations and to
stay in Nestorian communities en route, so a commercial caravan, which would have needed to move expeditiously, would
not have been suitable. Moreover, they had to be accompanied by men with the knowledge and experience to escort
them across the desert, mountains, and other inhospitable
terrains of Central Asia. Even if they made no lengthy stops,
the trip from Tai-tu to Persia might take six months or more,
and they would have to have funds to procure food, drink,
and other essentials for the entire caravan. Protection costs—
irregular levies demanded by some of the tribes and states en
route to guarantee the safety of the travelers—would have
been an additional financial burden.[6] The likelihood of en-
countering unforeseen obstacles or delays warranted obtain-
ing reserve funds for the journey.

The Nestorian community doubtless bore the major share of the costs, but the Mongol court also contributed funds to the expedition and helped pave the way for its speedy and safe passage. Inexplicably, however, Sauma's account of the two monks' travels fails to mention finances, and it omits any reference to Khubilai Khan and the Mongol government.

Two roughly contemporaneous Middle Eastern sources assert that Khubilai entrusted Sauma and Markos with a mission to visit the holy sites of Christianity on his behalf. The Hebrew physician Bar Hebraeus (1226–1286) wrote a world history which explained that Khubilai had sent the two Uyghur [*sic*] monks to worship in Jerusalem.[7] An Arabic Nestorian chronicle of the fourteenth century definitely states that Khubilai had ordered the monks to take the clothes he gave them, baptize the garments in the Jordan River, and drape them over Jesus' sepulcher.[8] If Khubilai truly expected Markos and Sauma to undertake this task, he would have subsidized part of their journey. The expense of an embassy that provided no economic return would have burdened private citizens, even the most devout Nestorians, but the court could justify such a mission on diplomatic or religious grounds.

Lending added credibility to these reports is Khubilai's grander strategy of representing himself as sympathetic to and protective of all the leading religions in his domains. He wanted their support to bolster his claim to legitimacy after his successful struggle for power with his younger brother. Moreover, winning their favor boosted his popularity and opened up opportunities for eventually recruiting clerics for his government. Because the Mongols had only limited experience in ruling an empire (conducting censuses, setting up a system of taxation, and so on), Khubilai had to seek literate and skilled foreigners to help him govern. Due to the fact that literacy and learning were most often found among the clergy, he frequently attempted to induce religious dignitaries to join his administration. He may also have had another,

Portrait of Khubilai Khan, painter unknown, ca. 1260.
From the National Palace Museum, Taipei.

more personal reason for wishing to please the Nestorians;
his mother had been one.

Another persuasive argument in favor of the accounts by
Bar Hebraeus and in the Nestorian chronicle is that Khubilai
reputedly entrusted Marco Polo's father and uncle with a similar responsibility when they returned to the West in 1269,
after their initial visit to the Mongol court. First, he requested
that they bring back oil from the lamp that burned above Jesus' sepulcher in Jerusalem. Then he urged them to return
with one hundred learned Christians, ostensibly to help him
convert Chinese and Mongols to Christianity but more probably because of his usual wish to obtain the services of educated men to help him administer his domains.[9] In 1275 the
Polos returned with young Marco and the holy oil but informed Khubilai that they had not been able to persuade one
hundred Christians to undertake the long trek to serve him.
Although the Great Khan was disappointed, he had fulfilled

Khubilai Khan presenting the letter patent to the Polo brothers. From an illuminated page of the Polo manuscript Reg. 19 D I folio 59v. (By permission of the British Library, London.)

part of his objective, which was to portray himself as a friend and patron of the Christians.

According to a somewhat tenuous interpretation once advanced by several scholars, Khubilai wished to use intelligence obtained from Bar Sauma and Markos for a projected military campaign to capture Jerusalem.[10] However, considering the rifts among the Mongol khanates in Asia, Khubilai could scarcely have believed that he could march his troops across lands inhabited by numerous enemies all the way to Jerusalem (not to mention the supply and logistical problems posed by such an expedition). Neither the Persian nor the Chinese official sources offer evidence of plans for such a campaign.

In any event, the Mongol court in Tai-tu must have given the two monks a license or letters patent (*p'ai-tzu*) to secure them safe passage and even a hospitable welcome in the other khanates and in lands friendly to or dominated by Khubilai.[11] The granting of these letters patent signified the court's and Khubilai's support for their mission. Sauma and Markos would need such guarantees. Indeed, they would have needed every conceivable advantage they could get.

With the blessings of the Nestorian community and the support of Khubilai, Bar Sauma and Markos could begin their journey. Sauma's narrative fails to mention a specific date for their departure. The two monks could not have gone after 1278, because they arrived in Persia by late 1279 and Sauma's account reveals that they spent six months in one town en route. They must have left after the Polo brothers' return with the holy oil in 1275; at that point the Khan would have assumed that, like the Polos, they could reach Jerusalem and hence have felt confident entrusting them with his assignment. A date closer to 1275 than 1278 appears probable, given their six-month stopover and the fact that the monks most likely tarried in other locations as well.

Once they had received court sanction for their mission,

Sauma and Markos began to prepare for the journey. They hired their own camel grooms, interpreters, baggage handlers, cooks, and guards and purchased the pack animals, food, and other supplies required for the first leg of the voyage. It is hard to know precisely how many men they employed for the trip; the figure could have varied from a dozen to thirty or forty at any given time. When the two monks arrived at major destinations and halted for several weeks or months, they would need to hire new escorts, because they could not afford to pay men simply to wait for them. Moreover, because the escorts would be familiar with specific legs of the journey, not the whole route across Eurasia, they would have to be replaced periodically in any case.

Sturdy camels were perhaps as important to the success and survival of the caravan as sound men. These beasts could carry more weight than any other available animal. The average camel could transport four to five hundred pounds, whereas the average mule, its closest rival for long-distance travel, carried approximately two hundred and fifty pounds. Camels required less water and less pasture than horses and mules, making them more suited to desert travel. Their hooves did not sink into the sand, and they could reputedly predict sandstorms and uncover underground springs in sandy areas, invaluable skills in the desert. Caravans used camel dung for fuel and camels as mounts for impromptu cavalries in case of bandit attacks. Yet the procurement, raising, and maintenance of camels required expertise. Their gestation period was long, and many of the beasts were sterile. Because the mortality rate for young camels was high, the rearing of camels was expensive and time consuming. All this, of course, pushed up the purchase price for the animals. Handling the beasts properly also called for special skills, and caravans thus required experienced and competent—and costly—camel grooms.

As the two clerics traveled from one oasis to another, they

would lodge at postal stations and garrisons.[12] Earlier Chinese dynasties had established postal stations to facilitate the transmission of government documents, but it remained for the Mongol Yüan dynasty to increase the number of stations and to join with Mongols elsewhere to extend the system to Central Asia. Although the stations primarily expedited the delivery of official mail, they also hosted traveling officials, military men, and foreign envoys; transported tribute to the court; served as guardhouses and beacons alerting the court to the movements of foreign troops; and functioned as inns for merchants and other travelers. Many stations lay on the major trade routes in China and Central Asia and thus facilitated commerce. Each of the stations, spaced about twenty miles apart, had for hire a specified number of horses, mules, ox-drawn carts, camels, or sedan chairs, depending on the topography of the region. The couriers, animal grooms, guards, and other employees at the station received their supplies from neighboring communities or, in some cases, farmed the land themselves and were responsible for supplying their own needs. Travelers found food, water, beds, and washing facilities for themselves and fodder for their animals in the sheds that served as postal stations. They also received valuable information about weather, terrain, and possible hazards. There were a considerable number of such stations in the Mongol domains: Manchuria alone had 146. There were also inns or other hostelries, but little is known about them.

Like earlier Chinese dynasties, the Mongols of this era stationed garrisons along the frontiers, and these too facilitated travel. The rulers of China intended for these garrisons, in addition to their other duties, "to provide a safe line of communication for the use of diplomats, trading caravans, and other travellers who were proceeding to the west."[13] They built watchtowers three-quarters of a mile to five miles apart and manned them with soldiers and a few convicts. The garrisons used smoke and flag signals to warn travelers of dangers; supplied them with food, water, lodging, and other necessities; and informed them of the distance to the next resting place. Serving in the garrisons and watchtowers was often unpleasant. Soldiers faced bandit raids, the intense heat of the desert, hazardous patrols beyond the towers, and poisonous scorpions and snakes. The isolation and loneliness contributed to the bleakness of such an assignment. Yet the soldiers' presence enabled voyagers such as Bar Sauma and Markos to travel more safely.

In addition to postal stations and garrisons, the Mongols in China had built quite a few roads. As Marco Polo observed:

> [Khubilai] has arranged that by all those main roads through the province of Catai [China] and through the neighbouring provinces, by which the messengers and the merchants and the other people go, he has had trees planted there beside the ways on either side two or three paces distant the one from the other . . . so that each may see the roads, that the merchants may be able to rest there in the shade . . .[14]

Roads in Central Asia was, however, a misnomer: *Trails* might be a more appropriate term for most of the paths on the trade routes to the West. They were difficult to traverse and by no means easy to follow. In some areas, poles or towers clearly marked their course, but in many regions travelers found no such assistance. Winter snows and summer floods occasionally obscured these trails or made them impassable.

Having made their preparations, Bar Sauma and Markos departed from Tai-tu. Their first stop was northeast of the great bend of the Yellow River in Markos's native town, Ko-sheng. The arrival of the two monks delighted the townsfolk, and Markos's family assumed that he was finally coming home. Escorting Markos and Bar Sauma into the local church, the leaders of the community made it plain that they hoped that the two monks would settle there, preside over their religious affairs, and lead services in the church. They were clearly chagrined to learn that Bar Sauma and Markos intended to depart shortly thereafter for Jerusalem.

News of the arrival of the saintly monks spread rapidly. The two most important Önggüd Christian leaders in the region, who lived in the steppes not far from town, dispatched messengers to invite and accompany Bar Sauma and Markos to their camp. These Nestorian princes were no ordinary rulers—one was, in fact, the son-in-law of Khubilai Khan. The Mongols often used marital alliances as a means of binding non-Mongols to them,[15] and Khubilai had earlier given his youngest daughter, Yüeh-lieh, in marriage to Ai Buqa, one of the two Önggüd leaders, while the other, Kun Buqa, was married to Yeh-li-mi-shih, daughter of the Great Khan, who had ruled from 1246 to 1248.[16] No doubt a strong bond existed between the Mongol court and the Önggüd princes, and the princes' attitudes toward the two monks might be expected to have reflected the official view of their mission.[17]

Ai Buqa and Kun Buqa welcomed Sauma and Markos. They probably wanted to use them as advisers and administrators and to capitalize on their prestige. Like the ordinary people in nearby Kosheng, they were disappointed when the monks informed them that they would soon be heading west. Ai Buqa and Kun Buqa attempted to persuade them to stay behind, emphasizing that the region desperately needed to lure knowledgeable Nestorian monks and fathers from the West (thus acknowledging that the real center of the Nestorian Church was in the Middle East) and that it made no sense to permit and encourage their own relatively few monks to leave. Despite this pressure, the two travelers would not be deflected from their mission. The Önggüd rulers implied at one point that they would not allow Sauma and Markos to continue their journey, but the Mongol court's sanctioning of the trip must have outweighed their misgivings about letting these valuable religious dignitaries go.[18]

Once they had accepted the inevitability of the monks' departure, the princes proved willing to help Bar Sauma and Markos on their way. When they offered the travelers gifts of gold, silver, clothes, rugs, and horses, the monks' response startled them. The account of this incident may reflect a touch of hagiography on the part of the editor-translator of Sauma's text. According to his version, Bar Sauma and Markos expected that Nestorians in the oases and towns en route would feed and shelter them, and therefore they politely spurned the princes' offer. They explained that they had renounced all possessions and did not need extra material goods. Their confidence would be borne out during their travels, for they encountered and received generous hospitality from Nestorian communities in nearly every major stopping place.

Overriding the monks' objections, the Önggüd leaders compelled them to accept the gifts they had offered. Ai Buqa and Kun Buqa did not call the two travelers naive, but they seem to have believed that they were true innocents. The Önggüd princes patiently pointed out that the trip was a long and costly one and that the monks would have expenses. To make Bar Sauma and Markos feel less beholden, the princes urged them to treat the gifts as a loan. If they did not use the funds, they could distribute them to the Nestorian monasteries in the West. This compelling argument persuaded the monks. They thanked their hosts for their generosity and returned to the road.

Following the course of the Yellow River southwest and along the Alashan mountain range, Bar Sauma and Markos reached the town of Ning-hsia, formerly part of the Hsi Hsia (or Tangut) Empire, which had been conquered by the Mongols in 1227. This segment of the journey could not have been easy, for it was just south of the Gobi Desert. Here again the two monks found a sizable Nestorian community, which greeted them warmly. Most of the inhabitants were Buddhists, but, according to Marco Polo, Muslims as well as Nestorians also lived in the town.[19] Learning of the monks' ambitious pilgrimage plans, many of the local Nestorians rushed out to meet them. Countless goods were showered upon them in spite of their protests. Both peasants and pastoralists brought supplies for the monks, hoping to facilitate their journey. The Nestorians of Ning-hsia were the first Christians who did not attempt to dissuade Bar Sauma and Markos from continuing their travels.

The two monks now faced another perilous part of their journey, which took them through the modern region of Southern Sinkiang in China. They followed the Southern Silk Road—so named because the caravans that took this route wound their way south of the dreaded Taklamakan Desert. Although they thus avoided the most dangerous section of the Silk Road, they still encountered a stretch of caravan trails that was not easily traversed, partly because of the proximity of desert. Entering the Tarim Basin, the monks' group first skirted the northern flanks of the K'un-lun Mountains, south of which lay India. Along the way, caravans often stopped in Miran, a site rich in historical relics. A second-century Buddhist shrine decorated with Greco-Indian designs and a Tibetan fort of the T'ang era, both still extant, confirm the town's heterogeneous character and its hospitality to foreigners. From Miran, travelers would head south and follow the Cherchen River for part of the five-hundred-mile journey to the next major stopping place, Khotan.

Two months elapsed between the monks' departure from Ning-hsia and their arrival in Khotan. Rabban Sauma's account indicates that they endured great hardships on this part of the trip, that it was "toilsome and fatiguing."[20] Journeys adjacent to or in the Taklamakan Desert were extremely hazardous; travelers on occasion had to walk across sand dunes as high as sixty or seventy feet. Vivid and frightening descriptions of sandstorms appear in the accounts of many who passed through the region, and Bar Sauma and Markos more than likely encountered such a flare-up. Marco Polo described another danger of journeys in the Taklamakan: "[If a traveler] chances to lag behind or to fall asleep or the like, when he tries to gain his company again he will hear spirits talking, and will suppose them to be his comrades. Sometimes the spirits will call him by name; and thus shall a traveller ofttimes be led astray so that he never finds his party."[21] Such hallucinations were not uncommon, particularly in the intense heat. In addition, the monks' caravan faced provisioning problems. It found potable water at only eight locations en route. Because lack of water limited the possibilities for agriculture, food was scarce along the way as well.

After they had survived these conditions, the two Nestorians arrived with great relief at Khotan, one of the most renowned oases in Central Asia. To the Chinese, Khotan's significance lay in its abundant supplies of white and black jade. The Khotanese had traded with the Chinese as early as the Han dynasty (206 B.C.–A.D. 220).[22] Its jade and its proximity to China and India helped earn Khotan fame as a trading center as far away as the Middle East. Moreover, because its position along the southern trade routes brought it in touch with India, the town became a vital thoroughfare in the spread of Buddhism. The Buddhist pilgrim Fa-hsien visited it around A.D. 400 on his way to India and found a population of three thousand Buddhist monks in one monastery and numerous other Buddhist monasteries as well.[23] According to a Chinese dynastic history of the sixth century, Khotan had "great throngs of temples, *stūpas*, monks and nuns."[24] The T'ang (618–907), a great expansionist dynasty, maintained garrisons there, an indication of the value they accorded the town.

Khotan depended on the river descending from the waters of the nearby K'un-lun Mountains. The Khotanese harnessed this river, the Khotan Darya, to create an elaborate irrigation system, which permitted them to cultivate wheat, millet, and oats and to grow fruit trees. Farmers, not pastoral nomads, dominated the region, although Khotan's renown derived from its craftsmen and merchants. Eurasian merchants prized its carpets, glass, and silk, and traders brought goods from Europe, the Middle East, and China to be exchanged and then transshipped either east or west.[25]

The religious and ethnic diversity of the merchants gave a special flavor to Khotan. Although Buddhism had dominated in the first millennium, by the thirteenth century Marco Polo maintained that "the people of that province all worship Mahomet."[26] However, when Bar Sauma and Markos visited, Khotan was a mélange of ethnic groups, including Persians, Uyghur Turks, Chinese, and Mongols, all of whom spoke different languages and represented different religious beliefs. In this respect Khotan was characteristic of nearly every town that travelers such as Bar Sauma, Marco Polo, and William of Rubruck passed through in Central Asia and Persia. Visiting foreigners could encounter, if they chose, inhabitants of similar linguistic or religious backgrounds in these communities, facilitating their relations with the local populace. Bar Sauma and Markos surely found Nestorians in Khotan and lodged with them during the six months they spent there. Bar Sauma's account barely describes their sojourn,[27] but since the two men stayed with monastic or Christian communities at nearly every site they visited, they doubtless did here as well.

It is interesting to speculate why the Nestorian monk's narrative gives such short shrift to the time he spent in Khotan. His record of his trip from China to Persia is in general often quite sketchy, omitting basic information about his and Markos's activities as well as about what he saw. Given his apparent interest in religious over secular matters, the editor-translator may have deleted most of whatever Sauma wrote on this leg of his journey about the spectacular landscapes and great buildings in and around the towns he passed through, as well as some of what he wrote about the monks' doings. Considering Sauma's own focus on religious concerns, perhaps he himself failed to mention many secular topics in the diary he was keeping. He may not have been as aware as he was in Europe that what he was writing had historic importance, and this too may have inclined him to give relatively minimal information about a number of matters that might interest the modern reader.

Although skimpy on the details of their stay, Bar Sauma's account does explain the reasons for the temporary suspension of their travels. Rifts in the Mongol hierarchy had generated turbulence and warfare. By 1269 Khaidu, Khubilai's cousin and enemy, had broken away from the Great Khan, and for the next few decades the two leaders fought over Turkistan. In 1271 Khubilai had sent his son Nomukhan to regain control over the Silk Road oases in the region and to crush Khaidu. The Pax Mongolica appeared to be unraveling. Although Mongol unity had been subverted even earlier, the turbulence now threatened the East-West flow of goods, people, and information.[28]

Bar Sauma and Markos were faced with what appeared to be insurmountable obstacles. The capture of Nomukhan by Khaidu's forces in late 1276, on what was probably the eve of the monks' departure from China, had exacerbated tensions along the route. Travel farther westward was hazardous, and the monks, who had only learned of Nomukhan's capture on reaching the area, now wavered. Finally, they embarked on a fifteen-day trek to Kashgar (virtually on the border of modern China), the meeting place for the Silk Road routes that proceeded north and south of the Taklamakan Desert. The two monks were appalled to find this major entrepot depopulated and devastated, particularly because it had been the site of a Nestorian Metropolitan see.

When Marco Polo had passed through the region just a few years earlier, he had found and described a flourishing, prosperous town:

> Much cloth and merchandise come there. And in this city they live by trade and by crafts and specially by working in cotton. And they have very beautiful gardens and vines

and beautiful closes of fruit trees. The land is fertile and
productive of all sorts of necessaries of life, because the
place is temperate . . . And from the country go out many
merchants who go through all the world doing trade.[29]

Bar Sauma and Markos did not see anything like this idyllic
site. In the interval between their visit and Polo's, the political
struggles plaguing Central Asia had taken their toll on Kashgar, and brigands had also plundered the town.[30] Such destruction clearly shocked the monks, but they did not give in
to fear. Trusting in their faith, they continued westward.

Nonetheless, they (or whoever escorted them) displayed
both astuteness and caution by selecting a circuitous route to
avoid some of the most dangerous areas along their way. Following a path northwest from Kashgar and fording the Syr
Darya, they managed to elude marauding armies and bandits, although they thus extended their trip by several weeks.
Their caravan halted at a spot off the traditional trade routes,
the historic town of Talas (within the borders of Kirghiz in
what was until recently the USSR). It had been the site in 751
of one of the greatest battles in world history, fought by the
two most powerful empires of that era, T'ang China and
Umayyad Arabia.[31] Now it was where Khaidu himself had his
camp. While there, the two monks had the opportunity to
meet with him and seek his assistance.

In dealing with the Mongol leader, Bar Sauma and Markos
faced a serious dilemma. They could not afford to portray
themselves as representatives of his enemy Khubilai. Nor
could they show any hint of fondness for Khaidu's other foes,
the Ilkhans of Persia, who remained close allies of the Great
Khan. They evidently chose to present themselves in apolitical terms, as monks on a personal religious quest. During
their audience with the Mongol leader, they wished Khaidu a
long life and offered a benediction for his "kingdom." Having
won his confidence, they requested letters patent that would
ensure safe passage throughout his domains.[32] Khaidu provided them with the documents.

No doubt this exchange typifies the way East-West trade managed to persist despite the warfare that plagued Central Asia. Like the two monks, the predominantly Muslim merchants who led caravans along the Silk Road would generally portray themselves as apolitical (which they usually were), distancing themselves from Khubilai. More often than not, they probably received permission to enter Khaidu's dominions and a guarantee of safe passage through them.

The next stretch of the monks' journey was extremely arduous. As they moved southwestward, they traveled through treacherous terrain. Heading toward K̲h̲urāsān, the region comprising northeastern Persia and part of modern Afghanistan, they underwent harrowing experiences that Rabban Sauma's account refers to but barely describes. It specifies only that this stage of the trip was exhausting and that they lost most of their belongings. They traversed rugged mountains and desolate and dangerous deserts not unlike the Taklamakan. Mountain travel was fraught with perils such as bitter cold, biting winds, thin ice, and avalanches. As late as the twentieth century, voyagers in the region reported cases of frostbite and more serious injuries. Albert von Le Coq, the early-twentieth-century German discoverer of Buddhist and Nestorian paintings and texts in Central Asia, cited "mountain sickness" as still another hazard. He mentioned that headaches, nausea, and delirium plagued climbers in these mountains. A few travelers even temporarily lost the power of speech.[33]

In addition to the rigors of mountain and desert journeys, the monks' party surely faced expropriations by so-called rulers and harassment by brigands. Fear of brigandage was so pervasive that the Mongols issued laws requiring the members of a caravan to join together against robbers and mandating severe punishment for anyone who helped robbers.[34] Moreover, hunger and thirst were frequent companions to travelers in this region. Many voyagers of this era observed the skeletons of camels and humans who had perished in crossing this forbidding landscape, and it is likely the two monks did as well. This was no journey for the fainthearted.

THE TWO MONKS REACH THE ILKHANATE

Having survived these perils, Bar Sauma and Markos finally crossed into Khurāsān, the easternmost region of the Ilkhanate of Persia. The initial Mongol assaults had inflicted terrible damage on Khurāsān, which probably suffered more than any other area in the Ilkhanate from the Mongol invasions. Although Persian historians doubtless exaggerated the devastation, their general observations on the earliest Mongol attacks were accurate. The Mongols spared inhabitants who submitted without a fight but massacred those who chose to resist. Intriguingly, they made an exception for craftsmen whose skills they prized.

Despite the brutality of their conquest of the region, and the oppressive nature of the administration they established, the Mongols relied on Persians to help them rule. The Ilkhans recruited mostly Muslim Persians, but several prominent Jews and Christians also served. The Mongol invaders recognized that deliberate ravaging of the land—the basis of the economy of Khurāsān as well as of other regions of Persia—would be counterproductive because it would lead to reduced tax revenues. Accordingly, the Ilkhans issued repeated injunctions to Mongol and Persian officials to treat the peasants well, but their efforts failed. Many peasants had fled during the early stages of the Mongol attacks. Others faced inordinate demands for taxes and service in postal stations and other types of corvée labor. Governors, tax collectors and tax farmers, and local officials, known as *basqaqs*, extorted huge sums, most of which did not reach the Mongol treasury.[35] Such corruption and misrule characterized the early years of Mongol control—at least until the accession of Ghazan Khan in 1295—despite the Ilkhans' attempts to limit excesses. Moreover, the Mongols needed to pasture their animals,

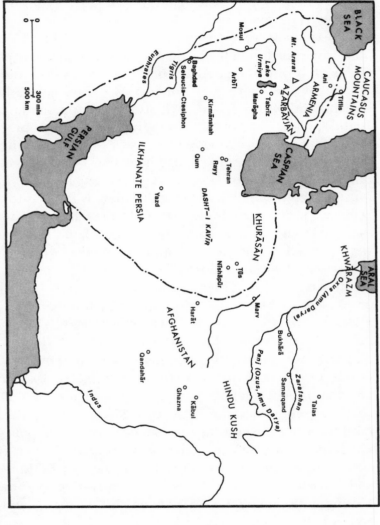

Ilkhanate Persia at the time of Rabban Sauma's arrival. (Copyright © 1992 by Morris Rossabi.)

which further reduced the land available to the peasants. In sum, the Ilkhans' plans for a sound government that might gain the approval or at least escape the hostility of Muslim Persians went awry.

The Mongols' religious policy also alienated Persia's Muslims, who constituted by far the largest segment of the population. Only one of the Ilkhans before the rise of Ghazan was a Muslim, and he reigned for just two years before being overthrown. However, the Ilkhans did not pursue an anti-Islamic policy. In accordance with the usual Mongol practice, they adopted an evenhanded approach toward the religions in the realm because they recognized that rulers of a multireligious empire needed to tolerate a variety of views. Many Muslims, however, believed that the Ilkhans favored foreign religions, particularly Buddhism and Christianity. It was true that the Mongols, surrounded by a large Islamic community, were pleased to have a minority of generally educated and prosperous Nestorian Christians to help them govern and conduct trade so that they would not have to rely exclusively on Muslims. The region's Muslims could also point out that Hülegü's son Abakha (r. 1265–1282), who was Ilkhan at the time of Sauma's and Markos's arrival, was a Buddhist, and that one of his wives, the daughter of a Byzantine Emperor, was an Orthodox Christian. However, in truth, Abakha did not discriminate against Islam or other religions, and no Ilkhan ever converted to Christianity.[36] Nonetheless, Muslims resented what they saw as the Ilkhans' prejudicial policy toward them. Mongol rule generally prevented Muslims from expressing overt hostility toward Christians or Buddhists— and Christians and Buddhists from expressing any toward Muslims—but antagonisms lay beneath the surface and, on occasion, flared up into nasty incidents.

These political and religious tensions deriving from foreign rule would have a significant effect on Bar Sauma and Markos, for they would spend most of the rest of their lives in the Ilkhanate. Because they had lived in Mongol-ruled

China, which faced tensions between Mongols and Chinese, the underlying hostility would not have startled them. Such political and religious antagonisms had not, in general, adversely affected them in China. Perhaps they anticipated a similar situation in Persia.

Having traveled through relatively uninhabited terrain, Bar Sauma and Markos reached a safer segment of their journey when they arrived at the town of Ṭūs (about thirteen miles northwest of Mashhad) in Khurāsān, probably early in 1280. The Mongols often treated Ṭūs as the capital of Khurāsān: One of the sons of the Ilkhan would frequently be appointed governor and stationed there. This renowned town was the birthplace of Firdausi (d. 1020), the author of the great Persian epic poem *Shāh-nāma*, which defined Persia in the same way that the Homeric epics defined classical Greece, and of Naṣīr al-Dīn Ṭūsī, the thirteenth-century theologian, astronomer, and government counselor. It was also the site of the tomb of the great Caliph Hārūn al-Rashīd (d. 809), whose court and reign were idealized in the *Arabian Nights*.[37] Despite its celebrated pedigree, Mongol troops had devastated the place sixty years earlier. According to the thirteenth-century Persian historian Juvainī, "nothing had been left of Ṭūs but the name and there were not more than fifty habitable houses in the whole town and even these scattered, one here, one there, in odd corners."[38] In 1239–40 an Uyghur named Körgüz, the Mongol-appointed viceroy of the region, had set about rebuilding the town, with elaborate mansions, a splendid bazaar, well-maintained channels for irrigation and water, and carefully planned gardens and parks. In 1247 one of his successors ordered the repair and restoration of the Saljuq Turk palace of Manṣūriyya, which added to the splendor and majesty of the place.[39]

Bar Sauma's account, as cut by the editor-translator, does not describe much of this splendor. It yields no information about the rebuilt center of Ṭūs, nor does it comment on the remaining signs of devastation the two monks might have witnessed around the town or in the region of Khurāsān. It merely mentions that their fellow monks in Ṭūs greeted Bar Sauma and Markos and that the two travelers immediately began to pray to show their gratitude to God, who, they believed, had protected them during their tortuous journey to Khurāsān. They asserted that their faith in the Divine had saved them. Sauma's account also notes that they lodged in a monastery on the outskirts of town.

While it describes meetings with Christians, it omits any mention of the much larger Muslim community. Shī'i pilgrims frequently arrived in Ṭūs, a revered religious center for Muslims because it was the site not only of the tomb of Hārūn al-Rashīd, the great Sunnī leader, but also of that of the eighth Shī'i Imām 'Alī al-Riḍā (d. 818).[40] According to the renowned Arab traveler Ibn Baṭṭūṭa, "when a Shi'ite enters to visit it he kicks the tomb of ar-Rashid [sic] with his foot, and pronounces a blessing on ar-Rida [sic]."[41] The tomb of 'Ali al-Riḍā was one of the holiest shrines for Shī'i Muslims, and nearby was a mosque of which one Arab geographer unequivocally said, "there is none fairer in all Khurāsān."[42] Many legends had grown up around these holy sites.

Did Shī'is resent the presence of the tiny Nestorian community in one of their holiest towns? Were the Christians, as a minority, fearful of the Muslims? The surviving account fails to say, but in fact, Mongol control generally maintained a surface peace among the diverse religions in the area.

Despite the warmth and harmony that Bar Sauma and Markos enjoyed during their stay in the monastery, they decided not to tarry. They had not lost sight of their objective, and asked Nestorian Persians to help them continue their voyage to the Holy Land by providing supplies. They departed, traveling via Āzarbāyjān and skirting the Caspian Sea to avoid the Dasht-i Kavīr Desert, which lay slightly to the south. They then intended to go directly south to Baghdad, the seat of the supreme leader of the Nestorian Church in Asia and the Middle East, the Patriarch Mar Denha. The Nestorian prelate was traveling, however, and happened to be in Āẕarbāyjān at the very time in the spring of 1280 that the two monks arrived in the region. He permitted them an audience in the town of Marāgha, the capital of the Ilkhanate under Hülegü and the site of the great observatory recently built by Hülegü for the renowned astronomer Nasīr al-Dīn Ṭūsī. Contemporaries described this observatory, located on a hill overlooking the town, as a "marvel" and "a treat to the eye." Its library contained 400,000 volumes, and the principal domed building, with a hole on top that allowed the rays of the sun to enter, offered a way to measure the mean motion of the sun and its elevation angle at various points in its trajectory. A visitor would also have found a vast and sophisticated array of astronomical instruments, including an armillary sphere and an azimuth ring (to measure angles of elevation) and would have met some of the world's most distinguished astronomers and mathematicians, whose achievements both the Chinese and the Europeans would come to envy. Wealthy Muslim benefactors had established a permanent endowment (*waqf*), similar to the special funding enjoyed by mosques, theological colleges, and hospitals, to support the activities at the observatory, still another cause for envy.[43]

This sophisticated city offered a fine setting for the first meeting between the two Nestorians and the leader of their Church. The encounter appears to have been very emotional: Bar Sauma and Markos bowed down before Mar Denha as soon as they saw him. Weeping profusely with joy, the monks were elated to have a personal interview with the head of their Church, and treated the Patriarch, or Catholicus, as almost a divine being. He in turn was moved by their faith and their obeisance. He was impressed to learn that they had come all the way from the land of the Great Khan Khubilai and that they wished to visit the holy sites in Jerusalem. He assured them that Divine Providence was with them and that they would reach their destination. Such harmonious dialogues characterized the meetings between the monks and the Catholicus over the next few days, offering the two travelers the stimulus and confidence to start on the last leg of their journey.

Bar Sauma and Markos naturally wished to visit the holy sites associated with Nestorianism in the area. They requested permission to tour the tombs, churches, and monasteries of Baghdad, the current center of the Nestorian Church, and the nearby town of Seleucia-Ctesiphon, the site of the oldest see in the Nestorian Church. With the Catholicus's blessing, they set forth town-hopping. Because they were now traveling in densely settled areas, they no longer required the sizable entourage of a caravan, and instead were escorted by a small contingent. Here again, though, Bar Sauma's account is preoccupied with religious sites, and the reader barely gets a glimpse of the secular features of the towns he visited, some of which had impressive bazaars, mosques, or gardens. Even the Nestorian buildings get relatively short shrift. They are merely mentioned, not described, perhaps because they were not as unusual and imposing as the Christian sites he would see and describe in Western Europe.

The fabulous capital of the 'Abbāsid caliphate, Baghdad, was the monks' first stop, but the account omits mention of the splendor of the city or of the damage it suffered as a result of Hülegü's and the Mongols' pillaging in 1258. It takes note only of the Great Church of Köke and the monastery of Mar Mari (ca. A.D. 300), named for one of the first missionaries of the Church and the founder of the see in Seleucia-Ctesiphon.[44] The narrative also ignores the Tigris River, on which Baghdad was situated, the mosques, the bathhouses, and even the Muslims.[45]

Similarly, the monks' subsequent travels to villages in the region bounded by the Tigris and Euphrates rivers produced merely a catalog of Nestorian monasteries, shrines, and tombs. The two went from one town to another, principally along the banks of the Tigris north of Baghdad. From there, Bar Sauma and Markos went to Beth Garmai to pray at the reputed tomb of the prophet Ezekiel. After a brief stop, they went to Arbil and Mosul, north of Baghdad along the Tigris and across the border from Armenia. Both towns had sizable Nestorian communities and many churches,[46] although Marco Polo had been scornful of the Christians of Mosul. He wrote, "they are the worst heretics . . . though they preach, they do not preach the truth in all things, but as heretics preach."[47]

The Nestorian communities in these areas welcomed the two monks, probably with more-than-usual warmth because hostilities had erupted between them and the larger Muslim communities.[48] Each side made incendiary remarks about the other, and Mar Denha in particular had alienated many Muslims by his enmity toward Islam.[49] In 1268 he had ordered his underlings to drown in the Tigris a lapsed Nestorian newly converted to Islam. In response, Muslims in Baghdad tried to kill Mar Denha and burn down his house. Three years later he and the Muslims blamed each other for an abortive attempt to assassinate the local governor. In 1280 tensions between the two communities in Baghdad and probably through much of Persia remained at a high pitch. So the Nestorians, who were decidedly in the minority, must have been heartened by the arrival of the two monks who appeared to have been sent by and thus have the favor of the Great Khan of the Mongols. Such support, even if only symbolic, gave hope to these isolated and outnumbered Christian communities. Nestorians in Mosul, which contained some fine churches and monasteries, and in Beth Zabdai, the northernmost town the monks reached, virtually on the border with modern Turkey, were hospitable, and the two monks responded by offering gifts and alms. Bar Sauma and Markos temporarily ended their travels at the monastery of Mar Michael of Tar'īl, near the town of Arbīl, the seat of a Nestorian Metropolitan.[50]

They returned to their monastic lives here and might have remained for a time, waiting for a propitious moment to continue their journey to Jerusalem. The Catholicus, however, had grander plans. Wanting to use them for his own purposes, he summoned them to Baghdad. He mildly reprimanded them for focusing on their inner peace while ignoring the needs of the larger community, saying, "We have heard that ye have been received into a monastery. This, however, doth not please us. For whilst the two of you sojourn in the monastery ye will be able to make perfect your own peace . . . and that is all that ye will do . . ."[51] With hypocritical piety, he urged them to minister to the secular world, but what he had in mind was essentially self-serving. He assigned them the task of traveling to the Mongol court and urging the Il-khan to grant letters patent to him—in effect, to confirm him as the Catholicus.[52] As a minority, Nestorians needed Mongol patronage, and they therefore sought the Ilkhans' blessing for newly elected Patriarchs. The reigning Ilkhan, Abakha, a Buddhist married to a Christian, was wary of alienating the Muslims in his domain and had not, as yet, blessed the anxious Patriarch.[53] It sometimes took several years after a Patriarch's election for the Ilkhan to confirm him, but in this case about fifteen years had elapsed. Very likely the drowning of the Muslim at the Catholicus's orders a few years after his election had contributed to the delay.

Mar Denha thus wanted to use the two respectable monks to help him gain legitimacy. Because Bar Sauma and Markos came from China and had credentials from the Great Khan Khubilai, the Catholicus probably believed that Abakha would grant their request for letters patent for him. The two monks undoubtedly understood his strategy. They politely asked for a quid pro quo: that Mar Denha provide an escort who would bring back the credentials while the two monks pressed forward toward Jerusalem. Sauma and Markos feared that the Patriarch would insist that they remain in the Ilkhanate, perhaps even in Baghdad. Thus their strategy: They would do him a favor if he, in turn, would facilitate their attempts to continue on their journey. A pragmatic, almost realpolitik element thus entered into their response to the Catholicus. So eager was he for the Ilkhan's blessing that he agreed to their condition. Sauma and Markos appeared to be on the way to fulfilling their religious mission.

The two monks now traveled with alacrity to the Ilkhanate's new capital, Tabrīz, about seventy miles from the former capital of Marāgha. It was the Ilkhan Abakha who had moved the capital to the fringes of Āẕarbāyjān. Although the ʿAbbāsid capital had been in Baghdad, in the south, the Mongols had never used it as their seat of government, a decision partly influenced by the conflict with their fellow Mongols of the Golden Horde. By establishing their capital in Marāgha (Arabic for "pastureland for horses") and then in Tabrīz, they guaranteed that a large military force would be stationed in the northernmost area of their lands and would thus be ready to repel incursions from the Khans of the Golden Horde.[54] In this way, they also laid claim to the rich pasturelands of Āẕarbāyjān, the main bone of contention between the two Mongol khanates. Besides, Tabrīz, situated in a plain dominated by Mount Sāhād, offered an appealing life-style to the Mongol rulers of Persia.[55] Mongol pastoralists could spend the winter in the elevated but protected valley of the Mūghān plain and move in summer to the less oppressively hot mountainous regions in Alatagh (in Armenia). Adding to Tabrīz's advantages was its location only about thirty miles from Lake Urmiya, the largest body of water in Persia, [56] giving the city a plentiful supply of water.

Another reason for the Mongols' choice of Tabrīz as their capital was the fact that, unlike Baghdad, which had fought desperately against them, it had not resisted the invaders from the East. Indeed, on three occasions its inhabitants had paid the Mongols off to prevent them from sacking the town, a type of transaction the Mongols sometimes made. As a result, the conquerors had not inflicted serious damage on Tabrīz.

By the time of the two monks' arrival, Tabrīz had replaced Baghdad as not only the political but also the commercial center of the Ilkhanate. Trade caravans that had earlier traveled through Baghdad now halted in Tabrīz, making Northwest Persia a key economic center. Bazaars flourished in the new capital. The Arab traveler Ibn Baṭṭūṭa, who lodged briefly in Tabrīz in 1327, was particularly impressed by its emporiums. He wrote that the city had "one of the finest bazaars I have seen the world over" and described the scene there as one in which his

> eyes were dazzled by the varieties of precious stones that I beheld. They were displayed by beautiful slaves wearing rich garments with a waist-sash of silk, who stood in front of the merchants, exhibiting the jewels to the wives of the Turks [the Persians were on good terms with some of the Turkic peoples], while the women were buying them in large quantities and trying to outdo one another.[57]

Since much of the city's commercial growth took place during the reign of the Ilkhan Ghazan (r. 1295–1304), Bar Sauma and Markos, who had visited Tabrīz before his time, saw a less splendid town than did Ibn Baṭṭūṭa. Yet Marco Polo, who had reached the city just a few years before the two monks arrived, also painted a portrait of flourishing international commerce transacted in its bazaars. He wrote too of the region's craftsmen who produced fine cloth with gold and silk, precious stones and pearls.[58] Merchants appeared to dominate the city to such an extent that one contemporary Arab geographer stated that "rich and poor alike occupy themselves with business."[59]

The vast array of goods for trade attracted merchants from throughout the known world, including Europeans. As early as 1264, a Venetian trader named Pietro Veglione (or Vilione) lived in Tabrīz and represented a group of European merchants.[60] By 1280 a small colony of Genoese merchants had set up temporary quarters in the town. In 1291 Pietro of Lucalongo, another Italian trader, would leave his commercial base in Tabrīz to escort the Franciscan missionary John of Monte Corvino to China to create a Western Christian presence in the Middle Kingdom.[61] Just as European merchants reached Tabrīz, so did Christian missionaries. When Bar Sauma and Markos visited, they found Dominicans and two Franciscan monasteries in the town.

A variety of Eastern Christian churches, including Byzantine and Armenian ones, also dotted the city. At least one Nestorian church had been constructed as early as 1262.[62] Marco Polo listed Armenian and Georgian Christians, Nestorians, and Jacobites as residents of Tabrīz. The Jacobites differed from the Nestorians, with whom they were often linked and on occasion shared a Patriarch, by challenging the doctrine of the two Persons of Christ, the divine and the human. In the Jacobite view, the so-called Monophysite interpretation, the two were fused into one Person. The Byzantine Empress Theodora, wife of the Emperor Justinian, had supported the efforts of the Jacobites' founder, Jacob Baradeus (d. 578; in Syriac, Ya'qub Bar-Addai) to disseminate the doctrine. An ardent Monophysite, she had both constructed churches and had clergy ordained. The Jacobites centered their activities in modern Syria and Iraq and, to a limited extent, Persia.[63] Unlike the Nestorians, they never spread farther east.

It seems fitting that it was in this cosmopolitan city—with its numerous Christian sects and Muslim orders and its mixed population of Europeans, Middle Easterners, and East Asians—that the meeting of the two monks and the Ilkhan Abakha occurred. The Mongol potentate took the arrival of the two foreigners in stride and inquired about their country of origin and then about the nature of their mission. They must have presented the credentials granted to them by Khubilai Khan and their letters patent from the Catholicus. His

uncle Khubilai's imprimatur surely affected Abakha's treatment of the monks, for he almost immediately fulfilled their
request that he bless Mar Denha as Patriarch. He gave them
letters confirming the Catholicus in his position and not only
permitted them to continue on their way to Jerusalem but
also ordered his officials to facilitate their journey.[64]

After their interview, which had succeeded beyond their
wildest expectations, Bar Sauma and Markos departed from
the Ilkhanate with strong support from the Mongol rulers of
Persia. Their first major stop was, not surprisingly, Ani,
which lay along a tributary of the Araxes River, in Armenia.
Ani was such a center of Christianity that it was "known as
the city of a thousand and one churches."[65] It had been the
capital of the Bagratid dynasty, which had ruled Armenia
from the late ninth to the early eleventh century. In 886 King
Ashot the Great had succeeded in securing Armenian independence from the Islamic 'Abbāsid rulers and founded the
dynasty, which supported a commercial, literary, and artistic
revival.[66] The Armenian churches in the town, which symbol-
ized liberation from the Muslims, had benefited from this
short-lived prosperity. However, internal rivalries among the
Bagratids weakened them and caused them to fall under Saljuq Turk and finally Mongol control from the late eleventh to
the early thirteenth century. The western region of the country, known as Lesser Armenia, had its own kingdom from
1080 to 1375 and generally managed to retain its independence. The Mongols briefly occupied Lesser Armenia in the
late 1230s and the 1240s but permitted the kingdom to continue in relative independence because it had not resisted
them.

Despite the political turbulence, commerce persisted for
much of this time, and wealthy merchants could and did provide funds for the construction of churches and monasteries.[67] Still, stability and peace did help make the region an
important thoroughfare in East-West trade from the 1240s
to about 1260, and the subsequent split between the Ilkhans

and the Golden Horde did intermittently interrupt commerce and would soon affect the plans of the two monks.[68]

Bar Sauma and Markos, in any case, capitalized on their
stay in Ani to visit the town's religious buildings, which included the great cathedral, the Church of the Redeemer, the
Church of the Holy Apostles, and the Church of St. Gregory
of Gagik. This remarkable town was a treasure trove of fine
architecture, in part because a late-tenth-century king had recruited the splendid architect who had also restored the Cathedral of Hagia Sophia in Constantinople. It was he who designed the Ani Cathedral, with its high dome, well-
proportioned semicircular arches in the wall of the apse, and
beautiful exterior columns. In the words of one specialist, it
"deserves to be classed among the more important examples
of medieval architecture."[69]

Once they had seen the most extraordinary of the buildings, the two monks left Ani, heading toward the Black Sea
ports. As they approached Georgia, however, they learned
that the road to these ports was treacherous because of robbers and the threat posed by both the Golden Horde and
their allies, the Mamlūks, who controlled Jerusalem and the
Holy Land and threatened the Christian strongholds of the
Outremer. Their Christian Armenian and Georgian hosts
dissuaded the monks from journeying any farther, probably
because of these dangers. Bar Sauma and Markos had no
choice but to accept the advice of those knowledgeable about
travel conditions. Thus they headed back to safety in the Ilkhanate.

By late in 1280 they were back in Marāgha, but, because
they were willing to bide their time, they were not discouraged. Their return delighted the Catholicus, who once again
wanted to use these prestigious emissaries for his own purposes. When he met with them, he began by commiserating
with them but concurring with the assessment offered by
their hosts in Armenia and Georgia. He noted that the journey to the Holy Land was perilous and that the routes had

often been severed because of the warfare and brigandage that afflicted the Middle East. Portraying himself as seeking to comfort them, he asserted that their sincere and pure-hearted veneration of the sacred relics and holy sites in his own Patriarchate was equivalent to a religious pilgrimage to Jerusalem. He slyly advised them to abandon their goal, but his motive for doing so had scant relation to any concern for the fulfillment of their spiritual mission.

His real motive emerged later in his discussion with the two monks. He announced that he wanted to appoint Markos, whom he now referred to as Rabban (or "Master") Markos, Metropolitan, or the leading representative of the Nestorian Church, in East Asia, and Bar (now "Rabban") Sauma as "Visitor-General" in China.[70] These appointments constituted rapid and dramatic promotions. Within Nestorian Christianity, the Patriarch or Catholicus was both head of the Church and a secular authority, leading an ascetic and celibate life while playing a political role in his domain. A Metropolitan ranked just below the Patriarch and held an extremely powerful and prestigious position. As the representative of the Patriarch, he was the most influential Church leader in the territory assigned him, which usually encompassed a sizable area.[71] In this era of rudimentary transport facilities, he was relatively independent of the Catholicus. He managed the bishoprics in his lands and had jurisdiction over the monks, priests, archdeacons, and deacons. Although the position of Visitor-General is not well defined in the sources on the Nestorian Church, it appears that the bearer of this title served as a principal assistant to the Metropolitan in his region.

Thus, the Catholicus was entrusting Marcos and Sauma with vital responsibilities and elevating them to exalted positions in the Church. Why did he make this precipitous decision? In the previous year he had appointed a bishop named Simon Metropolitan of China, but, even before setting forth for China, Simon had proved disloyal. He reputedly planned

to denounce the Patriarch to the Ilkhan and, on his arrival in
China, to Khubilai Khan. Mar Denha revoked his appointment and ordered him into a monastery, from which Simon
escaped only to be recaptured. Subsequently Simon and several of his followers were found dead, under mysterious circumstances, in the monastery. The Catholicus, on the one
hand, needed to divert attention from these potentially dam-
aging events and, on the other, had the opportunity to select
as his own legatees in China two monks known to and respected by the Mongols and the Chinese.[72]

Rabban Sauma and Markos attempted to fend him off.
First, they responded by flattering him, noting that his words
were equivalent to orders from Christ and that disobeying
him was tantamount to breaking a commandment. Yet they
pointed out that they had already endured a long and arduous journey from China. Moreover, they did not deserve
these promotions, and the new responsibilities were too bur-
densome for ordinary men like themselves. They wanted
simply to live in a monastery to serve Christ until their deaths.
The Catholicus replied that they were overly modest and
were indeed qualified to undertake the responsibilities with
which he had charged them. His tone indicated that he would
not countenance refusal, and Rabban Sauma and Rabban
Markos were compelled to comply.[73] Before they could return to their native land, however, Church authorities
learned that the war between Khubilai Khan and Khaidu had
heated up considerably, making the trip to China, via Central
Asia, extremely dangerous if not impossible. The Pax Mongolica was again disrupted, trade and travel were restricted,
and the two monks could not risk such a perilous journey.

Mar Denha nonetheless proceeded with the ceremonies
that accompanied such promotions in the religious hierarchy.
Emphasizing that the newly chosen Metropolitan needed a
proper Syriac name, the Catholicus had a good sample of
names written on slips of paper and placed on an altar.

Through divine intervention, according to Rabban Sauma's account of the monks' travels, one slip, with the name Yaballaha (or "God-given"), separated from the rest. Mar Denha added the term of respect *Mar* ("Your Lordship"), and Markos was thus transformed into Mar Yaballaha, the name by which he is commonly known.[74] The two monks received their credentials, but, unable to reach their assigned posts, they returned to the monastic retreat of Mar Michael of Tar'īl, as they had wished to do from the outset.

Their simple and ascetic yet apparently pleasurable life in the monastery ended abruptly with the death of Mar Denha in February of 1281. Sauma's narrative insists that Mar Yaballaha had premonitions of the Catholicus's death and of his own future role in the Church. Others in the Church hierarchy reputedly also had dreams and saw portents of the impending passing of their leader. Yet Yaballaha apparently did not at first take these signs seriously. Then, when he determined to obtain a pastoral cloak and staff, the symbols of his position as Metropolitan, from the Patriarchate in Baghdad, he encountered a friend en route who informed him that Mar Denha was indeed dead. He hastened to the Catholicus's church, entered, walked up to the bier, took off his coat, started to rip off his clothes, and wept inconsolably. Sauma's stereotyped account, as edited by the editor-translator, states that Mar Yaballaha fell to the ground like a dead man and had to be lifted to his feet by the rest of the somewhat more restrained mourners. After the mourners completed their rituals, the interment took place.

MARKOS BECOMES CATHOLICUS

The very next day, the leaders of the Church met in Baghdad to select a new Patriarch. After discussing the merits of several proposed candidates and candidly explaining their motives, the assembled notables unanimously chose Mar Yaballaha. Because political power was in the hands of the Mongols, a Patriarch such as Mar Yaballaha, who spoke Mongol, would have a decided advantage in dealing with the rulers of much of Asia. Mar Yaballaha was also familiar with and knowledgeable about Mongol customs, procedures, and laws, and this would in theory help him protect and advance the interests of the Church.[75]

Sauma's narrative portrays Mar Yaballaha as astonished at his nomination. He protested that he did not speak Syriac, the major and essential language of the Church, that he did not possess the eloquence required of a principal leader of the Nestorians, and that he was not well enough versed in the minutiae of Church doctrines. Church authorities regarded his response as a sign of befitting and laudable modesty and insisted that he was the most qualified candidate. With some misgivings, he finally accepted the nomination. Having done so, he returned to the monastery of Mar Michael of Tar'īl to inform his mentor of his election. Elated by the news, Rabban Sauma told his former student and traveling companion that his selection was God's will. The older man then demonstrated his political sophistication by advising Mar Yaballaha to seek the Ilkhan Abakha's blessing as soon as possible.[76]

Escorted not only by his friend and mentor but also by a representative group of monks and Fathers of the Church, Mar Yaballaha headed toward a mountain retreat near Tabrīz in Āzarbāyjān where the Ilkhan spent his summers. Since Mar Denha's anti-Islamic stance had embarrassed Abakha, the Ilkhan was doubtless relieved by the appointment of a Patriarch who had no discernible prejudices against Islam, and who had links with the Great Khan in Tai-tu to boot. When the monks asked his opinion of their nominee, he quickly blessed him, noting that "this purity [or sincerity] of thoughts and conscience is worthy of admiration . . . This man and his companion have come from the East to go to Jerusalem; this hath happened to them through the wish of God."[77] He gave the newly designated Nestorian Patriarch a cloak, a chair that resembled a small throne, a parasol identical to the one granted to and used by the royal family, a gold letter patent, and a great seal previously in the possession of Mar Denha, a symbol of the Patriarch's authority. He also confirmed that, as was customary, the Patriarch's commands were equivalent to law in the Nestorian community. Finally, to ingratiate himself even more strongly with these Christians, he provided Mar Yaballaha with funds to cover the expenses of his installation as Patriarch.[78]

Mar Yaballaha now prepared to assume his new role as the third Catholicus of that name, Mar Yaballaha III. He and Rabban Sauma traveled back to Baghdad, where his enthronement would take place. In November of 1281, Metropolitans from as far away as Samarqand, Lesser Armenia, and Tripoli witnessed and participated in the ceremonies.

At the age of thirty-six, Mar Yaballaha had come a long way from his native land and had attained the highest position in his Church. The mission of the two monks appeared to have reached its apex with this appointment. If later developments had not intruded, history would remember Mar Yaballaha as the more renowned of the two and would portray Rabban Sauma merely as the mentor of the Patriarch from the East. But there were more adventures in store for the older cleric. Meanwhile, political turbulence in Central Asia still prevented him from returning to China to take up his duties as Visitor-General, and Mar Yaballaha had already recruited him to manage the Patriarch's household.

Mar Yaballaha continued to enjoy good relations with the reigning Ilkhan. Abakha went south to Baghdad late in 1281 or early in 1282, after having learned of the Ilkhanate forces' disastrous defeat by the Mamlūks at the battle of Ḥimṣ in the fall. This conflict with the Muslims encouraged him to support as many of the non-Muslims in his domain as possible. Thus, with scarcely any prompting from Mar Yaballaha, the Ilkhan provided lavish gifts to the Nestorians and authorized their Church to levy an annual tax for the support of churches, monasteries, priests, and monks. Before it could actually collect the tax, however, the Ilkhan died. Having dispensed his patronage and spent an agreeable winter in the southern clime of Baghdad rather than the harsher environment of Āẕarbāyjān, he departed from the Nestorian Church's (and Mar Yaballaha's) center in early spring, perhaps to plan a campaign for revenge against the Mamlūks. Like many of the Mongol rulers in both Persia and China, however, Abakha was a heavy drinker if not an alcoholic, and after a prolonged and serious bout of drinking he collapsed and died on April 1, 1282.[79]

His death touched off the same kind of succession struggles that had plagued earlier Mongol leadership. Abakha's brother Tegüder and Abakha's son Arghun were the main contenders. After some testy deliberations, the Mongol nobility selected Tegüder as the Ilkhan in June of 1282, precipitating an extended armed conflict with Arghun's supporters that would last throughout his reign. Although he was the son of Hülegü, the ruler despised by the Muslims because of his conflicts with the Mamlūks, Tegüder had become a Muslim and had renamed himself Aḥmad.[80] He now adopted the title of Sultan, which distressed some Mongols and Nestorians.

Some scholars have suggested that their fears were unfounded, for the new Ilkhan did not initiate wide-ranging anti-Christian policies.[81] Yet his evident support of Islam and the Muslims surely aroused the apprehensions of these minorities in Persia. His reinstatement of Shams al-Dīn Juvainī, the brother of the historian 'Alā al-Dīn 'Atā'-Malik Juvainī, as Minister of Finance appeared to signal favoritism toward Islam. During Abakha's reign, Shams al-Dīn had been downgraded and was about to be severely punished because in 1280 he had been accused of having secret and traitorous dealings with the Mamlūks. His return to power and favor inspired great trepidation. Even more worrisome to Christians was Aḥmad's dispatch of two embassies to foster cordial relations with the Mamlūks. Ironically, both missions met with hostile receptions at the Mamlūk Sultan's court; the Sultan actually imprisoned the envoys on the second embassy. Yet Nestorians regarded even such preliminary and tentative efforts by the Ilkhan with great suspicion.

The new Ilkhan's brief reign certainly intimidated the Catholicus. The account of the two monks' travels discloses that Mar Yaballaha feared the Ilkhan and the advisers and ministers around him. Yaballaha named Shams al-Dīn Juvainī and the Ilkhan's confidant, 'Abd al-Rahmān (who eventually led the second embassy to the Mamlūks), as the Nestorians' and his main antagonists and persecutors.[82] According to the Catholicus, these officials denounced him to the Ilkhan as a supporter of his rival Arghun. In addition, they accused him of covertly sending letters to Khubilai Khan that offered devastating and perhaps incriminating appraisals of the Ilkhan.[83] Another prominent Nestorian, the governor of the region of Mosul, was also accused of being part of this conspiracy. Muslim ministers and sycophants at the Ilkhan's court joined in the surreptitious denunciations of Yaballaha and his allies.[84] So did two ambitious Nestorian dignitaries, a Metropolitan from the Ning-hsia region and a bishop from Arni, in Syria, who coveted the Patriarch's and governor's positions.

These fabricated accusations were persuasive enough that the gullible and, according to Sauma's doubtless biased account, unintelligent Ilkhan was duped into believing them. As a result, in the spring of 1283 he confiscated Yaballaha's letter patent and had the Patriarch, Rabban Sauma, and the governor of Mosul rounded up and escorted to a hastily convened tribunal. The three men immediately requested an explanation. Their escort responded that several Nestorian bishops, scribes, and counselors had come to the Ilkhan and accused them of plotting a coup and of defaming the Ilkhan, in letters to Khubilai Khan, as a renegade convert to Islam. The tribunal brought in each accuser separately, and each repeated the same charges against the three Nestorians. Yaballaha, demonstrating the quick-wittedness that had probably contributed to his selection as Catholicus, made a simple yet astute suggestion: He urged the authorities to dispatch a messenger to recall the courier who was traveling toward China with his letters to Khubilai. They could then examine the documents carefully for any evidence of sedition.[85] Pleased with this proposal, the tribunal requested that the Ilkhan follow this course. A messenger intercepted the courier, the letters were reread, and no seditious or defamatory passages were discovered.

Yet, according to Sauma's admittedly one-sided narrative, the Ilkhan still smoldered with resentment toward his captives. He detained them for forty days and sought any pretext that could be used to punish them severely. He was dissuaded from ordering their execution only by the strenuous efforts of some influential counselors and ministers and of his own mother.[86] A fervent Nestorian, she reputedly convinced him that he had nothing to fear from the Christian dignitaries, prompting him to release all three detainees and to return the letter patent to Yaballaha. Gratefully and quietly, Yaballaha traveled to the pleasant town of Urmiya, the seat of a small Nestorian community near Lake Urmiya, in the fertile region of Āzarbāyjān. While praying in a church there, he had a vision which revealed that he would never see the Ilkhan again.

Meanwhile, the Ilkhan Aḥmad pursued his campaign to quell the uprisings led by his nephew Arghun. In January of 1284 he first arrested and then executed one of his younger brothers who had secretly plotted with Arghun to overthrow him.[87] From January to July, he pursued Arghun's armies throughout Persia, finally overtaking, surrounding, and capturing his rival on July 11. Instead of immediately executing Arghun, he turned his nephew over to underlings while he returned to his home and his newest wife.

This decision proved an eventually fatal miscalculation. Aḥmad's personality and policies had aroused considerable opposition within his ranks. His attempted rapprochement with the Mamlūks, his high-handedness, his dismissal and thus alienation of several key officials, his empathy for fellow Muslims, and the growing suspicion that repressive policies against other religions were forthcoming had generated resentment even among his leading ministers. Within a few days of his precipitous departure from the front, a coup engineered by one of the disaffected officials whom he had ousted led to the freeing of Arghun and the resumption of hostilities. Aḥmad was now on the defensive. His enemies took heart that his own allies and ministers had betrayed him and immediately mounted a sizable force to pursue the Ilkhan. Once he learned of the well-organized detachments arrayed against him, he tried to seek sanctuary in the territories of the Golden Horde, the traditional rivals of the Ilkhanate, but it was too late. His tardiness in recognizing his precarious position doomed him, for his own followers prevented him from escaping and turned him over to Arghun. Under great pressure, the nephew reluctantly had his uncle executed on August 10.[88]

Arghun's victory and subsequent speedy coronation dramatically altered the lives and careers of both Yaballaha and Sauma. After the tribunal had cleared him and he had enjoyed his brief respite in Urmiya, the Catholicus had traveled to Marāgha, the center of the earlier Nestorian and Ilkhanate opposition to him and the site of Mar Denha's residence. Yet Yaballaha was uneasy, and Sauma's perhaps not entirely reliable narrative offers a justification for his fears. It asserts, without qualification, that Aḥmad had instructed dissident bishops to kill Yaballaha as soon as they learned of Arghun's execution.[89] There is no independent confirmation of this charge against Aḥmad; his defeat and death make it difficult to verify Sauma's account and perhaps vitiate the need to do so. Also unverifiable is Rabban Sauma's story of Yaballaha's dream. Before he learned of Aḥmad's demise, the Patriarch had a nightmare in which a young man appeared carrying a dish with a cloth covering a boiled head on it. Removing the

Arghun Khan in his garden. From a manuscript of Rashīd al-Dīn's fourteenth-century history of the world *Jami 'al-Tawanikh* in the Bibliothèque Nationale, Paris.

cloth, the unidentified man ordered Yaballaha to eat the head. Once Yaballaha had consumed most of it, the young man disclosed that it belonged to Aḥmad.[90] The account ends with the remark that just a few days later the Catholicus learned of Aḥmad's death.

His life and career saved, Yaballaha gathered his retinue and traveled to pay homage to the new Ilkhan, Arghun. He had an audience with the ruler and prayed for a long reign. Arghun, in turn, treated him with great deference, particularly when he learned of the trials and tribulations he had been subjected to by Aḥmad. Then, focusing his attention on the Nestorian religious dignitaries who had plotted against Yaballaha, Arghun ordered their execution. However, Yaballaha dissuaded the Ilkhan from killing the two errant Christians, arguing that the Church had its own punishments.

Having saved the lives of the plotters, Yaballaha now convened an assemblage of Church Fathers to look into the case. They advised him to strip the pair of their Church titles and offices and excommunicate them, advice he quickly implemented.

It now appeared that Yaballaha and Rabban Sauma, who had undergone so many adventures in journeying from their homeland, would spend the rest of their lives freely pursuing their religious vocations. They had already made their mark on history: through their daring and perilous trip across Asia, Sauma's account of their travels thus far (an invaluable source for future historians), their appointments to leading positions in the Nestorian Church, and their involvement in the political and military turbulence of the Ilkhanate between 1282 and 1284. They had earned the right to lead a peaceful life, focusing on their religious concerns and duties. But politics and diplomatic relations would soon intrude and offer Rabban Sauma an opportunity to undertake a delicate and significant assignment, one that had the potential to shape the future of Eurasian history.

3

THE MONGOLS, THE MUSLIMS, AND THE EUROPEANS

THE ILKHANATE AND A DIVIDED EUROPE

Rabban Sauma's new mission derived from European and Asian conflicts that stretched back several decades. At the time of Arghun's accession, the Ilkhanate was still surrounded by hostile neighbors. The Muslim Mamlūks were resisting the Persian Mongols in Syria and could potentially stir up fellow Muslims in Persia to overthrow Mongol rule; the Golden Horde was challenging the Ilkhanate in Āẕarbāyjān; Khaidu, the Central Asian ruler, was battling the Ilkhans over revenue and territory. Since the late 1260s, the Chaghadai Khan, whom Khaidu controlled, had been intermittently doing the same. The Mamlūks, standard-bearers for Islam, were seeking to dislodge the Outremer, the last remnants of the European Christian communities residing in the Middle East.[1] As before, these conflicts centered on land and control of taxes and tribute, with religious divisions also most likely serving to isolate the Ilkhans. The Mamlūks sought to maintain Islamic rule over the Middle East by compelling the Ilkhans to remain within Persia and perhaps even withdraw from Persia and move farther east. Moreover, much of the population within the Chaghadai domains consisted of Muslims hostile to the Ilkhans.

If the Ilkhanate's difficult relations with its neighbors had not changed much in the interval since Hülegü's death, neither had its means of dealing with the problem. It needed help from its allies more than ever. Khubilai Khan, however, remained preoccupied too far away, and Christian Lesser Armenia, though willing to help, still had too weak an army to be of much use.[2] Christian Europe, then, remained the likeliest prospect, in spite of the failure of Hülegü's efforts to secure an alliance.

When Abakha succeeded Hülegü as Ilkhan in 1265, he continued his father's policy of seeking to collaborate with the West against the Mamlūks.[3] Within a year of his accession, he dispatched an embassy to Clement IV (Pope, 1265–1268) to express an interest in negotiations and an alliance. Ambassadors in this and some subsequent Mongol embassies, aware of the Pope's interest in converting the "heathen," repeatedly assured the Christian dignitaries of the Ilkhans' desire for baptism and conversion. In his response, the Pope demurred about an alliance and made no reference to possible cooperation against the Muslim Mamlūks.[4] The Pontiff knew that the Ilkhan's mother and wife were Christians, and therefore mistakenly believed that Abakha was a convert to Christianity, but he still did not wish to promise European military assistance to the Mongols.

Part of his reluctance stemmed from conflicts within Europe itself and the inability even of his neighbors, the Italian city-states, to achieve unity. Venice and Genoa, the two leading commercial centers in the region, were hostile rivals, both eager to dominate Mediterranean trade. Sharply divergent policies toward the Byzantine Empire and the Outremer heightened the conflicts between the two cities. Venice, which in the Fourth Crusade had taken the Byzantine capital of Constantinople and had occupied it from 1204 to 1261, resented Genoese financial and military support for the Byzantine Empire. It also sought to exclude Genoa from trade and political involvement with the Outremer.[5] The Christian outposts in the Outremer suffered as a result of this conflict, because they did not have the concerted support of Christian Europe. Still fearful of the Mongols, they in turn had ruled out an alliance with the Ilkhans. Although a joint campaign by the Christian outposts and the Mongols might not have restrained Mamlūk expansion around the Holy Land, it might have averted the total collapse of the Outremer.

Contributing to the unrest and lack of unity in Italy was Charles of Anjou. The brother of St. Louis, Charles had been enthroned as King of Naples and Sicily with the blessing and support of the Pope in 1265. Charles had scant interest in the Crusades' objective of recapturing and "freeing" the Holy Land. His principal goal was to gain control over the Byzantine Empire so that he could shape Mediterranean trade to his own interest and profit, and he disdained cooperation with the Mongols of Persia because he believed that Abakha's marriage to a Byzantine princess ensured Ilkhanate alignment with the Byzantines. Thus, Charles and Venice frequently acted together against the Byzantines, whom the Genoese assisted.[6]

Prince Edward of England was the most enthusiastic advocate of a Crusade in his time. He was also deeply embroiled in Continental politics. As the grandson of Eleanor of Aquitaine, his father, King Henry III, had jurisdiction over Gascony and therefore owed fealty to the King of France. Thus the English monarchs of the period, including Edward, when he succeeded to the throne in 1272, had a stake in the Continent. Moreover, Edward was a first cousin of France's King Philip III (called "the Bold") (r. 1270–1285), because his mother's sister was St. Louis' wife and Philip's mother. Edward's desire to participate in a Crusade, like St. Louis', appears to have been motivated by religious zeal.

However, Edward was a complicated man, driven by contradictory impulses. At his death, contemporaries portrayed him as a great and noble patriot, but he was unstable and

Charles of Anjou. Statue by Arnolfo di Cambio. Palazzo dei Conservatore, Rome, late thirteenth century.

violent in his early years. In one particularly unpleasant incident, the young prince ordered his companions to cut off the
ear and gouge out the eyes of a youth who had offended him.
Although as King he improved administrative and financial
procedures in his realm and emphasized legislation by statute
rather than by fiat, his kingdom was beset by wars with Scotland, Wales, and France, which imposed severe strains on the
exchequer. An imposing six feet two inches in height, Edward was "a man of action" and "did not use the techniques
of persuasion and patronage with any real ease: his preferred
style was one of confrontation and compulsion."[7] Nonetheless, he was extremely pious and wished to promote Christianity in his own realm and throughout the world. He was an
ardent believer in proselytizing.[8] His devoutness also took
more unsavory forms. In 1290 he expelled Jews from England, in part to appropriate their wealth and assume the
debts owed them but also as a consequence of his religious
beliefs and consequent prejudices against the Jews.

Since the early thirteenth century, he and other members
of England's royal family had received many missives from
the Outremer communities requesting assistance against hostile neighbors.[9] Edward was eager to respond by taking the
cross. Helping ensure the security of the Outremer meant
contending with the Mamlūks and their Sultan, Baybars, who
were moving ever closer to the isolated Christian Crusading
communities.

In 1270, while he was still only England's Crown Prince,
Edward joined a Crusade sanctioned and called by Pope
Clement IV some years earlier but truly initiated by St. Louis,
who had been persuaded by his brother Charles of Anjou to
launch an assault against Tunis, a more vulnerable enemy
area than the Holy Land. Charles had ulterior political motives. He wanted to avenge himself on the Emir of Tunis, who
had supported the Hohenstaufens against Charles in a war
over Sicily. When Charles won, the Emir had refused to pay
annual tribute to Sicily.

A King, very probably Edward I. Early fourteenth-century painting on the Sedilia, Westminster Abbey. (By courtesy of the Dean and Chapter of Westminster, London.)

The Crusade did not fare well. The heat, unsanitary conditions, and infectious illnesses ultimately overwhelmed the invading forces, and St. Louis himself fell victim to disease late in the summer of 1270.[10] Edward meanwhile went to Tunis and was chagrined to learn that Charles and the Emir had negotiated an agreement, which ended hostilities and led to renewed Tunisian tribute payments to Sicily.

Though disillusioned by Charles's cynical suspension of the Crusade in return for material gain and distressed by news that his father was seriously ill, Edward decided to persist. On arriving in Acre, one of the remaining strongholds of the Crusader states, in May of 1271, he discovered, to his dismay, that Venetian merchants traded extensively with the Mamlūk enemy. Because he could not rely on other Europeans to continue to support his Crusade, he turned to the Mongols in Persia. He sent an embassy to Abakha to propose a joint campaign against Mamlūk positions in Syria, with the Ilkhanid forces to attack from the east.[11] However, the Ilkhans were preoccupied by conflicts with the Chaghadai Khanate. Abakha had to concentrate on his eastern frontier.[12] Although he earned a smashing victory against the Central Asians in July of 1270, he could not respond wholeheartedly to Edward's overtures.

Bereft of dedicated allies and with a relatively small force under his command, Edward nonetheless continued his campaign for about a year. After several skirmishes and standoffs, all sides were war weary, and in May of 1272 they negotiated a truce that guaranteed the security of the Outremer communities for ten years. The Mamlūk Sultan could thus concentrate on the Mongols while preparing for a later assault on the Crusader states. Edward returned home after being wounded in an assassination attempt on June 16 by a Muslim of the Ismā'īlī order. He left behind a tarnished image. As a recent biographer of Edward writes,

> He showed little real statesmanship . . . After the Tunis debacle, Edward showed remarkable obstinacy in persisting

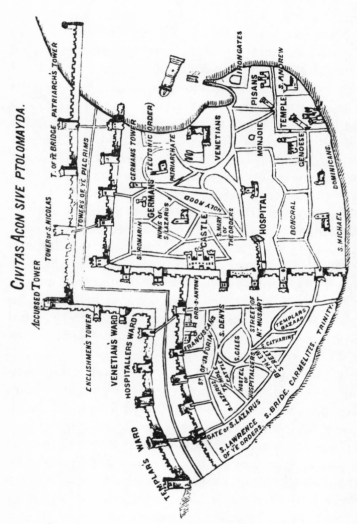

Modern reconstructed plan of Acre showing the locations of the residences of the Knights of the Hospital (Hospitallers) and the Knights of the Temple (Templars), as well as the sections for the various European groups based in the town. Whereabouts unknown.

in going on to the east with a totally inadequate force . . .
In Palestine, Edward's diplomatic efforts to obtain the cooperation of the Mongols achieved little, and in military
terms his troops were too few to achieve much.[13]

Meanwhile, Abakha recognized that the suppression of the
Mamlūks and the occupation of the Holy Land—which remained a Mongol goal—and other areas of the Middle East
required unity and concerted effort with the West. A new
Pope, Gregory X had been invested in 1272, and Abakha
hoped to interest him in joint maneuvers against the Mamlūks.[14] To this end, in 1273 Abakha dispatched a mission accompanied by David of Ashby, who had remained in Persia
after serving as a Western emissary to the Ilkhan Hülegü in
1260. The embassy arrived in Lyons as ecclesiastical and political leaders gathered there for an Ecumenical Council
called by Gregory X in 1274 (although the Khan's ambassadors met only with the Pope).

Having resided in Acre for a time, Gregory X was eager to
recapture the Holy Land and protect the Crusader states. He
hoped to persuade the European rulers to unite for a major
onslaught against the Mamlūks. Edward I, who had by this
time become King of England and was the only enthusiastic
proponent of a Crusade among Western Europe's monarchs,
did not attend because he did not return from the Crusade
in Tunis until August of 1274.[15] A representative from the
Byzantine Emperor, Michael Palaeologus, came to the Council to ask the Pope to induce Charles of Anjou to call off any
planned invasion. The Pope did urge Charles to lay down his
arms, and he evidently was persuasive; Charles temporarily
delayed any assault on the Byzantine Empire.[16] In return, Michael agreed to a union of the Eastern Orthodox Church
with the Catholic Church, a major coup for the Pope. But any
rejoicing proved premature; the union never took place. The
Pontiff was less successful in eliciting support for his proposed Crusade. He died in 1276, having been unable to re-

spond positively to Abakha's plea for a joint effort against the Mamlūks.

Like his father Hülegü before him, Abakha did not initially realize that Europe in many ways resembled the Mongol world in its fragmentation. He continued to try to secure an alliance with European Christians. In 1276 he sent two Georgian Christians, James and John Vassalli, to the Vatican to renew his proposal for cooperation, but John XXI, who became Pope that year, lacked Pope Gregory X's crusading zeal. Under Pope John, the Papacy reverted to its policy of welcoming the Ilkhan's envoys in the hope of converting the Mongols to Christianity but not committing itself to a political alliance.[17] The mission of 1276 was thus, for Abakha, an abject failure. Similarly, an embassy he dispatched in 1277 to European courts reached London but apparently did not have an audience with Edward I—or indeed any other European monarch—and failed to elicit pledges of alliance.

While the various Italian city-states, the Byzantine Empire, and the Outremer continued to pursue their own agendas—which left no room for an alliance with the Mongols—the European states, even more remote from Persia and the Holy Land, remained unable to respond favorably to Abakha's request. Edward I, still an enthusiastic proponent of a Crusade, was diverted by political challenges and wars in Wales in 1277. France's King Philip III, intent on acquiring additional territories in France through marital alliances as well as expropriation of the lands of local rulers who died, differed considerably from his father, St. Louis. Through the 1270s he betrayed scarcely any interest in the Holy Land or in alliance with the Ilkhans, showing more concern with developments in France as well as with promoting the success of his uncle Charles of Anjou in Naples and Sicily.[18]

This survey of European-Mongol diplomatic relations reveals some of the rifts among the Europeans that prevented them from accepting Abakha's overtures. Of course, it does not do justice to the complexities of the economic and political developments of that time and to the numerous intra-European pressures and distractions faced by secular and religious leaders. Each of the European rulers had differing objectives and interests, reducing the possibility of concerted action. A few of them even traded, usually clandestinely but occasionally openly, with the theoretically despised Muslims.

Given this evident inability to achieve cooperation, Abakha had little recourse but to avoid full-scale warfare. He could not, for example, take advantage of the death of Baybars in 1277.[19] He learned that the main Mamlūk force had retreated to Syria after a successful campaign against the Saljuq Turks, but he simply did not have a big enough army at his disposal to pursue and face them as well as the other Mamlūk troops, already in Syria, who would surely come to their assistance in case of attack. He also failed to capitalize on turbulence among the Mamlūks evidenced by the succession of Baybars's weak son Baraqa and Baraqa's subsequent overthrow by the Sultan Qalawun in 1279.

Thus, Abakha did not make a concerted effort to expel the Muslims from Syria until 1281. In that year he assigned his brother Möngke Temür to take charge of the 40,000 troops to be dispatched westward. Without the extremely able Abakha at its head, the expedition faced a difficult time. On October 30 the Mamlūk and Ilkhanate forces met in Ḥimṣ, a Syrian town just north of modern Lebanon. Before the day was out, Möngke Temür had been wounded and his forces routed, and he and the remnants of his army barely escaped.[20] Abakha died a few months later, without having avenged this humiliating defeat.

Because Abakha's successor, Aḥmad, was sympathetic to Islam, he did not, during his brief reign, conduct any campaign against the Mamlūks, nor did he dispatch envoys to Christian Europe to seek an alliance. Thus, Abakha's plans for an anti-

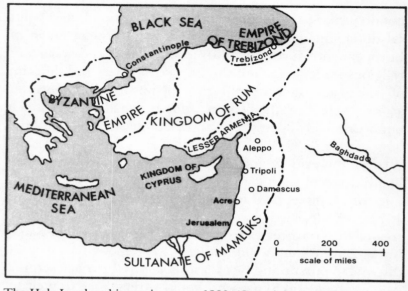

The Holy Land and its environs, ca. 1280. (Copyright © 1992 by Morris Rossabi.)

Mamlūk coalition to recapture the Holy Land were temporarily abandoned.

ENCOURAGING SIGNS IN EUROPE

Events in Europe during this time initially exacerbated the Continent's divisions but ultimately improved prospects for an alliance with the Mongols. By the early 1280s, the Ilkhans' longtime foe Charles of Anjou was on his way to losing his power. In October of 1281 Charles persuaded Martin IV (Pope, 1281–1285), a Frenchman, to excommunicate the Byzantine Emperor and abandon the union of the Catholic and Orthodox churches that had been negotiated at the Council of Lyons. He could thus portray an invasion of the Byzantine Empire as a Crusade against a heretic.[21] A successful attack on the Byzantines, however, would require supplies and financial resources, some of which had to be extracted from Sicily. The Sicilians already resented being ruled by the

French in general and Charles in particular, and the added burden of taxation finally provoked the insurrection known as the Sicilian Vespers. On March 30, 1282, they rose up and quickly took control of the island, a devastating blow not only to Charles but also to the Papacy, which had supported him. Peter III of Aragon, who supported the Sicilians, captured Charles's son in 1284. In the following year, Charles himself died of natural causes.

With Charles no longer involved in European politics, new alignments, which offered new opportunities for the Europeans as well as for the Ilkhanate, developed. It was possible that the remaining European rulers, who were less suspicious than Charles had been of the Ilkhanate, would be more willing to join with the Mongols in an anti-Mamlūk alliance. The death of Charles also prompted Venice to abandon its plans for an attack on the Byzantine Empire and, in 1285, to negotiate a treaty with the Christian Empire in the East, leading to a resumption of trade from the Adriatic Sea port to the port of Constantinople. Peace between the major powers in Italy—Genoa, Venice, and Naples and Sicily—and the Byzantine Empire also created prospects for a more united Southern Europe and Mediterranean.

Meanwhile, despite rebellions and other problems in England, Edward I remained a staunch supporter of a Crusade. Aside from his religious zeal, he may have had new political motives for seeking closer ties to the Mongols. He was contemplating a marital alliance with what he perceived as a Christian ruler among the Mongols of Persia.[22] Another political consideration was the current relatively vulnerable state of the Mamlūks. The Master of the Knights Hospitallers, a military religious order originally designed to care for pilgrims who became ill, informed Edward that the battle of Ḥimṣ had weakened the Mamlūks and the time was ripe for a new Crusade, particularly if the Mongols joined in an attack.[23]

Still, realpolitik dictated that Edward's first priority was maintaining control within his borders. In 1283 he was forced to divert funds allocated for a Crusade to the suppression of a revolt in Wales.[24] Nonetheless, his sincere desire to recover the Holy Land promised an opportunity for the Ilkhans.

The Vatican too underwent changes in the 1280s that offered possibilities for cooperation with the Mongols of Persia. The death in 1285 of Pope Martin IV, a supporter of Charles of Anjou and thus not a friend of the Ilkhans, and the subsequent election of Honorius IV (Pope, 1285–1287), a Roman who was not as adamantly anti-Mongol, resulted in a change in policies. The new Pope adopted a conciliatory attitude toward Italian city-states that had been alienated by Martin's strong sympathies with Charles. Because he shared little of Charles's animus toward the Byzantines and the Mongols, he was a more active proponent of a Crusade against the Mamlūks, which would naturally mesh with the Ilkhan's plans. To secure funding for and actual participation in a Crusade, the Pope appealed to Edward, the monarch most devoted to the dream of a Christian-controlled Holy Land.

Believing that he had an admirable negotiating position, Edward sought, in his reply, to elicit concessions from the Pontiff. He asked first to be appointed chief commander of the Crusader forces and second to be authorized to levy tithes to cover the expenses entailed by the Crusade.[25] Pope Honorius, fearful of alienating other princes and monarchs, delayed naming Edward as the proposed Crusade's leading standard-bearer but ordered him to head for the Middle East no later than Christmas of 1285. Edward's response was noncommittal. He still wished to take part in the Crusade, but he was realistic enough to want to gain as much revenue as possible, which he could, if necessary, divert to crush further outbreaks in Wales and Scotland. Despite this opportunistic stance, it seemed that Edward could be expected to respond favorably to an overture by the Ilkhan if no major rebellion within Britain erupted.

Continuing Mongol-European interchanges added to the renewed potential for cooperation against the Mamlūks. In 1278 Pope Nicholas III had sent a delegation of Franciscans to instruct the Great Khan Khubilai in Christianity, but they had halted in the Ilkhanate court, so the Mongols of Persia perhaps assumed that the mission was meant for them.[26] Similarly, early in 1285, after the turbulence occasioned by the reign of the Ilkhan Aḥmad, Arghun sent a letter to Pope Honorius. In the letter, which reached the Pontiff that May, Arghun assured Honorius that the Christians in the Ilkhanate had been granted exemptions from tribute payments and that he and his family, as long ago as the time of his grandfather Hülegü, had a heritage of tolerating and indeed favoring Christians. Emphasizing this attitude, he then proposed a joint attack on Syria.[27] Like his predecessors stretching back to the 1260s, Honorius was unwilling to make a political commitment to the Mongols of Persia. Moreover, he was already having a hard time persuading Europe's monarchs to unite in a crusading effort. Yet he did not reject Arghun's proposal out of hand, and there remained a glimmer of hope, at least in Arghun's eyes, that a joint campaign could be mounted.

Meanwhile, some private citizens were advocating greater involvement and cooperation with peoples outside Europe. Ramon Lull, one such influential figure, who was born in Mallorca around 1235, wanted to establish colleges for the training of missionaries that would emphasize foreign languages as well as theology. Although his contemporaries often labeled him a visionary or a fanatic, he persisted in his views, and in this critical period, between 1283 and 1285, he produced a work of fiction that embodied his "missionary spirit."

Blanquerna, his "thirteenth-century romance," proposes that the Pope "ordain that to all monks that had learning there should be assigned friars to teach divers languages."[28] Messengers would be dispatched to the lands of the "unbelievers" to entice some of them to come to Europe, where they could teach their tongues to the Europeans. Lull described the possibility of organizing groups of fifty "Tartars," i.e., Mongols, and ten friars who would teach each other their languages. He counseled Europeans to provide elaborate gifts to the Tartars before the foreigners returned to their homelands, in the hope that the Tartars would praise Christianity and Christians when they reached the courts of the Khans. He predicted that about thirty of each group of Tartars would convert to Christianity. According to his scenario, the Pope would then instruct the new converts, accompanied by five carefully selected friars, to return to the Great Khan's court to propagate the teachings of Christianity.[29] Lull's optimistic missionary program, as well as those of other like-minded Europeans, offered Arghun an opportunity. By parading the Mongols' toleration toward Christians and intimating that Christianity was making inroads among the "Tartars," he could conceivably ingratiate himself with the Europeans and lure them into an alliance against the Mamlūks.

4

An Embassy to the West

ORGANIZATION OF AN EMBASSY

By 1286 Arghun was prepared to dispatch a delegation to the West to seek help in defeating the Mamlūks and forcing them out of Syria and the Holy Land. He was feeling particularly hard-pressed not only by the Mamlūks but also by the Turks, Kurds, and other Muslims who often cooperated with the Mamlūks in attacking Nestorians and communities of other Christians in his domains.[1] He would try to secure the Europeans' assistance, indeed to persuade them to launch a Crusade; in return, he would offer them jurisdiction over Jerusalem and a guarantee of the security of the Outremer communities. He now believed that they might come to an agreement if his embassy sufficiently impressed them. Thus, the composition of the embassy was critical. Arghun would be best served if he could recruit a well-traveled, sophisticated, and admired envoy fluent in several foreign languages. Another useful, if not essential, qualification was that the envoy be a Christian. If possible, he ought to be highborn or at least in a respected occupation.

On every count, Rabban Sauma was an ideal choice. He had traveled extensively through Asia, from Tai-tu to Tabrīz, and had shown a courageous and intrepid spirit in undertaking a demanding, difficult, and dangerous journey to secure a glimpse of the Holy Land and other religious sites and relics. He was certainly sophisticated, having dealt with Chinese and Mongols in China, Turkic peoples in Central Asia, and Armenians and Persians in the Middle East. He was literate and had spent much of his early life in study and meditation. From childhood and early adulthood, his devotion to his faith and his scholarly work had earned him the admiration of the Önggüd community and had impressed Nestorian leaders as well as the secular hierarchy in Persia.

His skill in a variety of languages no doubt contributed to his reputation. His earliest languages were Turkic and spoken Chinese, he could read Syriac, and he probably knew Mongol as well. His years in Persia had given him the opportunity to become fluent in Persian. In fact, he would write his account of his travels in Europe in that language. A few Italian merchants as well as a few European ambassadors to the court of the Ilkhans had mastered Persian, so Rabban Sauma could readily find interpreters able to translate his Persian into the European languages. Because Arghun was eager to send a Christian to the Western Christian world, the monk's status as one of the leaders of the Nestorian Church in the Middle East also recommended him. Such an emissary would surely strike a responsive chord in Christian Europe. In addition, his closeness to the Patriarch made him an attractive candidate and would impress Europeans.

When Arghun requested from Mar Yaballaha the name of a suitable Nestorian ambassador, therefore, the choice was obvious. Yaballaha recommended his master, old traveling companion, and good friend Rabban Sauma as the "wise man capable of undertaking [such] an embassy."[2] Yet on the eve of Sauma's departure, Yaballaha was reluctant to have his indispensable helpmate leave. He said that without Rabban Sauma "my affairs will fall into a state of confusion."[3] Yaballaha would naturally have had misgivings about being separated from the comrade who had managed his household so well since he had been elected Patriarch. Rabban Sauma too must have needed to be convinced to undertake this mission. Doubtless one of its attractions for him was the possibility of visiting some of the holy sites and seeing some of the Christian relics in the Byzantine Empire and the West, and the opportunity to meet with leaders of the Catholic Church was of as much importance to him as the diplomatic objectives at stake.

Presented with these enticements, Rabban Sauma agreed to lead a mission to the West, an assignment that he never would have foreseen when he set forth from China about a decade earlier. He would be the first ambassador from the Ilkhanate to meet any European monarch, the first to write an account of his travels—and of course the first man from China to reach and write about Europe. Arghun gave him letters and oral communications to be delivered to the Pope, the Byzantine Emperor, and the Kings of France and England, as well as presents for the Pontiff and each of the monarchs. The Ilkhan also provided him with gold for his expenses, thirty good riding animals, and a letter-patent that ensured safe passage.

The account of Rabban Sauma's travels does not reveal the contents of the letters to the Western rulers. Nor does it describe the instructions given to Sauma.[4] What was he authorized to offer the Pope, the Byzantine Emperor, and the European monarchs in return for their support? What treatment should he consider unacceptable? Was he ordered to bring back a report on economic, social, and military conditions in the lands through which he traveled? Arghun and the officials at the Ilkhanate court no doubt told him to be as observant as possible and to record whatever would be of use to the Mongols of Persia.

We do know that on his return from Europe he submitted to the Ilkhan a report on the specifically diplomatic aspects of his mission, which has been lost. Perhaps he saved some of his remarks on such matters for this document, leaving them out of the other accounts he wrote as he traveled, the more general, inclusive report for his fellow Nestorians and his diary on the journey, both of which the Syriac editor-translator worked from. Perhaps this translator cut some material of this type. At any rate, these omissions from the narrative that has come down to us frustrate efforts to gauge the exact significance and success of Rabban Sauma's embassy. Nonetheless, a good deal of information on the diplomatic side of his journey is included, and a close examination of his account of his travels and observations of the people, customs, and circumstances he encountered yields insights into his attitudes and some of the goals of his mission.

Early in 1287, accompanied by interpreters, animal grooms, and other assistants, Rabban Sauma set forth, with high hopes, for the Byzantine Empire and the West. His travels this time would not be as perilous as his trip from China to Persia. The terrain was not as treacherous as the Gobi and Taklamakan deserts and the lofty mountains along the Silk Roads. And, because the regions he would now traverse were more densely populated than Central Asia, he faced less risk of thirst and starvation. The Mediterranean Sea was the most significant obstacle, because storms could so suddenly erupt there. One similarity of this trip to his earlier travels was the prevalence of bandits and protection costs along the way, but pirates navigating the Black Sea and the Mediterranean were an added source of concern. Another change would be that once he reached Europe, he would ride on horses and donkeys rather than camels.

Among those who accompanied Rabban Sauma were an Italian interpreter named Ughetto and a merchant and interpreter named Thomas of Anfossi, both probably returning to the West from China via Persia.[5] Thomas, who came from a Genoese banking family, apparently knew Persian as a result of frequent commercial forays into the Ilkhanate. A Nes-

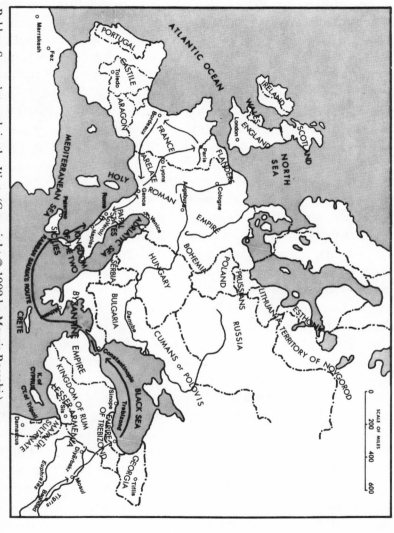

Rabban Sauma's travels in the West. (Copyright © 1992 by Morris Rossabi.)

torian named Sabadinus, who is otherwise unidentified, also
escorted Rabban Sauma, but it is unclear whether he served
as an interpreter, was a merchant, or was simply a cleric
brought along as an assistant.

Sauma's account does not describe the route that this mul-
tiethnic party traveled to the Black Sea, where it would embark for Constantinople. They probably went northward
along a well-established caravan road through Mosul, Jazīrat
ibn-'Umar, and Diyārbakr, in Mesopotamia and reached the
Black Sea and the Christian world at Trebizond. The trip was
uneventful, and the mode of travel and the pace were not
particularly demanding.

The unique Middle Eastern institution known as caravanserais, located approximately eighteen to twenty miles apart
along the major trade routes in the region, surely facilitated
their travels. Caravanserais often lay adjacent to water holes
or streams, because water was a vital prerequisite for these
stopovers. They offered provisions and rest for men and animals. The typical caravanserai consisted of a large central
court surrounded by walled-in areas, not quite rooms, for
lodging, bathing, and praying. The more elaborate ones also
included, on the one hand, mosques and, on the other, broth-
els and bathhouses. Some may have had prayer rooms for
Jews, Christians, and other non-Muslims. Defense was a
prime consideration in the construction of caravanserais. It
was probably for the sake of security that the buildings were
constructed around a central courtyard. Storytellers, danc-
ers, and other entertainers provided respite and amusement
for weary travelers. Many Arabic folk tales probably originated in such a milieu. Merchants, camel grooms, and escorts
met here and traded information on mundane matters as
well as on loftier political affairs.

The presence of caravanserais belies the archaic
nineteenth-century European view that one result of the
Mongol invasions was that "the oases, well known for their

fertility, lay barren and neglected; the trade in arms and jew-
ellery, in silks and enamels, so celebrated throughout Islam,
decayed for ever." Rabban Sauma and his companions no
doubt made use of and were grateful for these accommodations.[6]

At Trebizond, Sauma and his embassy boarded a ship for
their journey over the Black Sea. They did not experience
any delay in getting passage on a vessel, an indication that
boat traffic and commercial activity along the Black Sea were
lively. A regular and frequent ferry service was conducted
among the ports on what Sauma referred to as the "Sea of
Meka."[7] Arab and Byzantine sailors, renowned as great sea-
farers, transported merchants and other travelers to the west
on the Mediterranean as well as the Black seas, and to the east
on the Indian Ocean. Their ships, with hulls of Indian teak
and coconut wood and their planks stitched together rather
than fastened with nails, plied the waters along the coasts of
Africa, Asia, and Southern Europe. Unlike the Europeans of
the time, these sailors used the magnetic needle as a compass,
and their navigational skills were the envy of the world.

Yet long sea voyages were "full of hardship." The Byzantine ship that Rabban Sauma and his embassy boarded, with
its three hundred other passengers, was overcrowded. This
condition and the crude accommodations, with no bunks or
beds and hardly any food aboard, made for an uncomfort-
able journey. Storms accompanied by galelike winds and
huge waves were a great danger to travelers on the Black Sea,
and together with the hazards of reefs and shallows would
make "captain and crew" feel "only slightly less helpless than
the merchants."[8] The pirates of the Black Sea, with faster-
moving ships, also posed a threat. Fortunately for Sauma, the
trip to Constantinople would last only a few days.

He passed the time on the boat by delivering daily lectures
on the tenets of his faith. According to the editor-translator
of his narrative, his explanations charmed the mostly Byzan-

tine Orthodox passengers, and they respected him enormously. This characterization smacks of hagiography and doubtless exaggerates Sauma's abilities as a public speaker. Yet his later engaging conversations with the Catholic hierarchy and with the political leaders of Europe indicate that he could explain complex theological questions clearly and simply. At the very least, the passengers must have found his lectures a diversion from the tedium of sea travel. On this as on later legs of the voyage, Rabban Sauma also continued the diary that would be one of the centerpieces of his travel narrative.

IN THE BYZANTINE EMPIRE

Once the ship reached Constantinople, early in 1287, Rabban Sauma followed a pattern that he had established earlier and would continue in Europe: He attempted to make contact with the rulers of the land through which he traveled. When he reached the capital of the Byzantine Empire, he ordered two young assistants to go to the Emperor's palace gates and give notice of the arrival of an embassy from the Mongol court in Persia. The Emperor, Andronicus II (r. 1282–1328), quickly dispatched court officials to escort the envoys to the palace.

Andronicus directed that the Nestorian ambassador be greeted with great pomp and treated with suitable respect. The ceremonies welcoming him impressed Rabban Sauma, but, unfortunately, his account does not say much more about them. Nor does it describe the Great Palace of the Emperor, where they took place. It had been heavily damaged during the Venetian occupation of Constantinople. After the expulsion of the Venetians in 1261, Andronicus's father, Michael Palaeologus, had begun to restore it, rebuilding the walls that had been torn down and repairing the mosaics (depicting country life, the hunt, and other secular subjects) and the furniture in the interior.[9] The Great Palace differed from

Western European palaces in that it consisted of detached pavilions, not a single edifice, and was perhaps less imposing as a result. The architects followed a simple plan in designing it, and, in the view of a modern art historian, Byzantine palaces, the Great Palace among them, had "no very important architectural features of their own."[10] Nonetheless, for a contemporary like Rabban Sauma, the ceremonies and the building must have been impressive. At the conclusion of the rituals, the Emperor assigned Sauma and his attendants a place to stay in for the remainder of their visit. The envoys left the Emperor's residence for their own palace, where they would rest for a few days before returning for a more substantive conversation.

Rabban Sauma's dialogue with Andronicus is revealing in its omissions as well as in what was said. His account fails to record any attempt to broach the subject of an alliance against the Mamlūks. Keeping in mind the objectives of his mission, it seems unlikely that Rabban Sauma would have avoided the topic so entirely. Andronicus's response to such an overture must have been less than encouraging, if not wholly negative. Perhaps this is why Rabban Sauma's narrative omits any reference to political discussions or to gifts and letters presented to Andronicus, though the editor-translator's deletions may also have something to do with this fact.

The result, in any case, is that Sauma's conversation with the Emperor appears bland. The two men's first talk seems to have consisted largely of polite observations and concerned inquiries by the Emperor about whether Rabban Sauma had had sufficient rest after his long, arduous journey. His solicitude, however, encompassed nothing beyond perfunctory politeness and the granting of permission to visit Christian sites in the Byzantine Empire. Rabban Sauma's request to view religious locales and reliquaries deeply impressed Andronicus, whom a modern scholar has described as a "profoundly pious man."[11] His religious fervor and devotion to the Orthodox faith inspired a religious policy that diverged sharply from that of his dynamic and colorful father, the Emperor Michael Palaeologus. It was Michael who had been willing to form the union with the Catholic Church that was mandated in 1274 at the Council of Lyons. Andronicus would never have countenanced such a coalition. The Orthodox and Catholic religions were now distinct and competitive, making Rabban Sauma's task of securing an alliance with the entire Christian world difficult.

A further difficulty for Sauma was the fact that Byzantine Emperors had for some time been ambivalent about their relationship to the Ilkhanate court. Although his daughter Maria had been married to Abakha in 1265, Michael had not shared the Ilkhan's enemies. He had tried to steer a neutral course in the struggles between the Ilkhan on the one hand and the Golden Horde and the Mamlūk Sultanate on the other. For example, when a Mamlūk embassy reached Constantinople in the late summer of 1263, Michael welcomed them but refused to allow them to travel through his lands since Hülegü's ambassadors, who were at his court, would find out that he had done so.[12] Michael was unwilling to alienate the Ilkhans because he wanted their help in resisting anticipated assaults by Turkmen from Anatolia to his east and by Charles of Anjou from the west. Charles was also instigating the Bulgarians to attack Byzantine positions. However, the Sicilian revolt of 1282 defused the fear of an invasion from the west because it mired Charles in troubles in his own domain.

After Michael's death later that year, Andronicus continued his father's policy of maintaining commercial and diplomatic relations with the Golden Horde and the Mamlūks while resisting an alliance with the Ilkhans against the Muslim rulers of Egypt. He went on sending embassies to Mamlūk Egypt, sometimes dispatching them to accompany missions from the Golden Horde. Trade among all three states also persisted. The major difference between the concerns that faced Andronicus and those of his father was that, after the Sicilian revolt reduced the threat to Byzantium from the west, the significance of an alliance with the Ilkhans diminished somewhat. Andronicus would seek to cultivate good relations with the Mongols of Persia but would not favor a military or political alliance with the Ilkhans.

However, Rabban Sauma's religious mission evidently appealed to the Byzantine Emperor, and there was no reason not to grant the cleric's wish to tour the holy sites in and around Constantinople. Sauma was captivated by what he saw on this tour. Hagia Sophia riveted his attention, as it had that of most visitors who arrived after its construction in the sixth century. The Emperor Justinian had had it built to replace on a more grandiose scale the original church on the site, which had been destroyed in a fire in 532. Ten thousand workers had labored to construct the awe-inspiring church that Rabban Sauma visited. The dome, which soared to a height of 180 feet, rested on the four arches of the nave, and forty windows ringed its outer rim. Rabban Sauma mentioned the height and spaciousness of the dome, remarking on the difficulty of describing it well.[13] Although his account fails to take note of the lightness and brightness of the church—a feature that most other visitors commented upon—it does refer to the 360 columns scattered through the building.

The different colors and the high quality of the marble used for the columns captured Sauma's imagination. This material, in fact, dominated the decor. Natural green, white, and red marble was found in the columns, the walls, and the floors of the church. The beautiful slabs often created remarkable tableaux and, in the words of an art historian, "sometimes . . . were successive slices cut from a single block of marble, repeating one another to make continuous, symmetrical designs, and thus marrying nature with art."[14]

Rabban Sauma had no doubt never seen as grand a church

Dome, Hagia Sophia. Istanbul, sixth century.

Mosaic of the Virgin, Hagia Sophia. Istanbul, sixth century.

as Hagia Sophia; it was one of the architectural marvels of the Christian world. Besides, Christians were minorities in the regions where he had lived or through which he had voyaged, so they often did not have the resources to erect elaborate buildings. Marco Polo, for example, mentioned several Nestorian churches,[15] but he indicated that they were not grand and, in the words of a well-known historian, they "may perhaps have been lacking in ornaments."[16] Hang-chou, the capital of the Southern Sung dynasty of China and probably the most populous city in the world, had only one Nestorian church,[17] and most of the towns or cities Rabban Sauma had visited on his travels had only one or two, and these neither imposing nor ornate. Thus, Hagia Sophia dazzled him. It is the first church he described in detail in his narrative, although he had mentioned several monasteries and churches in passing and briefly discussed one church in Baghdad.

The contents of the church also overwhelmed him.[18] He saw many paintings and sacred relics and listed quite a number of the relics. The Venetians had looted many of the originals when they invaded Constantinople in 1204, so most of the objects Sauma saw were copies. However, he was either unaware or unconcerned that the so-called holy relics were not genuine. A mosaic of the Virgin, which he claimed was painted by St. Luke, thrilled him. His local escorts showed him what they identified as the hand of John the Baptist and parts of the bodies of Lazarus and Mary Magdalene. He also claimed to have seen the tombs of John Chrysostom and the Emperors Constantine and Justinian. According to his narrative, Constantine's tomb was made of red marble and Justinian's of green. However, Constantine was not in fact buried in Hagia Sophia, so Rabban Sauma appears to have been misinformed.[19]

Perhaps the most unusual site he visited was the tomb of 318 Orthodox Bishops in the Church of the Nicean Fathers at the Monastery of St. Michael, located just outside the city.

Sauma apparently believed the legend that their bodies had not deteriorated but remained pristine because of their service to the faith. Another purported relic he saw in the church was, in his words, the "stone which was laid on the grave of our Lord, when Joseph . . . brought Him down from the Cross. Now Mary wept on that stone, and the place whereon her tears fell is wet even at the present time; and however often this moisture is wiped away the place becometh wet again."[20] These were but a few of the many extraordinary things Rabban Sauma observed and commented on in Constantinople.

Both here and afterward, the narrative of his travels says very little about the ordinary life Rabban Sauma saw on his way from Persia to Europe or during his time in Europe. Later historians would certainly have been eager to know his views of the customs, clothing, products, and of course peoples he encountered. Was he intrigued by the prominent presence of women in public? Was he impressed by the high status of the Church and its role in politics? Was he dazzled or even interested by the goods and secular buildings he saw? Was he struck by the contrasts between marriage and funeral ceremonies, bathing customs, and the etiquette for conversations between social inferiors and superiors in the West and those in the Eastern lands from which he came? The deletions by the editor-translator preclude our ever having definitive answers to these questions.

Moreover, Rabban Sauma very likely tailored his observations to the audiences he was writing for. As indicated earlier, he would have focused on the details of his diplomatic mission for the now-lost report he was preparing for the Ilkhan. His fellow Nestorian clerics, for whom he was drafting the much more inclusive report on his trip to Europe, would naturally have been most interested in the religious buildings, relics, and rituals he observed. Because they would have supported the political objective of forging an anti-Mamlūk coalition, since they feared the growing power of the Muslim dynasty, they would have wanted to know something about his diplomatic transactions. They would also no doubt have been at least somewhat curious about how he had fared in general. Details about foreign cultures and societies, on the other hand, would probably have been less likely to concern them. Even what Rabban Sauma wrote in his diary might have been shaped by these considerations of his audiences' preferences, since he drew on it in drafting these reports.

Still, his stress on religion and diplomacy may well have simply reflected his own interests. His account of his trip to Persia had not suggested that he was particularly concerned with daily life in the cities he visited, although of course the editor-translator's deletions or simply the fact that Rabban Sauma was on less exotic and thus, to him, less intriguing ground may explain this. Nevertheless, it seems natural that, while he was in the West, Rabban Sauma's attention would focus, to the exclusion of much else, on remarkable religious sites of the sort he had so long wished to see and on his momentous negotiations with Christian monarchs. Given the nature of his mission, he would, in any case, have spent most of his time with those in power and with the clergy, and therefore have had relatively little contact with ordinary life.

Moreover, his guides in Constantinople and in Western Europe probably tried to steer him toward churches and monasteries and limit his contact with a variety of local people. First, they were proud of the magnificent sites they had to show. Second, they doubtless assumed a monk would be most interested in religious monuments. Third, they may have feared that the Ilkhan had sent Rabban Sauma to gather intelligence about the West, and so might have diverted him as much as possible from observing secular and, certainly, strategic sites.

It is hardly surprising, then, that Rabban Sauma dealt most frequently with the local elite and with the Church hierarchy,

An Embassy to the West ♦ 115

and evidently had or took few opportunities to meet with
people of different occupations and social groups in the cities
he visited. This pattern was not an unusual one for medieval
travelers, even unofficial ones. For example, William of Rubruck and John of Plano Carpini, the envoys from the West,
and Marco Polo, the merchant from Venice, met and con-
versed primarily with the Mongol elite when they reached
Mongolia and China.[21] Similarly, the fourteenth-century
Arab traveler Ibn Baṭṭūṭa generally talked with men in the
Muslim elite during his voyages to Asia and Africa.[22] It
would, in fact, be surprising to find that Rabban Sauma had
other than the most perfunctory contact with ordinary
people in the West.

Thus far, Rabban Sauma had fulfilled many of his religious
goals. Freely visiting the holy sites west of China was precisely
what he had aspired to from the very beginning of his journey. He doubtless realized, however, that it was useless to try
to pursue his diplomatic aims further in Constantinople. Andronicus was not about to ally with the Ilkhanate against the
Mamlūks; indeed he maintained trade and diplomatic relations with the Muslim rulers of Egypt after Rabban Sauma's
departure just as he had before. It was time for the Nestorian
envoy to move on.

Rabban Sauma had one final audience with Andronicus,
during which he expressed gratitude for the Emperor's hospitality and explained that the Ilkhan Arghun had ordered
him to go to the territory of the Franks, his term for Western
Europeans. The Emperor granted him permission to leave,
but not before providing the Nestorian cleric with gold and
silver to help cover the expenses he would incur. These gifts
would be useful, for his small entourage was about to embark
on a long sea voyage, and Sauma would need to purchase
passage and supplies, cutting into the subsidies granted him
by the Ilkhan.

In mid-April of 1287, Rabban Sauma and his embassy were

prepared to head toward Western Europe, with Naples as the first port of call. Before they set out, however, they visited just one more holy site. As he was about to board ship, Rabban Sauma learned of the Church of Saints Sergius and Bacchus, which housed some revered relics, and decided to see them for himself. At the church he viewed what were purportedly the heads of John Chrysostom and of Pope Sylvester, who he was told had baptized the Emperor Constantine. In fact, the so-called genuine head of John Chrysostom had been conveyed to Western Europe much earlier, so it must have been another head that Rabban Sauma saw.[23] Moreover, there is no evidence that it was Pope Sylvester who had baptized Constantine. Again Rabban Sauma's credulity led him astray.

In this, he was not unlike many medieval Christians in the West, who were uncritical in investigating and assessing religious objects and so-called sacred relics. Medieval travelers were often gullible too; Marco Polo wrote about humans with tails.[24] Rabban Sauma's status as an outsider makes his unquestioning attitude more understandable. He was traveling for the first time to some of the holiest sites of the Christian religion, having what must have been emotionally riveting experiences, during which doubts might be suspended or, even if felt, rarely expressed. As a Christian from a region relatively remote from the center of his religion, Sauma would not challenge much of what he was told. Moreover, he believed in a form of Christianity that emphasized cults of martyrs and pilgrimages to sites associated with them. Their tombs, their remains, and their possessions were objects of veneration.[25] Thus, the sacred relics and the pilgrimage sites in the West fascinated him. Indeed, his emphasis on seeing and describing such relics may have reflected a desire to obtain some, perhaps as gifts for Nestorians in the Ilkhanate. He certainly enjoyed viewing relics as much as he did fulfilling the diplomatic and political responsibilities of his mission.

After his detour to see these relics, Rabban Sauma boarded

a boat for what he described as a hazardous voyage to Naples. He wrote that many travelers had died trying to cross the seas to Europe, presumably as a result of shipwrecks and storms but also because of a "great serpent" that posed a threat to voyagers. En route, he was startled to witness the eruption of a volcano. His narrative implies that the volcano's site was surrounded by water (ergo, it was a small island), which might lead to an identification of the volcano as Mount Stromboli in the Lipari Islands, north of Sicily in the Tyrrhenian Sea. Yet it was the volcano at Mount Etna, on the island of Sicily, that erupted on Monday, June 18, 1287, and Rabban Sauma's description indicates that he saw an active volcano. Mount Etna, then, is no doubt the site "from which smoke ascended all the day long, and in the night time fire showed itself on it."[26]

ARRIVAL IN ITALY

After two months of travel, Rabban Sauma arrived, exhausted, in Naples. It is curious that the journey took so long. The distance from Constantinople to Naples is less than 1,500 nautical miles; assuming a relatively slow speed of 2.0 to 2.5 knots, the trip should have taken less than a month. Did the ship stop in a Mediterranean port en route? Was it simply anchored at night? Rabban Sauma's account does not provide any details.

When he reached the city, he no doubt anticipated a brief respite from the hazards of his trip before he continued on to Rome. True, a stop in Naples might appear to entail a certain risk, because the recently deceased ruler Charles of Anjou was no friend of the Ilkhanate. Yet Naples was not at war with the Mongols of Persia. Moreover, both the Mongols and the Europeans considered the person of an ambassador inviolable. In any case, Sauma cannot have been prepared for the devastating battle in the Bay of Naples on June 24, which he witnessed from the roof of the mansion that had been set aside for his party by the ruling House of Anjou.

The battle was yet another episode in the struggle between the Angevins and the Aragonese that had originated in the Sicilian Vespers revolt against Charles of Anjou. Since Charles had died in 1285 and his son Charles II (called Charles of Salerno) was imprisoned in Aragon, it must have been Charles of Salerno's son Charles Martel who was Rabban Sauma's host and one of the combatants in this battle, although the narrative inaccurately names Charles of Salerno as the leader of the Angevin forces. The Aragonese simply overwhelmed Charles Martel's troops, and Sauma wrote that 12,000 of Charles's men perished.[27] This figure seems improbably high for one day's casualties; it would have been impossible in any case for Rabban Sauma to gauge the numbers. Because, as a cleric, he had surely observed few if any battles, the military details he offered are suspect. His observation that the combatants did not attack civilians, however, carries more weight. The Mongols, the group that Rabban Sauma was most familiar with, often engaged in total war, in which they did not make distinctions between combatants and noncombatants. The razing of a town that staunchly resisted the Mongol advance had not been uncommon in Central Asia. Thus, the guarantees provided for ordinary subjects in this battle startled Rabban Sauma. He found the restraint of the combatants remarkable and impressive. Since he and his entourage watched the battle from some distance, they were personally never at risk, but the experience must still have been unsettling.

Sauma's narrative reveals nothing else about Naples. It does not even describe churches and monasteries, sites that Sauma always mentioned in covering the other European cities or towns he passed through. It seems likely, therefore, that he remained in Naples for the briefest of stays before setting forth for his most important destination in Italy, the Vatican. On horseback, his party and their Italian escorts traveled northward, where he was struck by the absence of barren terrain. He seemed surprised that they "found no land which was destitute of buildings."[28] This situation apparently made for a sharp contrast with many of the regions in Asia, particularly Central Asia, through which he had traveled. Much of the terrain on his voyage to Persia, including that along the Silk Road, was inhospitable and unpopulated, and he had traveled for days, perhaps weeks, without seeing a single permanent building. Italy, with its arable but less extensive lands, presented a very different picture. Vast empty spaces were simply uncharacteristic of the regions through which he voyaged in Southern Europe. No major desert impeded his travels, as it had in Central Asia.

The Nestorian cleric hoped to persuade the Pope to call upon the monarchs of Europe to initiate a Crusade, which would coincide with a Mongol attack on the Mamlūks. En route to the Vatican, however, he learned about an event that could disrupt his mission. Pope Honorius IV had died on April 3, approximately two and a half months before Rabban Sauma had landed in Naples. Knowing this, Sauma must have felt more eager than ever to reach Rome quickly. He naturally hoped to be among the first to converse with the just-elected Pope.

Rabban Sauma was, however, to be sorely disappointed. Upon his arrival in Rome sometime in July, he learned that no Pope had yet been chosen, although twelve Cardinals were meeting for the purpose. Had he known that many of the recent Popes had been preoccupied with political issues closer to home than those involving the Mamlūks, he might have been less optimistic about attracting papal support for a Crusade. But Sauma was happily ignorant of all this when he sent word to the Cardinals that he was an official ambassador from the court of Arghun, the Ilkhan of the Mongols.

The Cardinals responded by inviting him to their meeting place, which was off limits to all outsiders other than their own assistants.[29] Ironically enough, Rabban Sauma's reception was in some ways similar to that accorded foreign envoys in China. Like the representatives of the Ministry of Rites who instructed ambassadors on etiquette for an audience with the Chinese Emperor, Sauma's Italian escorts coached him on correct manners for his meeting with the Cardinals.[30] They urged him, for example, to kneel before the altar in the room where the Cardinals were gathered and then to greet each of the Church leaders.[31] They also told him that the Cardinals, being of a higher status, would not stand when he entered, and they advised him not to take offense at what he might have perceived as a slight.

When Rabban Sauma met the Cardinals, therefore, he was well prepared to make a good impression. The prelates had convened at the palace of the recently deceased Pope near the Church of Santa Sabina, which still stands across the Tiber from the Vatican. Honorius III (Pope, 1216–1227) had only recently given the church to St. Dominic, to be turned into a convent and cloister for the Dominican order.[32] The distance from the Vatican offered the Cardinals greater privacy during their deliberations. Despite the relatively calm and secluded setting, however, they could not come to an agreement. According to one contemporary source, the delay in selecting a Pope was "due perchance to the fact that each of them wanted the papal dignity for himself."[33] Tensions rose in this closed environment. By the end of the long, hot summer, five or six of the Cardinals would die. The arrival of Rabban Sauma thus offered a welcome diversion from the debates and grinding deadlock that would persist until early the following year.

Recognizing the distance he had traveled, the Cardinals were worried that Rabban Sauma's fatigue might lead to illness. Although he tried to assure them that he was well rested, they continued to express their concern. With a certain urgency, Sauma explained that the Mongols and Mar Yaballaha had sent him to meet with the Pope and to convey letters concerning the liberation of Jerusalem. Evidently, however, the Cardinals were in no mood to consider a serious issue. Instead, they insisted that Rabban Sauma rest, a course of action that would coincidentally give them more time to reflect upon his arrival and to deliberate upon possible responses to his mission. He was, after all, the first cleric ever to have been sent as an emissary from the Mongols.

RABBAN SAUMA'S DESCRIPTION OF HIS FAITH

When the Cardinals called him back, they had evidently decided on the proper path: to lead the discussion to a consideration of theological questions and to do their best to avoid inquiries about politics. Rabban Sauma ought to have been disappointed by this turn of events, and toward the end of their conversation he did show some irritation that a principal issue had barely been discussed. Yet religious questions naturally appealed to someone with his training and bent, and he seems to have relished the dialogue with the Cardinals. His narrative shows that he was absorbed in the conversation and eager to describe the main tenets of Nestorianism to his audience. No doubt he was also delighted with the opportunity to be center stage, expressing his views to this elite group.

The discussion started with questions and answers. Rabban Sauma and his interlocutors had to rely on interpreters to translate between Persian and Latin. Some of these interpreters were part of his entourage, but the Vatican recruited others. The Cardinals first asked about his native land and the object of his mission, and, though he replied, the narrative does not record what he said.[34] After this very brief preliminary exchange, they requested information about his Church, and he responded that the seat of his Church was Baghdad and that he himself held the position of Visitor-General in China and supervised the Church's disciples. Trying to discover how Christianity had spread to Rabban

Sauma's lands, the Cardinals questioned him about the identity of the Apostles who had preached there. He mentioned St. Thomas, one of the Twelve Apostles, who had left Palestine and led a peripatetic life, preaching the Gospel among the Parthians and Persians and traveling all the way to India. Upon Thomas's death, his disciples returned his relics to Edessa (modern Urfa in Turkey), which became a center of the Nestorian Church.[35] Rabban Sauma also mentioned Addai (Aramaic for Thaddaeus), one of the seventy evangelists and a twin of St. Thomas, who spread the Word in Mesopotamia and Persia, and his disciple Mari, who was credited with establishing a Nestorian bishopric at the Sasanian capital of Seleucia-Ctesiphon. The Cardinals were impressed by Rabban Sauma's obvious familiarity with the early leaders of the Church. They were also delighted that the Mongols had selected such a knowledgeable Christian as an ambassador. As they said, "it is a marvelous thing that thou who art a Christian, and a deacon of the Throne of the Patriarch of the East hast come upon an embassy from the king of the Mongols."[36]

Rabban Sauma capitalized on the good impression he had made. It seems clear that he wanted to convey a positive image of the activities of his Church. He informed the Cardinals that the leaders of the Nestorian Church had traveled far and wide to spread the Word to the Mongols, Turks, and Chinese. His narrative credits them with converting many Mongols. Rabban Sauma was proud, in particular, of the conversions of the children of the Mongol elite. He asserted that Christians were respected in Mongol realms and that some Mongols had constructed churches even in their military camps.

Now that he had established that the Mongols favored Christianity and that a few of their leaders were ardent Christians, it was a propitious time to bring up the objective of his mission. He told the Cardinals that the Ilkhan, who was a staunch friend of the Catholicus Mar Yaballaha, sought to dislodge the Mamlūks from Palestine and Syria and hoped for European assistance in recovering Jerusalem for the Christian world. He also pointed out that the Mongol rulers of Persia had selected him to lead the mission because, "being a Christian, my word will be believed by you." [37]

Without a Pope, however, the Cardinals could not make a commitment to such a scheme. Moreover, they probably doubted that they could persuade the European monarchs to spearhead a military campaign against the Mamlūks. The late Pope Honorius IV had been a proponent of an attack on the Mamlūks but had been unable to elicit commitments for a Crusade from the most fervent Christian monarchs, including Edward I of England. The current leaders of the Church, recognizing the disunity of Europe and the awesome obstacles to persuading its rulers to cooperate in mounting still another Crusade, were less sanguine about the prospects of a joint military campaign with the Ilkhanate. They therefore immediately shifted the conversation to theological issues.

Trying to determine if the doctrines of the Eastern Christianity he represented and of Catholicism had much in common, the Cardinals asked him if his beliefs resembled those of the Pope. Rabban Sauma replied, with remarkable ingenuity, that no Catholic envoy had arrived in the East in earlier times and that Eastern knowledge of Christianity derived from the teachings of the Apostles he had named earlier in their conversation. The Cardinals then requested a detailed statement of his beliefs.

The way in which his words were now interpreted was critical. The interpreters from his own entourage may have attempted to mute the differences between the views Rabban Sauma expressed and those of the Catholics because they hoped to avert controversy and maintain harmonious relations. He, too, undoubtedly hoped to find common ground with his audience. The narrative indicates that he described the Nestorian attitude toward the Trinity ambiguously, and it is not hard to guess why. Had he presented it starkly, the Cardinals would surely have been more distressed than they were by some of his observations.

His responses, as reported in the narrative, started with an affirmation of his belief in One God and in the concept of the Father, the Son, and the Holy Spirit, views that the Cardinals shared. He asserted that the Son in his *divine form* derived from the Father and in his *human form* derived from Mary, a sentiment that would not have antagonized his audience. Yet there was a hint here of a belief in two distinct *personae*—one divine and the other, the human Jesus.[38] The Cardinals would certainly have disapproved of the concept of, in effect, two Jesuses. From their standpoint, both natures were fused in one Christ. The Cardinals, however, did not react to this whiff of heresy, probably because it was presented so vaguely and in such a low-key way by both Rabban Sauma and the interpreters.

Next, the Cardinals focused on an issue, the origin of the Holy Spirit, that had divided the Catholics from the Orthodox Church, although there had been encouraging efforts to resolve their differences at the Council of Lyons in 1274. In the Cardinals' view, the Holy Spirit was coequal to the Father and the Son, and they wanted to know where Rabban Sauma stood on this matter. He responded with an elaborate and detailed analysis, which, again, might have generated controversy but in the event did not offend his audience.

The Cardinals opened this section of the dialogue by asking whether the Holy Spirit derived from the Father or the Son or was a separate entity. Rabban Sauma then engaged them in a Socratic dialogue, with each side querying the other and asking leading questions to elicit the responses sought. The Cardinals were vastly impressed by his erudition and intelligence as he affirmed the primacy of the Father, who begot both the Son and the Holy Spirit. According to the narrative of his travels, he stated that "the Father is the cause of the Son and the Spirit and that both the Son and the Spirit are causations of His."[39] He argued by analogy, pointing out that the sun causes light and heat but that heat does not cause light. The sun, he implied, is the primary cause, just as the Father "is the cause of the Son and the Spirit."[40] In essence, he was suggesting that the three natures of the Divine were not co-equal, a challenge to the orthodox views of the Cardinals. Yet his audience passed over this heretical opinion and attempted to head off possible disputes by asserting that they themselves merely wanted to test Sauma's originality and his knowledge of theology. Obviously, the Cardinals were not eager for controversy.

Rabban Sauma helped them to avoid any by seeking to end the theological discussion. He said that he had come to Rome not to teach or discuss his faith but rather to convey the proposals of the Ilkhan and the message of the Catholicus to the Western Christians, to secure personal blessing from the Pope, and to see as many churches, religious sites and shrines, and relics as he could. It was time for the interview and interrogation to come to an end. Rabban Sauma recognized that the absence of a Head of the Church meant that he could make no progress on his primary objective. Moreover, continuing the conversation might generate a controversy, which he would not relish and which might jeopardize hopes for an agreement for cooperation in the future. Turning to a lower priority, then, Rabban Sauma suggested that the Cardinals select a man to guide him around the most celebrated religious sites in Rome. Doubtless eager to return to deliberations leading to the election of a Pope, the Cardinals quickly consented. They ordered several monks to escort the Nestorian cleric on a tour of Rome's fabled churches and monasteries.

TOUR OF THE ETERNAL CITY

The first and most impressive site Rabban Sauma visited was the old Basilica of San Pietro (St. Peter's) in the Vatican.

Needless to say, what he saw was not the celebrated basilica built during the sixteenth and seventeenth centuries to designs by Michelangelo, Bernini, and Bramante. Even so, it overwhelmed him, for he had rarely seen a religious building constructed on so monumental a scale. As he wrote, "the extent of that temple and its splendors cannot be described . . ."[41] He did not refer to the mosaics that surrounded the facade, focusing instead on the interior of the church. His attention was drawn to the 180 pillars built during the Emperor Constantine's time to support the basilica. He also saw the altar where only the Pope could celebrate the Mass and its bench on which only he could stand.

Also impressive was the Chair of St. Peter, made of wood and said to have been used by Jesus' disciple. This chair, also referred to as a throne, was in the apse, and, again, only the Pope could sit on it. Bernini would encase in bronze the remains of the chair, which had been embellished with ivory; this constitutes the Throne of St. Peter now found in the basilica.[42] Rabban Sauma's narrative does not mention the bronze statue of St. Peter by the contemporary artist Arnolfo di Cambio, which he may have seen. However, its omission from this narrative perhaps indicates that, although we know it had already been finished, it was not installed until later.[43] His escorts did conduct him to the tomb of the saint, which was directly beneath the Throne of St. Peter. The sarcophagus, made of gold, was encased in still another coffin, of bronze, on top of which was a gold cross weighing approximately 150 pounds. The whole assemblage was, in turn, surrounded by an elaborate grill of gold.[44] This sacred relic was certainly one of the most significant and ornate that the Nestorian cleric had seen during his travels.

It was not the only one in the basilica that impressed him, however. He was also struck by an image of Jesus on a fine linen cloth. The legend about this item, which his narrative does not relate, tells that Abghan, the King of Edessa, had

Tomb of St. Peter. Basilica of San Pietro, the Vatican.

sent a painter to make a portrait of Jesus but that the painter, overwhelmed by the supernatural light emanating from Christ, could not fashion his image. According to the legend, Jesus responded by picking up a shroud and wiping his face on it, where the imprint of his features remained. This unusual relic was brought back to Edessa, but centuries later it wound up in Constantinople and was ultimately taken to Rome.[45]

Still another object Rabban Sauma mentioned in his narrative was an altar where the Popes had enthroned the Holy Roman Emperors. He noted a curious custom, which his hosts must have described to him: He said that the Pope picked up the crown with his feet and placed it on the new Emperor's head, an act that signified the primacy of the religious hierarchy over the political leadership.[46] This description of the ceremony is decidedly inaccurate, perhaps because Rabban Sauma misunderstood his interpreter's account. In fact, on receiving his crown, the Emperor would customarily kneel down and kiss the Pope's feet, a ritual that no doubt was intended to emphasize the superiority of the clerical over the secular leadership. In fact, as a result of the hostile relationship between the Popes and the Holy Roman Emperors, this custom had lapsed by the time Rabban Sauma arrived in Rome—a time when even the French monarchy was mounting challenges of its own to Papal authority.[47]

Having completed his tour of the Basilica of San Pietro, Rabban Sauma was, at his request, guided to several other churches. His escorts took him to the Church of San Paolo Fuori le Mura (St. Paul's Outside the Walls), on the outskirts of Rome. This magnificent basilica had been constructed on the site of the tomb of the Apostle Paul. After his execution Paul had been buried in a cemetery adjacent to the Ostian Way. A memorial tablet had marked the precise location of the tomb, and the Emperor Constantine had ordered the construction of a church to commemorate the saint's martyrdom. The church, which housed the remains of the disciple, was completed early in the fifth century but unfortunately was largely destroyed in a fire in 1823.[48] Because the present structure is a reconstruction, it is difficult to verify, in toto, Rabban Sauma's description of the church and the relics he saw. Some of the relics he mentioned are no longer extant, and whether they were in any case genuine is impossible to establish.

Rabban Sauma's narrative starts by noting that the church was built on Paul's tomb, which was under the altar. His account does not describe the architectural style or the exterior of the building nor, in fact, does it refer to notable features such as the frescoes illustrating the life of Paul, the imposing series of columns leading to the apse, and the cloister that had been constructed early in the thirteenth century. It also omits any mention of the spectacular tabernacle designed by Arnolfo di Cambio and installed in 1285, just two years be-

Tabernacle, Basilica of San Paolo Fuori le Mura, Rome. Fashioned by
Arnolfo di Cambio in 1285.

fore Rabban Sauma's visit.[49] As the most recent addition in the church, the tabernacle would certainly have been shown to him, by his guides and by the doubtless proud clerics who staffed the church. In the words of a modern art historian, the tabernacle has "the characteristically elegant gothic line," though the "sculptures . . . bear the stamp of . . . contact with Roman art."[50] Four columns sustain triple arches replete with mosaics, statuettes, and even a replica of a temple topped by a cross. The gold decorations, the statue of Paul holding a sword, and the mosaics depicting deer and other animals would surely have caught the eye of the visitor, but Rabban Sauma seems to have been more interested in the sacred relics and other marvels that his guides showed or told him about.

The church was apparently a storehouse of the body parts of great martyrs and venerable leaders of early Christianity. In addition to St. Paul's tomb, the Nestorian cleric's escorts showed him the purported head of St. Stephen, the first deacon and a martyr of the Christian faith who had been stoned to death for his heretical views of Moses and the God of the Old Testament.[51] In the fifth century, his body was disinterred and brought to Rome for reburial. It was ironic and singularly appropriate that the Church leaders had buried his head next to Paul's remains, for the Apostle, before his conversion to Christianity, while he was still known by the name Saul, had consented to and witnessed the execution of Stephen.[52]

Similarly, it was fitting that the hand of Ananias, another sacred relic that Rabban Sauma saw in the church, was venerated in a church named for Paul, because the lives of these two Christian leaders had been intertwined. Saul had been struck blind on his way to Damascus to take charge of the pacification of the Christians there, and Ananias gave him back his sight, brought him to the Christian faith, and baptized him with the Christian name Paul.[53] In listing the won-

Chains of St. Peter. Church of San Pietro in Vincoli, Rome.

ders in the church, Rabban Sauma mentioned Paul's staff, not perhaps as exotic as Ananias's hand but evidently intriguing. Also part of his list were the chains used in transporting Paul to the execution grounds. Here Rabban Sauma must have been confusing the Church of San Paolo Fuori le Mura with the Church of San Pietro in Vincoli (St. Peter in Chains), for it was the chains that had shackled St. Peter in Palestine that were preserved in Rome and that the Nestorian probably saw there.[54]

On leaving the Church of San Paolo Fuori le Mura, Rabban Sauma and his escorts proceeded to the reputed place of Paul's martyrdom. Sauma's narrative records as fact the legend his guides related to him: When the executioner severed Paul's head, "it leaped up thrice into the air, and at each time cried out 'Christ! Christ!'" Three fountains gushed from the three places his head had landed, and Rabban Sauma's guides claimed that the water from these fountains had curative powers.[55] Adjacent to the fountains, Rabban Sauma came across, depending on the translation of a term in his narrative, a shrine, a cemetery, or a sepulcher laden with the bones of martyrs and early Church leaders. His whole group stopped to venerate these remains before continuing their tour.

The next great monument visited by Rabban Sauma's party was the Church of San Giovanni in Laterano (St. John Lateran). Erected by the Emperor Constantine in the fourth century as the cathedral of Rome and the seat of the archbishopric of the city, the original structure, seen by the Nestorian cleric, burned down in 1308. The present building dates in part from the Baroque era and in part from the eighteenth century. It is therefore difficult to verify whether objects and relics listed by Rabban Sauma were actually to be found in the church. Again, his account scarcely mentions the church's unique architectural and artistic attributes and, even more remarkably, ignores the huge statue of Constantine on the porch, emphasizing sacred relics instead.

Rabban Sauma wrote that he saw a seamless tunic worn by Jesus and a table on which Christ had celebrated the Eucharist and which he had then given to his Apostles. His guides told Rabban Sauma that the Pope came to the Church to conduct the Mass on this table around Eastertime. They also showed the apparently delighted Nestorian cleric the basin of black polished stone in which the Emperor Constantine had been baptized.[56] He wrote that he saw as well the exact location in the church where St. Peter debated Simon Magus, the magician who tried to convince the Apostle to sell him spiritual powers. Many of these claims cannot be judged, and it may be that his guides took advantage of Rabban Sauma's credulousness and misled him about these objects. Or they may have believed everything they said about the articles and sites they showed him. We do know that one of the few things in his account of the church that can be verified—his description of four columns of gilded bronze that can still be found in the Chapel of the Holy Sacrament—is accurate,[57] although his claim that the columns were brought from Jerusalem is suspect.

The final recorded stop on his itinerary of holy sites in Rome was the Basilica of Santa Maria Maggiore (St. Mary Major). Like his comments on the other Roman churches, his description of this church focuses on the reputed relics preserved in it. He was particularly impressed by the crystal reliquary that contained some of Mary's clothing and some wood from Jesus' Crèche. Along with these relics, he saw a silver reliquary in which the head of St. Matthew was reputedly kept, as well as the foot of Philip the Apostle and the arm of another Apostle, St. James the Great, whose brother St. John was the youngest of the Twelve.[58]

Rabban Sauma went on to tour other religious sites in Rome, but the narrative does not mention any of them. In any case, by the time he was done he had truly had his fill of churches and sacred relics. It was clearly the marvels and the relics that captured his interest most. The text of his narrative scarcely alludes to the aesthetic appeal of the buildings and their appurtenances, the intellectual interest of the doctrines, and the stimulus to meditation of the sites and ideas to which he was exposed, and, even allowing for his editor-translator's possible deletions, this seems significant. The primary objective of his pilgrimage was evidently not intellectual. His account gives the impression that seeing and venerating sacred relics was, in his view, a means of securing divine blessing and that he was thus fulfilling a religious quest.

Rabban Sauma must have been frustrated, however, at not having fulfilled his diplomatic objectives. Still, he had hopes that he might do so in future. He may have mistakenly assumed that only the absence of a Pontiff prevented the cementing of an alliance against the Mamlūks. Lacking knowledge of the serious political fragmentation of Europe, he probably believed that, because the Mongols of Persia and the Europeans were both enemies of the Mamlūks, it was only a matter of time before an agreement could be reached.

At any rate, Rabban Sauma certainly was aware that his political mission would be held in abeyance until a Pope was elected and that weeks, perhaps months, might elapse before this happened. Since he had seen the principal religious sites in Rome, his continued stay in the Eternal City would not have been particularly productive. Besides, waiting for an election would squander whatever time remained for his stay in Europe. Thus, Rabban Sauma decided to travel to the territories of the two European monarchs whose support was essential for an alliance and a Crusade. He wished to have audiences with the Kings of France and England, so he set out on a journey to the north.

A BRIEF STOP IN GENOA

En route to France, Rabban Sauma's principal stop was in Genoa, which he reached early in August. He knew that he would receive a warm welcome in this port city. Genoa had maintained a lively trade with the Ilkhanate, and Genoese merchants had traveled to Persia, thus forging strong links with the Mongols. The fact that one of the interpreters who had accompanied Rabban Sauma on his travels from Persia was a Genoese increased the prospect of a cordial reception. The Genoese people did not disappoint the Mongols' envoy. His narrative tells us that he was received enthusiastically and treated with great respect.

Because the Genoese, having developed a thriving international commerce, could boast an exceptionally cosmopolitan society, Rabban Sauma's arrival did not upset their equanimity. Genoese merchants traveled everywhere from Morocco to India and China. Unlike the merchants of Naples, they even traded with Sicily and Aragon, dread enemies of many of the Italian city-states.[59] According to one perhaps somewhat exaggerated estimate, the value of goods passing through the port doubled from 1214 to 1274, then quadrupled from 1274 to 1293.[60] With 60,000 to 70,000 inhabitants, one of the largest populations in Europe, Genoa was at the height of its prosperity. Its merchants had earned reputations as independent and sharp-witted if somewhat rapacious, and its men of learning were perceived as creative yet pragmatic, contributing to knowledge of navigation, herbal medicine, and other practical areas of study. In 1284 the city's military forces had defeated Pisa, and in the 1290s they would overwhelm the Venetians. Yet, by the second decade of the fourteenth century, Genoa would be characterized "by violent changes of regime, expulsions of defeated factions, and downright civil wars."[61]

Its politics had simply not kept pace with its flourishing trade. It first established, in 1099, a commune governed by consuls. The nobility and the rich merchants dominated the commune, but various factions within these groups repeatedly fought over control,[62] leading in 1191 to the establishment of a system in which a non-Genoese, known as a *podesta*, was selected as chief executive. In 1218 the Genoese once again changed their political system in order to quell continuing factionalism and its attendant conflicts. Now a Genoese, to be called the *capitano del popolo*, would act as chief executive of the city and be responsible for mediating among the factions of the old nobility, the wealthy merchants, and the petty tradesmen and maintaining order. The conflicts among these groups doomed the system within three decades after Rabban Sauma's visit.

On his arrival in Genoa, the *capitano* or perhaps the chief abbot of the town greeted Rabban Sauma with great fanfare and with a sizable crowd in tow. Because he had scant knowledge of the government of the Italian city-states, it came as a surprise to Sauma that Genoa had no King or Emperor. Since his narrative fails to record any conversations with the city's leaders, there is no indication that he broached the possibility of an alliance; indeed, it seems probable that he did not.[63] In any event, Genoa was embroiled in commercial rivalries and hostilities with Venice, so its leaders would not have made commitments that would have led to other conflicts. Moreover, they would not have wished to alienate a potential trading partner, the Mamlūks, by appearing to favor the Muslims' enemies. Thus, even if Rabban Sauma had proposed an alliance, he surely would have faced a polite though firm rebuff.

His visit to the Cathedral of San Lorenzo (St. Laurence) was, from his viewpoint, the highlight of his stay in Genoa. The cathedral, which had been constructed earlier in the century, was named for the third-century martyr who had died with Pope Sixtus II at the hands of the Romans. The saint was condemned to death for having distributed to the poor the Church's wealth, which would otherwise have gone to the Romans. He was executed by roasting on a gridiron and is most often depicted in Christian art with a palm, symbolizing martyrdom, and the instrument of his death.[64] A bas-relief above the door in the Genoese cathedral portrays him precisely thus. Lying on the gridiron in a beatific pose, he is surrounded by fantastic animals, monsters, and mourners.

Because the cathedral was in an elevated part of town, it must have had a commanding view of the port.[65] Black and white marble from the immediate locality gave the facade an attractive and elegant checkerboard appearance. Otherwise, because the present apse, nave, and bell tower all date from the Renaissance or later, it is impossible to say just what the building that Rabban Sauma saw actually looked like.

Once again, his extant account mentions nothing about the site except the sacred relics purportedly found there. It fails to describe the mural of St. George and the Dragon, which was obviously influenced by Byzantine models, or to mention the Byzantine crosses, evidence of the contact between the Byzantine Empire and Genoa. Rabban Sauma did, however, write about his glimpse of the silver coffer in which the body of St. John the Baptist had been placed. The cathedral still contains a Chapel of St. John the Baptist, in which his purported remains are kept. Still another marvel that Sauma described was an emerald dish said to have been Jesus' plate when he celebrated the Last Supper (or, in Sauma's words, the Last Passover) with his disciples.[66] The Treasury of the cathedral still preserves this so-called six-sided paten, later discovered to be made of glass and to have been brought back to Europe by the Crusaders in the twelfth century. Unscrupulous merchants in the Middle East must have palmed it off on the credulous Crusaders as the Holy Grail.

Rabban Sauma also described a curious conversation with some unidentified local people. He had learned that they did not fast during the first week of Lent. He asked why they deviated from the practices of other Catholics. They responded that when their forebears had been converted to Christianity they were too weak to fast. Thus, those who converted them gave them dispensation to fast for "only" forty days a year.

This unusual dialogue requires explanation. By "fasting" Rabban Sauma and the Genoese probably meant not eating meat rather than taking on a Ramadanlike abstention from all food. The lengthy period of fasting they cited was more in line with Nestorian traditions than with those of the Christian West. Nestorians abstained from meat not only at Lent but also at six other times during the year and on every Tuesday and Saturday,[67] so that the total number of fast days in the Nestorian calendar considerably exceeded forty. Hence Rabban Sauma's surprise at the paltry number of fast days among the Genoese. Because he did not arrive in Genoa during the regular fasting period, it may seem curious that the topic came up at all, but the fact that his visit in early August coincided with one of the major Nestorian fasts provides a likely explanation.

Having seen the major religious sites in Genoa and Rome and transmitted the Ilkhan's messages to the authorities in the Vatican, Rabban Sauma had no further need to stay in Italy. It is no accident that while there he had visited the two cities that had the closest links with the Mongols but did not travel to Venice, most probably because it had until recently been in conflict with the Byzantine Empire and thus had limited relations with the Ilkhanate. Still, his stay in the cities he had visited had been politically unproductive. He had received a cordial reception everywhere but had not secured a commitment to a joint military campaign. His mission was not at an end, however. He could still entertain hopes of persuading the monarchs of France and England to join in the proposed alliance.

5

Paris, Bordeaux, Rome, and Return

In the middle of the thirteenth century, France's ruler St. Louis had been among the most pious of the Christian monarchs of Europe and had played a prominent role in two Crusades. His son and immediate successor, Philip the Bold, was, however, less concerned with a Crusade than with consolidating control over France, supporting his uncle Charles of Anjou in Naples and Sicily, and trying unsuccessfully to help his own son Charles of Valois mount the throne of the Kingdom of Aragon. He lacked both the religious fervor and the breadth of vision of his father and was perhaps less intelligent as well.

The accession of Philip the Bold's son Philip IV (the Fair) in 1285, just two years before Rabban Sauma's arrival in France, aroused hopes that the new monarch would be more receptive to an effort to expel the Muslims from the Holy Land. The King was not even twenty years old, and his youth promised the possibility of a new course and new policies. Would he follow the example of his revered grandfather or that of his more calculating and political father? It appeared likely that the educated, ambitious, and handsome Philip the Fair would want to emulate the grandiose visions of St. Louis rather than the stolid achievements of Philip the Bold. This was a propitious time for a proposal that required energy, commitment, and zeal, all qualities that a newly enthroned monarch might find appealing.[1]

Rabban Sauma arrived in France in late August of 1287. Here seemed a golden opportunity to fulfill the tasks with which he had been entrusted. Unlike the leaderless Vatican, France had a vigorous and assertive ruler. The reception accorded Rabban Sauma, in addition, boded well for his success. Philip sent a large detachment of men to meet and escort the Nestorian cleric as soon as he arrived at the French border. At the end of September, they reached Paris. There they were greeted with great pomp and ceremony, and Philip offered Sauma a splendid place in which to lodge.

The Nestorian cleric was exhausted after the rigors of his journey. The arduousness of his travels is perhaps difficult to comprehend in an age of high-speed transport over well-defined and generally well-maintained routes, comfortable accommodations in hotels and inns, and cuisine catering to travelers from distant lands. Rabban Sauma had been voyaging for more than six months since his departure from the Ilkhanate, using various modes of transport. The strain of riding on horses, camels, and donkeys in the Middle East and horses and donkeys in Europe and of crossing rough seas on flimsy boats certainly took its toll. As in Central Asia, *trails* would have been a more accurate term than *roads* for the routes across the terrain Rabban Sauma traversed during this segment of his journey. Riders often had to wear masks and goggles to protect themselves from the dust and mud that caked the roads. Maps barely existed, and, if they did, were often unreliable.

Travelers needed to buy fodder and shoes for their horses and food and medicines for themselves before setting forth, although they could purchase some provisions along the way. They stayed in inns or hostelries of considerably varied quality. A few doubtless offered beds and good meals; others, in more rustic areas, provided merely the ground to sleep on and sparse and stale fare to eat. Many offered no food at all, so that travelers had to rely on what they had brought or obtain their own. Experienced travelers carried their own blankets, for, if there was bedding to be had in the more primitive inns, it was changed only infrequently and likely to be full of vermin. In the shadier establishments, the maids often served as bedmates, but Rabban Sauma probably did not make use of their services.

Brigandage threatened Sauma throughout his voyage. Feuding in various regions and states in Europe created unsettled conditions, which unscrupulous vagabonds and bandits capitalized on.

The dangers and discomforts that Rabban Sauma faced on his travels from China to Persia about ten years earlier had been more severe. Yet now he was in his early sixties, so the hardships and perils he faced were undoubtedly even more wearying. He had also just endured the heat of an Italian summer, although the arrival of autumn had presumably brought some relief. Still, some aspects of the trip must have been enjoyable. Rabban Sauma doubtless encountered wandering entertainers such as jugglers, musicians, and acrobats, and he probably met merchants and pilgrims, which would have diminished somewhat the tedium of his voyage.

Well aware of the fatiguing journey that his guest had just concluded, Philip left the Nestorian cleric alone for three days. Only after Sauma had refreshed himself did Philip dispatch an official to invite his visitor to an audience. Once Rabban Sauma arrived at court, Philip rose to greet his guest, treating him as an equal instead of requiring a symbolic acknowledgment of obeisance or vassalage. The French monarch immediately inquired about the object of the Nestorian cleric's visit. Why had he come and who had sent him? Rabban Sauma responded with alacrity and without any attempt to veil even temporarily the aims of his mission. After replying that he was an official envoy from the court of Arghun, the Ilkhan of Persia, he broached the subject of an alliance to recover Jerusalem. Delivering the letter from the Ilkhan, he invited the French King to join in a mighty campaign to crush the troublesome Mamlūks. He concluded his presentation by handing over Arghun's gifts. These probably consisted of jewels or beautiful cloth, luxury items of great value but little bulk. Voyagers who did not travel with large merchant caravans could not carry heavy items over such long distances and on such overcrowded, heavily laden ships as Rabban Sauma had had to contend with.

According to Rabban Sauma's account, the Mongols' determination moved Philip. He said that if they, who were not Christians, were so concerned about the recapture of Jerusalem, then it was incumbent upon the Western Christians to gather their forces with enthusiasm and join in the struggle to regain the Holy Land.[2] Now it was Rabban Sauma's turn to be moved by Philip's devotion to his faith. The Nestorian cleric expressed delight with Philip's words of support. His mission appeared to have borne fruit.

However, Philip's exuberance belied his primary goals, which did not encompass the Crusade that Rabban Sauma envisioned. The French King was more interested in gaining control over English domains within France or at least in having the English King treat him as a suzerain. In May of 1286 King Edward I, who ruled his domain in Gascony under Philip's suzerainty, had come to Paris to do homage to the French monarch, but, despite this conciliatory gesture, Philip still mistrusted Edward. The hostility between the two rulers would lead to full-scale war from 1294 to 1298. Exacerbating tensions between them was Edward's effort to mediate in the conflict between Philip and the Aragonese, the principal enemies of Philip's great-uncle Charles of Anjou, a conflict intensified by Philip's carrying on his father's efforts to place Charles of Valois, Philip's brother, on the throne of Aragon.

In July of 1287, just a few months before Rabban Sauma's audience with Philip, Edward had met with King Alphonso II of Aragon to seek the release of Charles of Anjou's son, Charles of Salerno, from captivity in Aragon.[3] Because Charles of Salerno was his cousin, Edward was naturally concerned about his welfare, and he was willing to make concessions to secure his freedom. The treaty he signed at Oloron-Sainte-Marie was extraordinarily generous to Alphonso and alienated Philip. One of the clauses that most enraged the French King was Edward's consent to the Aragonese occupation of Provence, over which both France and Aragon claimed jurisdiction, if peace was not made within three years of the release of Charles of Salerno—consent the English King, of course, had no right to give, since he had no authority over the region.[4] Both Philip and, eventually, Pope Nicholas IV, who would be enthroned in 1288, denounced the treaty, thus continuing the tensions along Philip's southern and western borders, with Aragon and England respectively.

Philip's northeastern frontiers were also unsettled. He and the Holy Roman Emperor were competing to expand into and annex Flanders. However, because of its weaving industry, Flanders wished to retain its independence in order to keep its commercial links with the wool merchants across the English Channel. Thus, Philip was once again frustrated in his attempt to secure his frontiers and increase the size of his realm.

He also became embroiled in controversies with the Church. Needing funds for his foreign campaigns and his efforts to incorporate all regions in France under his direct control, he collected tithes from the Church's revenues in his domain. His feudal vassals were financially troubled, so he could not expect to obtain much money from them by increasing their tax burden. The Church was vulnerable because much of the revenue raised by the French clergy was turned over to the Vatican. Philip could arouse nationalist sentiment by arguing that French wealth was enriching the coffers of the Papacy in Rome. Emphasizing this reasoning, he would eventually ban the export of gold and silver from the country, embroiling himself in a critical dispute over secular versus clerical authority with Boniface VIII, who was elected Pope in December of 1294.[5]

These concerns weighed heavily on Philip, making it difficult for him to focus on a Crusade. His dramatic response to Rabban Sauma was probably sincere. Like many Christians, he wished to dislodge Muslim control over Jerusalem and no doubt supported the Outremer communities as a base from which to regain the Holy Land. Yet he was compelled to consider more immediate and pressing matters before turning his attention to the pledge he had made to Rabban Sauma.

Having elicited what he believed was a strong commitment from the French monarch, the Nestorian cleric turned to the more personal objectives of his mission. Again, his greatest interest was in being escorted through the most renowned shrines and churches in the area, as well as being shown relics of saints. When he explained this interest, Philip responded enthusiastically. He assigned several of his officials to escort Rabban Sauma through some of the spectacular sites in Paris, and he held out to his foreign visitor the tantalizing prospect of seeing even greater treasures, remarking cryptically, "afterwards I myself will show [him] what I have."[6]

First, however, Rabban Sauma wandered around Paris and was struck by the large number of students in the city. His narrative states that there were 30,000 of them. According to an expert on medieval universities, "it is virtually impossible to be exact either about student numbers or the social classes from which they were drawn,"[7] but 30,000 is clearly excessive. An accepted figure for the late fourteenth century is 3,000 to 3,500. In the pre-Plague times of the thirteenth century the number may have been higher,[8] particularly because there were fewer cities in Northern Europe competing for students in the 1200s, but nothing nearly as high as 30,000. Widely accepted estimates placing the total population of fourteenth-century Paris at 100,000 to 120,000 cast further doubt on the figure cited by Rabban Sauma.[9] The population had probably been slightly higher in the century before the Plague, but even so, by Rabban Sauma's count something like one-fourth of the city's inhabitants were students, which seems, on the surface, unlikely.

Yet did Sauma's observation (or his transmission of his informants' observation) have any basis in reality? An examination of the university system in Paris in the thirteenth century may account for his seemingly exaggerated estimate. The university, initially associated with the cathedral school at Notre-Dame, was composed of informal communities of faculty and students and had scarcely any property. Theology had been the original focus of studies during the cathedral school days, but throughout the thirteenth century these communities were moving toward independence from the Papacy and incorporating more nontheological and nondoctrinal subjects into the curriculum. They turned to the French monarchy for support, and Philip proved a strong advocate and protector of university interests. Because he was trying, in any case, to limit the Church's power, he naturally capitalized on the university's appeal to him. Thus, Philip "confirm[ed]—and indeed extend[ed]—the university's privileges" as an independent institution and took steps to ensure that foreign students coming to and from Paris be protected from bandits and hostile natives.[10] The pupils at the university were well provided for: Rabban Sauma maintained that they received stipends from the King, and Philip did subsidize some of their expenses to keep masters and students in Paris. A large-scale exodus to another city was certainly a possibility at the time, given that the university was not lodged in sturdy, immovable structures but consisted simply of masters and students discussing intellectual and vocational subjects. In any event, Paris became a magnet for students from throughout Northern Europe, with quite a few spending months or perhaps years there. It must have appeared to be a city of students, and this makes Rabban Sauma's estimate more comprehensible.

Sauma also commented briefly on the subjects taught at the university. He noted that students could study not only the Scriptures and theology but also philosophy, rhetoric, and mathematics. In addition, the curriculum included the science of astronomy and the art of healing. What is known from other sources about developments in the curriculum at Paris during the thirteenth century generally confirms his observations. Concern for theology and grammar and rhetoric was shifting to a growing emphasis on logic and law, in part derived from the interest Aristotle's newly translated works on logic and science were arousing. The emphasis on medicine that Rabban Sauma mentioned conforms with today's prevalent view that "universities in the thirteenth and fourteenth centuries were essentially places of vocational training,"[11] although the liberal arts continued to be taught. As the university in Paris became more organized, separate faculties of law, theology, medicine, and the arts developed, a scheme that reflected the principal interests of masters and students.

As an educated man, Rabban Sauma was naturally intrigued by the educational system in this city that seemed to be a mecca for students. His native land did not have formal universities, but, thanks in part to the influence of Confucius, scholarship and the scholar-official class had long played important roles in Chinese society and continued to do so, despite the contemporary Mongol rulers' abolition of the traditional Confucian civil service examinations, the main objective of (and stumbling block for) students in earlier times. Because Chinese tutors focused on study of the Confucian classics and did not emphasize practical pursuits such as medicine, prospective doctors were introduced to their profession through apprenticeship. Only Chinese students preparing to become priests or monks studied theology. Muslim students in the Ilkhanate, Rabban Sauma's second homeland, did study Islamic theology, just as students in medieval Europe studied the Christian equivalent. Like the Europeans, the Muslims also emphasized practical subjects such as astronomy and medicine at special institutes (for instance, the great observatory of Marāgha). Having now traveled in three worlds, Confucian and Buddhist China with its small Nestorian community, Muslim Persia, and Christian Europe, Sauma had at least two educational systems to compare with the university in Paris.

Having taken note of student life on his rambles, Rabban Sauma visited the Church of Saint-Denis, where many of the French Kings were buried. Philip's officials escorted him to this majestic structure. Construction of the building may have begun as early as the seventh century, but it was completed in 1281, only six years before Rabban Sauma's visit, with funds and impetus provided by the monarchy. Because the church had been finished so recently and was perceived as the ultimate in architecture and decoration for its era, it was only natural that his proud escorts would take Rabban Sauma to see it.

St. Louis had ordered that several tombs be placed at the middle of the crossing adjacent to the altar. Along with these, a sizable transept was built to accommodate a large mausoleum. The crypt contained the tombs of the earlier Capetian Kings as well as the only recently dug graves of the deceased young sons of St. Louis.[12] The first thing Rabban Sauma's narrative mentions is the gold and silver effigies of the Kings atop their coffins and tombs in the crossing. These statues are no longer extant, having been melted down in the desecrations of the French Revolution.[13] Rabban Sauma could relate to these funerary sculptures because such figures were customary in China. Yet he was probably startled that monarchs

A portal of the Church of Saint-Denis, Paris. Thirteenth century.

would be buried with what he would have seen as relative simplicity in a church. The Chinese Emperors of great dynasties such as the T'ang were not buried in temples or monasteries, and their tombs were much better secured, less readily accessible and thus less vulnerable to desecration, than the coffins of the French Kings. The Chinese Emperors' tombs were often quite deep underground (or, if aboveground, in tumuli that were similarly difficult of access) and were set with elaborate traps to deter potential intruders and grave robbers. Accompanying the bodies of the Emperors were artifacts that they prized—jewelry, porcelains, furniture—as well as the coffins of their principal wives.[14] Compared with these tombs, those of the French Kings at Saint-Denis were far from opulent, aside from the effigies (and some of the Kings' clothing, armor, and crowns) on top of some of them.

In describing the church, Sauma's narrative unfortunately fails to mention one of the glories of medieval art: the exquisite stained-glass windows, including large and magnificent rose windows, which allowed an abundance of light into the building.[15] The narrative does, however, remark on the many monks at Saint-Denis. Rabban Sauma wrote that five hundred monks prayed at the tombs of the French monarchs and that the Kings paid their expenses.[16] A monastery was adjacent to the church and may well have been the residence for this number of monks. It appears unlikely, however, that such a large number would have been needed to worship at the tombs. The Kings no doubt subsidized them to act as caretakers as well as to pray continuously for their ancestors and for earlier royal families.

Rabban Sauma spent a month touring the city, but, curiously, his narrative fails to mention Notre-Dame, even though it refers to the neighboring site of Sainte-Chapelle. The omission of Notre-Dame, certainly the most majestic and eye-catching church in Paris, is extraordinary. Ever since the bishop of Paris had initiated the construction of the church about a century earlier, it had clearly aroused the national pride of the French and, for many, it was already a vital symbol of the city. Rabban Sauma must have seen at least its exterior, particularly the tower, which was visible from most parts of the city, and his hosts probably escorted him to this dominating site.

Why then his silence? Like Marco Polo's omissions (for example, the Venetian traveler's not mentioning the bound feet of many Chinese women),[17] it gives rise to several explanations and much speculation. It may be that Rabban Sauma simply forgot about the building when writing his account, although this is the least likely explanation. Or the editor-translator may have deleted Sauma's description, also an unlikely scenario, because as far as we know he did not eliminate references to other religious sites. Or, finally, as a good Nestorian Christian Sauma may have been embarrassed by the attention accorded the Virgin Mary, in particular the naming of a cathedral in her honor. This explanation is highly speculative, yet Sauma's beliefs are a constant refrain in his account, and throughout his narrative he avoided making sharp distinctions between Nestorianism and Western Christianity. Why emphasize the cleavages between the two forms of Christianity in an account meant to portray Westerners in a favorable light and in the course of a mission designed to forge an alliance between East and West? With so little information available, it is difficult to sort out Rabban Sauma's intent, and his lack of attention to Notre-Dame will likely remain a mystery.

Having ended his monthlong tour of Paris, he had his final audience with Philip in the celebrated Sainte-Chapelle. The King had treated Sauma with great cordiality during his stay in the city, giving sumptuous banquets and staging elaborate festivities in his honor. Philip now had one last pleasure in store for Rabban Sauma, viewing the "greater treasures" he had alluded to at the conclusion of his first audience with the

Stained-glass medallion depicting Judith with the head of Holofernes.
Sainte-Chapelle, Paris, thirteenth century. (Arch. Phot. Paris/S.P.A.D.E.M.)

Nestorian cleric. Philip inquired whether he had seen all the sites he wanted to, and Rabban Sauma responded, with gratitude, that he had been escorted to the city's principal religious buildings and shown its most important sacred relics. Philip then led him into the exquisite upper chamber of the chapel, still renowned for its remarkable array of stained-glass windows. Because they had just been completed, their colors were bright and vivid. As a group, they tell in a series of vignettes the history of the world from a Biblical standpoint, with each window incorporating a number of scenes. Starting with the creation of the Earth from the Book of Genesis, they include representations of the Passion and of events from the Books of Esther, Judges, Joshua, and others. Polychrome statues of the Twelve Apostles as well as wall paintings in the chapel contribute to the bright appearance of the interior, which has often been compared to a dazzling jewel box.[18]

Philip lifted from a case an object reputed to be Jesus' Crown of Thorns, as well as a piece of wood from the cross.[19] After showing these precious articles to Rabban Sauma, he told him that they had been obtained in the Holy Land during the Crusades. Some of the reputed sacred relics in Paris had, in fact, been brought to Europe by soldiers sent to recapture the Holy Land. The so-called Crown of Thorns, however, which is now lodged in Notre-Dame, was not taken as booty. Instead, Philip's grandfather St. Louis had bought it and several other relics in the Byzantine Empire four decades earlier.[20] The pious Christian ruler had constructed Sainte-Chapelle to house the great treasure he had secured for France.

Because Philip and much of the Parisian population surely knew of the origins of Sainte-Chapelle, it is baffling that he gave Rabban Sauma the explanation he did of the provenance of the so-called Crown of Thorns. Sauma may either have garbled the conversation or misinterpreted one of Philip's general observations about the capture of sacred relics by Crusaders as a reference to the means by which the crown had come to be in Paris. Or Philip may have intentionally misled Rabban Sauma in order to show the value the French placed on sacred objects they could obtain from the Holy Land and by implication to prove their commitment to the Crusade the Nestorian cleric had proposed. Although he undoubtedly knew that his other domestic and foreign concerns temporarily precluded his active involvement in such a Crusade, Philip evidently still wanted to impress on Rabban Sauma the notions that he and the French had a strong motive for resuming attempts to recapture the sites associated with the origins of Christianity and that he was sincere in his determination to join with the Ilkhan in an alliance against the Mamlūks. Certainly his behavior throughout Rabban Sauma's visit seems to have been consistent in this regard. To further demonstrate his commitment, he sent an envoy named Gobert de Helleville, with a letter for the Ilkhan Arghun, to accompany Rabban Sauma on his return to Persia.[21] Moreover, he tried to ingratiate himself with his visitor by rewarding him with clothing and other gifts of "great price." The pious and abstemious Nestorian did not record his impressions of these lavish presents.

MEETING WITH THE KING OF ENGLAND

Assuming that he had gained the support of the French King, Rabban Sauma next attempted to win over Edward I of England. Fortunately for the Nestorian, Edward happened to be visiting his domain in Gascony. Rabban Sauma somehow learned that Edward was not far away and that a sea voyage would be unnecessary. After twenty days' journey, he arrived in Bordeaux in mid-October of 1287. The town's inhabitants, apparently less sophisticated than the Parisians, were startled by his arrival. When they asked him to identify himself, Rabban Sauma responded that he was the ambassador of both the Catholicus and the Ilkhan of the Mongols. When he learned who his visitor was, Edward immediately granted him an audience. Rabban Sauma presented him with a letter from Mar Yaballaha and the letter and gifts that the Ilkhan Arghun had sent. Like the presents given Philip, these probably included jewels and silk and other textiles. Edward was gracious in his acceptance of these items, but he became truly animated when Rabban Sauma raised the subject of the recapture of Jerusalem and the Holy Land.[22] Earlier that spring Edward had vowed to take the cross, and he now reaffirmed his intention of embarking upon a Crusade.[23]

Although Edward was probably sincere, other pressing preoccupations would soon divert him from this commitment. Among them would be further rebellions in Wales and his own continuing efforts to secure the release of Charles of Anjou's son from the Aragonese now that Philip and the Pope had both rejected the Treaty of Oloron-Sainte-Marie.[24]

Yet his unambiguous affirmation to Rabban Sauma that "[w]e the kings of these cities bear upon our bodies the sign of the Cross, and we have no subject of thought except this matter"[25] surely impressed the Nestorian, who once again assumed that his diplomatic mission had been crowned with success. Both Philip the Fair and Edward I appeared to be ardent supporters of a Crusade and to be willing to place the considerable resources of their respective kingdoms at the disposal of a concerted effort to oust the Muslims from the Holy Land. Rabban Sauma had seemingly persuaded two of the most important secular rulers of Europe to forge an alliance with the Ilkhans.

Edward's next words no doubt reinforced the Nestorian cleric's assessment of his mission's success. The English monarch invited Rabban Sauma to conduct a religious ceremony at court. Sauma celebrated the Eucharist, and Edward, along with several other court officials, ate the wafer and drank the wine offered by his visitor. The celebration, which preserved the old components of the Church liturgy and followed Syriac tradition, differed from its Western equivalent, but its essential elements, the consecration and the communion, were sufficiently familiar to the audience that they could follow the proceedings. When the rite was over, an elaborate banquet was held, principally to honor and welcome the visitor from the Mongol world. The narrative fails to describe the festivities, but, judging from other accounts of Edward's feasts, the English King did not stint. At one banquet Edward provided his guests with ten oxen and fifty-nine lambs; at another an unspecified amount of veal, 1,742 chickens, twenty-two pheasants, seventeen dozen partridges, and vast quantities of bread, ale, and wine, among other victuals, were served.[26] By receiving his visitor with such an audience and feast Edward appeared to be signaling that an agreement had been sealed.

Believing he had earned a remarkable diplomatic victory, Rabban Sauma turned to his private concerns. Following what was by now his standard practice, he asked Edward for permission to tour the churches and shrines in the King's domain on the Continent. However, he used a new rationale to justify his request. For the first time, he suggested that he wanted to tour these sites in order to report on them to his coreligionists in the Middle East.[27] Edward gave his blessing for this tour, but he was more concerned about transmitting a message to the Ilkhan. He wanted Rabban Sauma to inform the Mongol ruler that Europeans believed in one creed and that all European Christians confessed to Jesus alone. They were not plagued, he suggested, by the sectarianism that divided Christianity elsewhere. Did this remark imply that Edward was aware of the tensions among Orthodox, Jacobite, Nestorian, and other churches, not to mention rival religions such as Islam and Buddhism? Had Rabban Sauma described the difficulties encountered by Christians in the East and thus elicited Edward's views? The text of his account tells us nothing more about this curious speech. Nor, oddly enough, does it make any further reference to Rabban Sauma visiting the religious sites in Edward's domain in France. It merely concludes by indicating that the English monarch provided supplies and funds to help Rabban Sauma's embassy defray its expenses.

By late November of 1287, Rabban Sauma believed he had accomplished two-thirds of his mission. He had elicited pledges from the pious English monarch and the young French King to partake in a Crusade against the Mamlūks. The armies of two of Europe's most powerful monarchies were thus, in theory, poised to join with the Ilkhanate in a three-pronged attack. Yet the spiritual leader of Europe had not given his imprimatur to such an expedition. Without Papal sanction, the campaign would lack the religious legitimacy that would attract and retain the support of a united Christian Europe and strengthen its challenge to the Muslim rulers of the Holy Land. Rabban Sauma could not return to his religious sanctuary in Persia without having secured a Papal audience and made a concerted effort to persuade the Pope to induce the other secular leaders of Western Christianity to support an expedition led by the monarchs of France and England. By the end of the year, however, the College of Cardinals had still not settled on a new Pontiff.

A WINTER SOJOURN IN GENOA

Having completed his audience with Edward and beginning to feel the onset of winter in France, Rabban Sauma elected to move south. The climate of his native region near Tai-tu was harsher and colder than France's, but his eight-year sojourn in Persia had accustomed him to warmer weather. Thus, he decided to go back to Genoa to await the election of a new Pope. By mid-December he had reached the prosperous Italian port where he proposed to pass the winter months. Once again Church dignitaries and the *capitano del popolo* proved hospitable. Sauma's description of Genoa shows that the mild climate and beautiful surroundings captivated him.[28] He compared the town to a garden paradise that experienced no extremes of temperature. The vegetation was lush the year round, and the trees were never bare of leaves. The vines produced grapes seven times a year, a fact that made a lasting impression because the Nestorian was accustomed to far fewer annual crops.

Despite this idyllic environment, Rabban Sauma became increasingly unhappy as the winter wore on. He wanted to present Arghun's proposal to the religious leader of the Western world, but the Cardinals had still not elected a Pope. Homesickness must also have entered into his growing disenchantment. He doubtless wished to return to more familiar surroundings to live out his last years. Few close associates or fellow clerics had accompanied him to the West, and he would have missed the companionship of people with whom he could converse easily, without having to wait for a translation. The fact that he had been separated for about a year from Mar Yaballaha, his intimate friend and confidant for nearly three decades, surely contributed to his feeling of isolation.

Rabban Sauma expressed his frustration at having to remain so long in Europe to a Papal legate who passed through Genoa that winter. This envoy, John of Tusculum, had been dispatched by Pope Honorius IV in 1286 to negotiate the conditions for the enthronement of Rudolf of Hapsburg as Holy Roman Emperor. After the enthronement, on learning of the death of the Pope, the envoy had departed from Würzburg for Rome. Rabban Sauma must have been something of a curiosity for Europeans, because, when John arrived in Genoa, he was immediately escorted into the presence of the Nestorian cleric.[29] The two men greeted each other affectionately, and the Papal envoy said that he had heard of Rabban Sauma's desire to revisit Rome. Sauma now poured out his feelings, explaining that he had waited a year for a Pope to be elected. How, he asked, could he return to his Mongol overlords without any response to their proposal from the spiritual leader of the Western world? According to the text, John understood and empathized with Rabban Sauma's dilemma, and he assured the foreign envoy that on his return to Rome he would bring the matter up with the Church hierarchy. He intended to urge the Cardinals to end their stalemate and elect a new Pope.

On John's arrival in Rome, he found that no such prompting was required, for the Cardinals had selected a Pope: Jerome of Ascoli, renowned as a pious, modest, and learned man. When the College had first elected Jerome, on February 15, 1288, he had refused the honor. The Cardinals then reelected him on February 22 and persuaded him to accept the position. On March 1 he had been enthroned and assumed the name of Nicholas IV.[30]

The choice of Jerome of Ascoli augured well for Rabban

Sauma's mission. The new Pope was well traveled and sophisticated. In 1272 he had been sent to Constantinople on a Papal mission to seek unity or at least closer cooperation between the Eastern and Western churches. Although the attempts at union finally proved abortive, his travels had made him sensitive to the concerns of the Eastern branch of Christianity. Aware of the Eastern Christians' fear of the Mamlūks, aware that the Muslims posed a threat to the Outremer as well as other Christian communities, he might look with favor on the Mongols' proffered alliance against them. His election thus appeared to hold out the prospect of a successful conclusion to Rabban Sauma's mission.[31]

MEETING WITH THE POPE

The initial sequence of events seemed promising. On learning that the Nestorian cleric was still in Genoa, the Pope immediately dispatched an emissary to invite him to Rome. As soon as he received the invitation, Rabban Sauma packed up his belongings, said his good-byes, thanked his Genoese hosts, and set forth for the Eternal City. After a two-week journey, he and his traveling companions reached the outskirts of Rome, where they were met by a bishop and a group of religious dignitaries sent by the Pope. Rabban Sauma inquired about the identity of the new Pontiff and was delighted to learn that the spiritual leader of Western Christianity was one of the prelates with whom he had had a lengthy exchange during his last audience with the College of Cardinals.

Elated that the conditions for his visit seemed to be optimal, Rabban Sauma went, with great esprit, to have an audience with the new Pope. Ushered into Nicholas IV's presence, he bowed low and on his hands and knees kissed the Pontiff's hands and feet. Then he straightened up and walked backward with his hands crossed on his chest, perhaps a Nestorian tradition. Having made this gesture of submission, he addressed the Pope, extolling the Papal office as well as its current occupant. He thanked God for allowing him the opportunity to appear before the Pontiff.[32] How much of this was sincere and how much was simply fulfilling the demands of ceremonial or ritual protocol is impossible to tell, although the Nestorian's delight and pride at having a personal audience with the Pope ought not to be discounted. After delivering his encomium, he gave the Pope the gifts and letter sent by the Ilkhan and a letter and presents from Mar Yaballaha. Neither letter has survived, but Arghun's dispatch surely proposed that the Pope call a Crusade and that Western and Eastern forces cooperate against the Mamlūks. Mar Yaballaha's letter is more problematic. Did the Nestorian Patriarch merely convey his greetings and salutations and sketch a description of his form of Christianity, or did he suggest the possibility of a union between the two churches? Good arguments could be adduced for either alternative, but, without access to the letter, neither can be confirmed or ruled out.

The Pope was, in any case, impressed by the gifts and messages and treated Rabban Sauma far better than ordinary envoys to the Papal court. He insisted that his Nestorian visitor spend Easter with his fellow Christians in the West. Rather than having to travel during the Holy Week, Rabban Sauma thus had an opportunity to conduct the proper religious rituals in a Christian community. The Pope also provided his visitor with comfortable lodgings, offering him a place nearby to stay and assigning servants to cater to his needs. With all his creature comforts cared for, Rabban Sauma could concentrate on the ceremonies associated with Easter.

Rabban Sauma recorded these ceremonies in detail. A short time after his initial audience with the Pope, he requested permission to celebrate Mass, because he wished to show Western Christians how it was conducted in the Nestorian Church. The Pope not only granted permission but also professed himself extremely interested in seeing Rabban

Sauma celebrate the Eucharist. He was not, however, the only fascinated observer. On the appointed day, a sizable crowd appeared, as Rabban Sauma noted, "in order to see how the ambassador of the Mongols celebrated the Eucharist."[33] When Sauma had done so, the general response of the Catholic prelates was that, although the language was different, the actions were the same as in their own Mass. They rejoiced at this and indicated that they would not be distressed if Sauma continued to conduct religious services for the next few weeks. The Pope too was willing and appeared to be captivated by his visitor. After the Mass, he expressed to Rabban Sauma his hope that God would receive the offerings made during the services, would bless him, and would absolve him of his sins. Grateful for the Pope's words, Rabban Sauma nonetheless made one more request. He asked to receive communion directly from the Pontiff, and the Pope assented immediately, with Palm Sunday set as the day for the celebration.

Palm Sunday turned out to be perhaps even more magnificent than Rabban Sauma had anticipated. An enormous crowd gathered to take part in and witness the ceremonies. Rabban Sauma's narrative tells us that thousands upon thousands of worshippers—so many that they were impossible to count—gathered around the Papal throne in San Pietro. The scene probably resembled similar celebrations at the Vatican today. The faithful brought olive branches, which the Pope blessed and offered as gifts first to the Cardinals, bishops, and others in the religious hierarchy and then to the city's secular leadership, including the nobility. Finally, he threw the remaining blessed branches to the multitudes.[34] After casting the olive branches, the Pope descended from his throne and went to a secluded area near the church's altar where he changed his vestments. Now wearing an ankle-length purple robe woven with gold threads and encrusted with precious stones, he walked past the altar to the pulpit and addressed and instructed the crowd. He then celebrated the Eucharist and offered communion first to Rabban Sauma, absolving the Nestorian cleric and his fathers of their sins. Sauma was greatly moved. Weeping with joy, he thanked the Lord and exulted in his good fortune.

The ceremonies continued on the day of Passover (Maundy Thursday). The Pope left his residence in the Lateran Palace to go to the nearby Basilica of San Giovanni in Laterano, the center of the archbishopric of Rome, which Rabban Sauma had visited during his previous stay in the city. It must have been as spacious then as its rebuilt version is now,[35] for Sauma wrote that a throng of devoted Christians had flocked into the church long before the Pope's arrival. According to his account, so many people had squeezed into the basilica that when they responded "Amen" to the Pope's prayers the ground shook.[36] The crowd was so vast that the Pope's words could scarcely be heard beyond the small group clustered around him.

Rabban Sauma's account does not reveal the contents of the sermon. It does tell us that, although the Pope's voice and message were barely audible, he elicited a strong response from the crowd. Finishing his prayers and sermon, he descended from the pulpit, offered communion before the devout crowd, and consecrated the oil that would be used in extreme unction. He then went to an adjacent large building where he rewarded each of the Church Fathers he regarded most highly with gold sheets and silver coins. He concluded the ceremonies by bringing together everyone in his household, including the servants, and ritually washing their feet. Taking note of this evidence of Papal humility, Rabban Sauma described the washing and drying ceremony carefully. All these rituals ended by midday, and when they were done the Pope held an elaborate feast for approximately two thousand people to celebrate such a successful Passover. The festivities lasted until, as Rabban Sauma wrote, "only three hours of the day were left."[37]

On the following day, Good Friday, the Pope once again led

a contingent to worship. Donning a black cloak, he was accompanied by similarly clad Church dignitaries, who, like him, walked barefoot to the Church of Santa Croce (Holy Cross). On reaching the church, the Pope took in his hands a purported fragment of the True Cross and paid homage to and kissed it. The Emperor Constantine's mother had reputedly brought this piece to Rome on her return from a pilgrimage to Jerusalem, and after her death her son had turned her palace into a church to house the relic. Whatever the actual provenance of the fragment, the Pope and other Church leaders obviously accepted it as genuine. The Pope allowed each of the Church dignitaries to handle and kiss it, then held it high for the throng that had followed his procession to see. As soon as they glimpsed it, most of the people in the crowd doffed their hats, bowed down, and prayed before this sacred object. The Pope preached to the crowd, then made the sign of the cross in all four directions. Having fulfilled his public obligations, he took some of the Paschal Offering, food that had been brought by the faithful and that he had earlier consecrated, supplemented it with wine, and dined alone in the church. Rabban Sauma wrote that, on this day commemorating the Passion, Western Christians did not ordinarily practice the ritual of communion; thus, the Pontiff ate and meditated by himself. After this somber meal, the Pope returned to his own palace.

On the Sabbath of Light (Holy Saturday), the Pope, accompanied by Rabban Sauma, returned to the church for additional services. He read aloud from the Books of the Prophets, in particular the prophecies concerning Jesus as the Messiah. He then arranged the baptismal font, consecrated the water, baptized three children, and made the sign of the cross over them. Finally, he went to the apse and changed into elaborately decorated and extremely expensive robes to conduct the Mass.[38]

On the Sunday commemorating the Resurrection, Easter

Day, the Pope continued to carry out his official duties. Escorted by a large entourage of Cardinals and bishops, he traveled to the Basilica of Santa Maria Maggiore, still another of the great churches built at the time of the Roman Empire that Rabban Sauma had visited during his first stay in Rome. Again, Nicholas offered communion to the assembled leaders of the Church, with all the participants embracing to seal the sacredness of the occasion. The Pope further affirmed his religious and personal harmony with his entourage by organizing a fabulous banquet for them. On the next Sunday, he conducted extravagant ceremonies once again. This time he performed the laying on of hands, then ordained three bishops.

Not surprisingly, Rabban Sauma witnessed all these celebrations, rituals, and festivities with great interest. He probably still perceived himself as being as much a religious pilgrim as an ambassador and recognized that Mar Yaballaha and his other Nestorian brethren would be most intrigued by his description of religious observances in the Western Church. They would await with great anticipation a report on Western religious ceremonies and doctrines by perhaps the first Christian cleric from the East to have an opportunity to observe these practices closely.

Now that he had taken part in a concentrated period of religious rituals, witnessed a variety of Church observances, and delivered Arghun's letter proposing an alliance, Rabban Sauma wished to return to his own people and land. After the Easter ceremonies, therefore, he requested permission to travel back to Persia. The Pope demurred and invited the Nestorian cleric to stay on in the West. Rabban Sauma responded that he would like to remain for a time but that a higher objective would be served by his return. If he told his own people about the exceptional treatment he had received in Europe, good feelings would be generated between the Western and Eastern churches. Peace would prevail in the territories where Persia and the European states interacted. Had Rabban Sauma concluded his reply at that point, he would have left without raising an eyebrow. But he went further, asking for a gift of sacred relics.

Doubtless annoyed by the brazenness of the request, the Pope nonetheless responded with aplomb. He said that if the Church made a habit of offering relics to each foreign visitor, then, even if it possessed mountains of such sacred objects, none would remain. However, in recognition of the tremendous distance Rabban Sauma had traveled, the Pope would magnanimously provide a few relics. He gave Rabban Sauma a scrap of Jesus' clothing, another scrap of the Virgin Mary's kerchief, and miscellaneous relics of various saints. He also transmitted to Mar Yaballaha via Rabban Sauma a crown of pure gold adorned with precious stones, a purple sacred robe lined with gold threads, socks and footwear festooned with small pearls, and one of his own rings.

At least as important from Rabban Sauma's viewpoint was the fact that, according to his narrative, Nicholas provided a letter patent investing the Nestorian Patriarch with authority over all Christians in the East, then gave Rabban Sauma a similar letter patent, confirming him Visitor-General in the East, presumably meaning Central Asia and China. Neither investiture is, however, mentioned in a letter to Arghun that the Pope gave to Rabban Sauma, and Rabban Sauma may have misinterpreted the Pope's words. In any event, the Pontiff's issuing such letters patent would have implied that he had authority over the Nestorian Church. Rabban Sauma did not object, probably because he did not wish to jeopardize any possibility of political alliance and religious cooperation. Finally, at the close of their conversation, Sauma received a substantial sum of "red gold" for his traveling expenses.[39]

Subsequently, the Pope also asked Sauma to bring the Il-khan Arghun presents and the letter from him. A copy of this letter has survived in the Vatican Archives, and it reveals a

great deal about the Vatican's objectives as well as the shrewdness of the Pope himself. It begins by praising the Mongol
ruler of Persia. The Pope noted with satisfaction that the Ilkhan was well disposed toward Christians living in his domains and had extended the bounds of Christianity. Indicating his appreciation for Arghun's efforts on behalf of
Christianity, the Pope also expressed gratitude for Rabban
Sauma's embassy and the message it brought him. He praised
this message for its respect for Christianity and Western
Christians.[40]

All these flattering remarks led up to Nicholas's real message, that both the Mongols and the Nestorians should accept
Papal authority. He devoted the next part of his letter to a
reaffirmation of the centrality of Jesus in the Christian message, writing,

> We are eager for it to be revealed to your understanding
> that the lofty King, son of the Highest King, went forth
> from the heights of the poles and to the depths of this
> world, so that he might free man, whom he had formed
> according to his image and likeness from the mud of the
> earth, from the bonds of slavery into which malicious ad-
> vice had fastened him.

He went on to note that the Messiah had given the keys of the
kingdom of Heaven to Peter, from whom the Popes derived
their authority. His aim apparently was to show and capitalize
on the direct relationship of the Papacy to Jesus, to cite
Christ's words and actions in order to sanction the Pope's
ecclesiastical power.

Nicholas was thus asserting his own primacy over the Nestorian Patriarchs. He emphasized that the Western form of
Christianity was the "true faith" and urged Arghun to recognize it as the one authentic and legitimate religion. He then
counseled the Ilkhan to be baptized and to embrace the
Christian faith as his own. Without such a conversion, he said,
the Ilkhan would jeopardize his chance for salvation and risk

entering the gates of Hell. With a rhetorical flourish, Nicholas advised,

> Consider also that no one is exempt from the law of death
> ... no one escapes its limits, no exception to death is
> granted by the Lord; accordingly, rise up readily, present
> yourself, make ready and approach the recognition of the
> Christian faith ... so that after the workhouse of the pres-
> ent life you may be freed from the gate of hell.

He indicated that Arghun would be a champion of Christianity if he accepted Papal authority.

Nicholas added a postscript to preclude any possible accusation that he had ignored Arghun's proposal for an alliance. Unlike Kings Philip of France and Edward of England, the Pope was unwilling to commit himself even verbally to a Crusade. As the religious leader of Europe, he, rather than the secular monarchs, would be the one to call the Crusade, although secular leaders had initiated Crusades with only the most perfunctory Papal support, as in St. Louis' and Edward's Crusade in Tunis around 1270. Still, the Pope was the one likely to be held responsible for the success or failure of such a venture, and he thus had reason to be more cautious and less prone to grand gestures than Edward or Philip. Knowing that European support was in doubt, Nicholas was unwilling to entangle himself in a perhaps futile attempt to recover the Holy Land.

In his postscript, the Pope assured the Ilkhan that he knew that the Mongol ruler desired to be reborn in the city of Jerusalem by being baptized[41] and asserted that Arghun ought to reverse his priorities. If the Ilkhan were baptized immediately, his recovery of Jerusalem and the Holy Land would be facilitated. The Lord would give him the strength to defeat and oust the Mamlūks if he pleased Him by accepting baptism. Moreover, his baptism would not only ensure his own salvation but also serve as a model for others in his domain. Nicholas implied that such mass conversions would further strengthen the Mongols of Persia in their attempt to occupy the Holy Land. By pleasing the Lord, the people of the Il-khanate would secure His blessings for their campaigns against the infidels.

Nicholas thus neatly sidestepped the question of active European support for such a campaign. He implicitly encouraged a Mongol assault on the Mamlūks but refrained from pledging an alliance. He failed to mention the fate of the Outremer communities and did not promise to urge Kings Philip and Edward to collaborate with Arghun. Instead of tangible political and military aid, he offered the possibility of salvation. Nicholas had his own agenda, and complying with the Ilkhan's proposal was not part of it.

The Pope's letter surely distressed Rabban Sauma. He had hoped for a more ardent Papal commitment to Christian control of the Holy Land. Similarly, he must have been disappointed by the Pope's letter, which he was also asked to carry, to the Ilkhan Abakha's widow, who had been a Byzantine princess. Nicholas praised her Christian zeal and encouraged her to be like a bee with honey and spread the word of the Lord among her people, but again he made no mention of a Crusade or an alliance against the Mamlūks.[42]

Another letter the Pope confided to Rabban Sauma, addressed to Mar Yaballaha, would not be expected to deal with an alliance. Dated five days after the letter to Arghun, it opens with an expression of gratitude for the Patriarch's own missive. Nicholas praised Yaballaha for his excellent treatment of the Franciscans who passed through or lived in his domains. Then the Pope somewhat condescendingly lectured the Patriarch on Church doctrine and faith. He described the Trinity, the concept of sin, and the Seven Sacraments, and went so far as to "inform" the Patriarch that bigamy, which the Nestorians practiced, was unacceptable for Christians.[43] The spiritual leader of the Nestorian Church in the East certainly would not require (or appreciate) a lecture about the main tenets of Christianity, in particular one that did not give any credence to or even discuss those of Nestorianism as compared with those of Catholicism.[44] The body of the letter is undoubtedly tactless, and the concluding paragraph, an affirmation of the supremacy of the Roman Church, is equally so.

The Pope took advantage of Rabban Sauma's imminent departure to entrust him with several other letters, including one addressed to a number of Europeans residing in the Ilkhan's court. Some of these were merchants, while others were interpreters and counselors to the Mongol rulers of Persia. They were clearly not agents of the Church. Individuals such as Hugo Gantelmes and Peter of Molina were men of affairs, looking out for their own or the Ilkhan's interests. Yet here again the Pope wanted them to take on religious tasks— that is, to act as missionaries in the East and "to extend the boundaries of the Christian faith." These works would make them "more pleasing to [the] Savior."[45] There is no record of the reactions of these Europeans to the religious duty suddenly thrust upon them by the Pope. It is also impossible to know if Rabban Sauma actually delivered this letter. Suffice it to say that none of these Europeans made a mark as a Christian missionary among the Mongols of Persia.

The Pope's final letter was a personal message to Bar Sauma, a Nestorian bishop in Persia who by pure coincidence shared the name of the traveler to the West. This missive adopts the same condescending tone as the Papal correspondence with Mar Yaballaha. Once again it opens with praise, commending Bar Sauma for having been enlightened by the Christian faith and accepted baptism. It urges the Nestorian cleric (as if he needed urging) to "enlarge the bonds and extend the limits of the faith"—that is, to proselytize and seek converts. Nicholas called upon him to strive to bring his own people from the "cloud of infidelity to the brightness of the Christian faith and from the wilderness of error to the path of righteousness."[46] Thus far, the Pope's message is basically exhortatory and could not have been regarded as offensive. The remainder of the letter, however, is not diplomatic. Nicholas had the temerity to instruct Bar Sauma on the principles of Christianity, regaling him with a description of the Christian religion much like what he had written for Mar Yaballaha.

Despite the note of condescension in these letters, Rabban Sauma did not show any rancor on taking leave of the Pope. Instead he thanked the spiritual leader of the West for all his gifts and for the fine treatment he had been accorded during his stay in Rome. The two men embraced and parted on a very cordial note. Rabban Sauma was no doubt relieved and excited to be heading home.

RETURN TO PERSIA

Since the Pope's letters to the Ilkhan, the Patriarch, and the Europeans in Persia are dated in early April of 1288, Rabban Sauma must have left shortly thereafter. Philip of France's ambassador Gobert de Helleville accompanied him to deliver a personal letter to Arghun. Departing from Rome, the Nestorian cleric seems to have returned to the Ilkhanate via the route he had taken before, but his narrative offers few details on his journey. He deviated slightly from his initial itinerary by stopping briefly in Veroli, a town about seventy miles southeast of Rome. Visiting the Cathedral of San Andrea (St. Andrew), he met three archbishops and ten bishops, who were delighted by his arrival. No record of their meetings or their conversations has survived. However, still extant is a fifteen-line text, written on parchment, which records the granting of indulgences—remissions of the punishments for sins—by the Western Christian dignitaries and Rabban Sauma to those who confessed, took communion, or provided alms to the cathedral for its construction, maintenance, or ornamentation. Curiously, contrary to the usual Catholic

practice of that time, it omits mention of Christ as the source
of mercy, focusing instead on God the Father. The Church
authorities may have wished to skirt the doctrinal issues that
might reveal disparities between their faith and the Nestorianism of Rabban Sauma, which of course emphasized the Father and not the Son. The document contains a bland assertion that God gave more privileges to his servants than to
others and that indulgences encouraged the faithful to pray
with greater fervor and to participate wholeheartedly and
generously in Church activities.

Why did the authorities in Veroli allow their Nestorian visitor to join them in offering indulgences? They must have
known that Rabban Sauma was not an orthodox believer. It
seems unlikely that he could have made a substantial contribution to the cathedral, which might have persuaded them to
permit him to grant indulgences. Perhaps their willingness
derived partly from his celebrity and partly from a desire to
foster more cordial relations with the Nestorians of the East.

Whatever their motives, eight of the Church leaders joined
with Rabban Sauma in placing their seals on yellow and red
silk at the bottom of the parchment. Rabban Sauma's was in
red wax and featured an image of a haloed figure, perhaps
representing Christ, with his left hand on his chest and a star
in his right hand. Measuring fifty by thirty-five millimeters,
the seal also bore an inscription designating him "Barba-
zoma/Tartarus/Orientalis," or Bar Sauma/Tartar/from the
Orient, in Latin. It is remarkable that Rabban Sauma had had
a seal produced during his brief stay in Europe, but the imprint, now found in the Vatican Archives, is unquestionably
authentic.[47]

After his brief stop in Veroli, he "crossed the seas" and
reached Persia by late September of 1288. There he was almost immediately escorted into the presence of Arghun. He
transmitted the various gifts and letters sent to the Ilkhan
and supplemented these tangible items with oral and written

reports on the diplomatic mission Arghun had entrusted to him. The written report was turned over to a court archivist but, as we know, subsequently lost.

Meanwhile, he handed over to his fellow Nestorians the second, more comprehensive unofficial report, which described the remarkable things he had done and sights he had seen in the West. A copy was found among his papers when he died, though the original disappeared at some point. Also among his papers (which went to the Nestorians on his death) were his diaries and memoirs, including his account of his years in the Ilkhanate after his return from Europe. The Nestorian cleric who translated these documents into Syriac about twenty years after Sauma died not only carried the traveler's story through to his death, but appended a report on the persecution of Nestorian Christians after the accession of Ghazan as Ilkhan in 1295, and concluded with a survey of Mar Yaballaha's career. As indicated earlier, he also added occasional comments of his own to Rabban Sauma's narrative and edited Sauma's entire account. He wrote that, since "it was not our intention to relate and set out in order all the unimportant things which Rabban Sauma did and saw, we have abridged very much of what he himself wrote . . . and even the things which are mentioned here have been abridged, or amplified, according to necessity."[48] Because the editor-translator was chiefly interested in theological questions and in Rabban Sauma's relations with clerics in the West, the "unimportant things" were largely secular matters, and Sauma's religious concerns and activities became the central focus of the narrative. This is no doubt the reason that Sauma himself has been accorded relatively little attention by later historians. Church historians and specialists on Nestorians have been the principal students of his work and have often tended to slight its political and diplomatic significance.

According to the account Rabban Sauma wrote about the period after his return from Europe, Arghun was delighted with what he saw as the success of the mission. After all, the Kings of England and France had pledged to join in a Crusade against the Mamlūks. Although the Pope had not committed himself to such an expedition, he had called for closer religious ties. Pleased with such striking results, Arghun treated the Nestorian cleric with particular graciousness. He apologized to Rabban Sauma for the many hardships he had imposed on him by having him undertake this valuable assignment. Determined to reward his envoy, he pledged to care for him in his old age and to build him a church near the Ilkhanate palace. After thanking Arghun, Rabban Sauma responded by requesting that the Ilkhan order Mar Yaballaha to come to the court to receive the gifts the Westerners had sent him as well as to visit and consecrate the site of the church to be built for Sauma's retirement. The Ilkhan consented and sent messengers to invite the Patriarch to the capital.

When Mar Yaballaha reached Arghun's court, the Ilkhan had a temporary, tentlike structure built as a church for special services and functions such as feasts. He then organized an elaborate banquet, which lasted for three days. Mongol taste had by now become sophisticated. Thus, in addition to dining on traditional fare such as roast lamb, broths and soups produced by boiling the meat in a caldron, wild onions and other vegetables, and berries, the Mongols supplemented their diet with Chinese and Middle Eastern foods. Turkic steamed, stuffed breads, Chinese noodles, Middle Eastern sweet drinks (*sharbat*) made of red currants, and tea with milk added variety to Mongol meals and banquets. Feasts were occasions for sustained and immense consumption of alcohol—the traditional *koumiss* as well as the brandies, wines, and beers of the civilizations with which the Mongols came into contact—though it appears unlikely there was much drinking in this case.

The Ilkhan personally served the Nestorian Patriarch and

Rabban Sauma, repeatedly dishing out food and pouring drinks for Mar Yaballaha and his entourage. Arghun encouraged the company to continue their prayers when they were not at the feast. They all joined in a chant: "Blessed be the Lord Who hath made us rich! The Lord hath visited His people, and hath made for it redemption."[49] The Ilkhan then commanded that prayers be recited on behalf of Rabban Sauma and made the Nestorian cleric the head of the church adjacent to his palace. In short, the grateful Arghun showered Rabban Sauma and the Nestorians with attention and gifts.

About one year later, in September of 1289, the Ilkhan went to the seat of the Patriarchate in Marāgha. He brought his eight-year-old son to be baptized and to receive absolution for his sins from Mar Yaballaha. In 1289, he also appointed a Jewish physician, Sa'd al-Dawla, as his vizier and granted him great leeway in controlling the country.[50] Judaism and Nestorianism, with Ilkhanate patronage, were surging in Mongol-ruled Persia. Almost at once, however, especially after Arghun became ill late in 1290, Muslim opposition to the growing prominence of Christians and Jews would arise.

Arghun remained confident that Rabban Sauma's mission would lead to an alliance against the Mamlūks. In 1289 he sent a letter, via a Genoese named Buscarel de Gisolf, to Edward I and Philip the Fair in response to Philip's dispatch of Gobert de Helleville. In his missive, he referred first to Philip's and Edward's respective pledges that if the Ilkhan's troops campaigned against Egypt their own forces would join in the military effort. He challenged the French and English Kings by alerting them that in January of 1291 his army would attack Damascus. Indicating that he expected Philip and Edward to send troops, he in turn promised to hand Jerusalem over to the Europeans once they had expelled the Mamlūks. He reminded the monarchs that promptness was essential and that the dispatch of auxiliary troops after the proposed date would be of little use. Finally, he requested some valuable goods, gerfalcons and precious stones of various colors, for which he promised to reward the Kings who sent them and the envoys who brought them.[51] The Western rulers' response to this letter was equivocal. Philip's letter has not survived, but Edward's reply, which has been preserved, makes no pledge to join in a campaign. The English monarch flattered Arghun and praised him for proposing an expedition to recover the Holy Land, but he sidestepped the Ilkhan's call for European troops to join in the attack. He instructed Arghun to seek a Papal commitment for a Crusade.[52]

Despite his clearly stated intention, Arghun's plans for a military expedition never materialized. Instead, he was diverted by threats from the Mongol Khanate to his north. In the spring of 1290, the Golden Horde raided his lands from South Russia. Simultaneously, he faced a rebellion in Khurā-sān, the easternmost province of his territories. Confronted with these double threats, he could not consider a campaign to the west. Adding to his difficulties was the illness that came upon him in the winter of 1290, apparently aggravated by his consumption of potions prepared by a so-called Buddhist priest. He died in March of 1291, and with him perished his plans for a coalition with the West.[53]

From this time on the Ilkhanate, the principal supporter of such an effort, abandoned the notion of cooperation with the Christian European states. Political turbulence, which resulted in the accession of three Ilkhans between 1291 and 1295, fiscal problems, and the conversion of the Ilkhan Ghazan (r. 1295–1304) and many other Mongols to Islam in the 1290s diverted them from concerns about the Mamlūks. In 1300 Ghazan's forces defeated the Mamlūks in Syria, but they withdrew shortly thereafter and the Mamlūks returned. This campaign was the sixth launched in Syria by the Mongols over the last four decades, none of them successful, and it would be the final one. The Mongols were never able to wrest control of Syria or the Holy Land from the Mamlūks.

The European monarchs themselves remained tentative about participating in such a campaign. Philip the Fair and Edward I had pledged to join in an attack on the Mamlūks, but they still faced either foreign threats or internal disturbances that diminished or destroyed their ability to fulfill their promise. Although in principle they supported an expedition against the Mamlūks, they must have known that they could not provide resources for such an operation. Meanwhile, Europe in general was plagued by disunity. In the words of one well-known historian, "already the West as a unit had ceased to exist, and consequently unified action was no longer possible. The Pope alone remained as the last evidence of the great Western idea."[54] And he was somewhat ineffectual at that, as Rabban Sauma's experience confirms. It was evidently not a time for concerted action.

The failure of the European monarchs to mount an effective campaign against the Mamlūks proved disastrous for the Outremer. Without protection and support from their fellow Christians, they were vulnerable to Muslim attacks, which had begun even before the Mongols and the Europeans had given up hopes for an alliance. By 1289 the Christian community in Tripoli had fallen to the Mamlūks, and by 1291 the Muslims had destroyed the last Outremer outpost at Acre.[55] There would be no further attempts at an alliance between the Mongols and the Europeans. The European monarchs had lost a golden opportunity to recover the Holy Land and maintain contact with the Mongol world.

What of Rabban Sauma himself? In his midsixties by the time of Arghun's death, he still had no permanent church of his own, as Arghun had not yet fulfilled his promise. Sauma had grown weary of following the Ilkhan, of having his church be a constantly moving appendage to the Ilkhan's constantly moving court. The Mongol rulers had not abandoned their nomadic ways, and Rabban Sauma could no longer sustain such migrations. As soon as Arghun's brother Geikhatu ascended the throne, therefore, Rabban Sauma requested that he provide him with funds for the construction of a permanent church building. He chose Marāgha, near the site of Mar Yaballaha's private residence, as the location for this church. Although Persian hostility to Judaism and Christianity continued to grow, Geikhatu, according to Rabban Sauma's account, favored the leaders of both religions and acceded to his request. Over the next three years, Geikhatu built an elaborate church to house the numerous sacred relics in Rabban Sauma's possession. During his travels, Sauma had accumulated the bones, clothing, and paraphernalia of a number of saints and martyrs. These treasures could now be kept in a secure building, which was also under the patronage of the Ilkhan.[56] Mar Yaballaha assisted in the efforts to construct the church and raise funds for its maintenance. An endowment similar to the Muslim *waqf* was established to provide for repairs, upkeep, and possible expansion of the church and its collection of artifacts.

Meanwhile Rabban Sauma expended enormous effort in raising funds and conducting religious services at the church even before it was finished. He repeatedly presided at the Eucharist for the pious and prayed in private in his cell. His dedication to the Nestorian Church and devotion to the Christian faith were manifest. Here was a man spending his last years doing precisely what he wanted and what he had prepared for. His account makes it plain that he was extremely happy in his new life, particularly with the opportunity to devote himself fully to his religious pursuits.[57]

During the years that elapsed before the church's completion, the Ilkhan Geikhatu was, according to Rabban Sauma's narrative, exceptionally supportive of the Nestorian cleric's religious activities. On two specific occasions, he traveled to Marāgha to meet with the Nestorian leaders. As characterized in the text, these meetings were not only amiable and joyous but also offered tangible rewards, for the Ilkhan presented the Patriarch with gifts and money. The Mongol rulers of Persia continued to favor the Nestorians until the Ilkhan Ghazan converted to Islam.

After Rabban Sauma's church was completed in October of 1293, he had more time for other concerns, the most important of which was to spend as many of his remaining days as possible with Mar Yaballaha. Toward the end of the year, although he was ill and in pain, he journeyed from Marāgha to the Patriarch's seat at Baghdad to spend the winter. He then traveled quite a distance to attend a banquet in honor of Mar Yaballaha. Arghun's cousin Baidu, who eventually attempted to depose Geikhatu as Ilkhan, was giving an elaborate feast to show his respect for Mar Yaballaha, and Rabban Sauma was determined to participate in this important ceremony for the friend with whom he had been closely associated for more than three decades. Fever and weakness on his arrival did not deter him from attending the reception. He appears to have fallen down once during the festivities but recovered sufficiently to get through the evening.

On the following day he headed back toward Baghdad. Before leaving he said his last farewells to Baidu and on the way made a brief stop in Arbīl to "settle" unspecified "urgent affairs."[58] We learn this from the editor-translator, who supplied the account of Rabban Sauma's last days. After he arrived in Baghdad, Sauma grew weaker. Pain spread throughout his body, and his ailments worsened, but he was determined to live until Mar Yaballaha, who was absent on Church business, returned. When the Patriarch arrived, the two clerics said their good-byes, both fervently believing they would meet in the afterlife. Having husbanded his strength for the meeting with Mar Yaballaha, Rabban Sauma began to fade after this emotional reunion. The editor-translator of his narrative wrote of his last days that "his disease waxed heavy, healing took to flight, his life was despaired of, and he departed from this world of nothingness and tribulations to the world of holiness and to the City of the Saints, Jerusalem which is in the heavens . . ."[59] In January of 1294, a month before the death of Khubilai Khan, Rabban Sauma succumbed to the disease wracking his body. He was buried in the church of a monastery, adjacent to the tombs of some of the great Patriarchs of the past. Despite his faith, Mar Yaballaha was grief-stricken and could not control his tears for some time. He mourned his friend and mentor for three days before returning home. There he received many of the pious, who tried to console him. In the years to come, Mar Yaballaha continued the correspondence with the Catholic Church that his friend had helped him begin, sending letters about purely religious matters to the Popes Boniface VIII and Benoit XI as late as 1302 and 1304.[60] However, his later life was marred by the Ilkhans' conversion to Islam and the growing antipathy toward Nestorians in Persia. When he died in 1317, Nestorianism was in decline throughout Persia and Central Asia.

Rabban Sauma's story was over. Similarly, his remarkable mission, which might have changed the history of the Middle East, Europe, the Ilkhanate, and the whole Mongol Empire, had come to nothing. Still, it had been potentially one of the critically significant embassies in Eurasian history.

As a leading historian of the Crusades has written, "had the Mongol alliance been achieved and honestly implemented by the West, the existence of Outremer would almost have certainly been prolonged. The Mamlūks would have been crippled if not destroyed; and the Ilkhanate of Persia would have survived as a power friendly to the Christians and the West."[61]

If Christian Europe and Ilkhanate Persia together had succeeded in crushing the Islamic dynasty in Egypt, the aims of the Crusades would have been fulfilled. The Holy Land would have been recovered by the Western powers; Europeans would have had a base in the Middle East; the lack of a powerful dynasty to protect Islamic interests would have

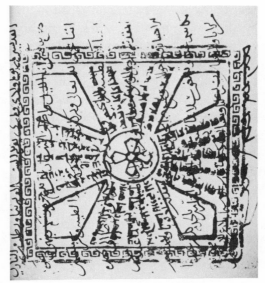

Mar Yaballaha's seal in the form of a crucifix, on a letter to Pope Boniface VIII, 1302. From the Vatican Library.

made the rest of the Middle East and North Africa vulnerable to attacks from both East and West. We can speculate endlessly about the relationship that would have developed between the Mongol Empire and the various Christian countries. Europe and Asia would have been more closely linked, increasing the opportunities for cultural, political, and economic interchanges. Some influential Mongols, like some of their cousins in China who embraced Buddhism, would probably have converted to the Western form of Christianity, and such conversions would surely have had profound implications for the future. This was clearly a critical turning point in world history.

Such speculation, however, is not essential to an appreciation of Rabban Sauma's career. He was an intrepid adventurer and traveler, a gifted linguist, a pious and learned man, and a skilled diplomat and negotiator. Although he was ultimately unable to forge an alliance between the Mongols and

Christian Europe, his embassy was an extraordinary early example of geopolitics on a modern scale. From his perspective, it was a resounding success: His most cherished goals were religious, and as a religious pilgrimage his journey to the West was deeply rewarding. Rabban Sauma, the first person to travel from Peking to Paris, the man entrusted with a delicate mission that could have changed history, had ample reason to be satisfied with his achievements. He had brought the very different worlds of Christian Europe and the Mongol Empire closer, if only for a moment.

NOTES

Chapter 1. Setting the Stage

1. Donald F. Lach, *Asia in the Making of Europe*. Volume 1: *The Century of Discovery*: Book 1, 39. It should be noted, however, that he was a Turk born in China and was not ethnically Chinese.

2. The earliest and best translation of this account is found in J. B. Chabot, "Histoire du Patriarche Mar Jabalaha III et du moine Rabban Çauma," 1: 567–610; 2:73–142, 235–304. Other translations are found in E. A. Wallis Budge, *The Monks of Kûblâi Khân, Emperor of China*, and James A. Montgomery, trans., *The History of Yaballaha III, Nestorian Patriarch and of His Vicar Bar Sauma*, which offers only a partial translation. Paul Pelliot, *Recherches sur les chrétiens d'Asie centrale et d'Extrême Orient*, provides an evaluation of the relative merits of these translations. For a fine Russian translation, see N. V. Pigulevskaia, *Istoriia Mar Iabalakhi i Rabban Saumy*. Excerpts from the Budge translation are found in Jeannette Mirsky, ed., *The Great Chinese Travelers*, 175–200. Even earlier than Budge's work is Norman McLean's study "An Eastern Embassy to Europe in the Years 1287–88," 299–312. For the discovery of the Syriac manuscript in 1888, see Pigulevskaia, 10–12.

3. David Morgan, *The Mongols*, 187.

4. On these Chinese porcelains in Fusṭāṭ, see G. T. Scanlon, "Egypt and China: Trade and Imitation," in D. S. Richards, ed., *Islam and the Trade of Asia*, 81–95.

5. Friedrich Hirth and W. W. Rockhill, trans., *Chau Ju-kua: His Work on the Chinese and Arab Trade in the Twelfth and Thirteenth Centuries, Entitled Chu-fan-chi*, 195–97, 224–26; Edward H. Schafer, *The Golden Peaches of Samarkand*, 58–73, 170–71, 173, 188–89.

6. On the significance of protection costs, see Niels Steensgaard, *Carracks, Caravans, and Companies: The Structural Crisis in the European-Asian Trade in the Early 17th Century*, 31–42, and my "The 'Decline' of the Central Asian Caravan Trade," in James D. Tracy, ed., *The Rise of Merchant Empires*, 357–63.

7. An excellent, recent survey of the Mongol conquests may be found in Morgan, *Mongols*, 61–73.

8. Vsevolod Slessarev, *Prester John: The Letters and the Legend*, 4; see also George Lary, *The Medieval Alexander* (ed. by D. J. A. Ross) and the somewhat eccentric L. N. Gumilev, *Searches for an Imaginary Kingdom: The Legend of the Kingdom of Prester John* (trans. by R. E. F. Smith), 107–28.

9. Denis Sinor, "Un voyageur du treizième siècle: Le Dominicain Julien de Hongrie," 589–602, asserts that Julian made only one trip toward the Mongol camp. Igor de Rachewiltz, *Papal Envoys to the Great Khans*, 41, argues that Julian went in 1234–35 and again in 1237.

10. A. A. Vasiliev, *History of the Byzantine Empire, 324–1453*, 527–29, discusses the link between Frederick II and the Byzantines in opposition to the Pope.

11. For St. Louis, see the renowned work of Jean Sire de Joinville, *Histoire de Saint Louis, Roi de France*, or his *Histoire de Saint Louis*.

12. The best edition of the original Latin is found in Anastasius van den Wyngaert, *Sinica Franciscana*, 1.

13. Christopher Dawson, ed., *Mission to Asia*, 75–76.

14. Joseph Fletcher, "The Mongols: Ecological and Social Perspectives," 14.

15. Dawson, *Mission*, 83–84.

16. Leonardo Olschki, *Marco Polo's Precursors*, 44. For a useful study of the tradition of travel writing, see Mary Campbell, *The Witness and the Other World: Exotic European Travel Writing, 400–1600*.

17. Dawson, *Mission*, 8.

18. Dawson, *Mission*, 16.

19. Denis Sinor, "The Mongols and Western Europe," 520; Paul Pelliot, *Les Mongols et la Papauté*, Section 3, for Andrew's embassy.

20. Jean Richard, "The Mongols and the Franks," 48–49; Simon of Saint-Quentin joined Ascelinus's embassy and wrote an account of their travels; on Simon, see Gregory G. Guzman, "Simon of Saint-Quentin and the Dominican Mission of the Mongol Baiju: A Reappraisal," 232–49; "Simon of Saint-Quentin as Historian of the Mongols and the Seljuk Turks," 155–78; and, "The Encyclopedist Vincent of Beauvais and His Mongol Extracts from John of Plano Carpini and Simon of Saint-Quentin," 287–307.

21. Bernard Lewis, "Egypt and Syria" in Bernard Lewis, P. M. Holt, and Ann K. S. Lambton, eds., *The Cambridge History of Islam*, 1:208.

22. Constantin Mouradgea d'Ohsson, *Histoire des Mongols, depuis Tchinguiz-khan jusqu'à Timour-Bey ou Tamerlan*, 2:236–41; Eric Voegelin, "The Mongol Orders of Submission to European Powers, 1245–1255," 379–80.

23. Sinor, "The Mongols," 522; Steven Runciman, *A History of the Crusades*. Volume 3: *The Kingdom of Acre*, 225–58.

24. de Rachewiltz, *Papal Envoys*, 122–23.

25. William W. Rockhill, trans., *The Journey of William of Rubruck to the Eastern Parts of the World*, offers a translation of his account of his journey. A new translation is Peter Jackson and David Morgan, eds., *The Mission of Friar William of Rubruck*, which also offers an excellent bibliography that should be used to supplement the one in this book.

26. Jackson and Morgan, *Mission*, 46.

27. Jackson and Morgan, *Mission*, 48.

28. See Robert Bedrossian, "The Turco-Mongol Invasions and the Lords of Armenia in the 13th–14th Centuries," 22–41; see also John A. Boyle, "The Journey of Het'um I, King of Little Armenia, to the Court of the Great Khan Möngke," pp. 178–79.

29. John A. Boyle, ed., *The Cambridge History of Iran*. Volume 5: *The Saljuq and Mongol Periods*, 349. Another version of the Caliph's demise is that Hülegü allowed him to starve to death surrounded by his vast stores of gold and silver. This account is highly suspect. A useful study of the subject is John A. Boyle, "The Death of the Last 'Abbāsid Caliph: A Contemporary Muslim Account," 145–61.

30. For the implications of this struggle for succession, see Morris Rossabi, *Khubilai Khan: His Life and Times*, 46–62.

31. John Masson Smith, "'Ayn Jālūt: Mamlūk Success or Mongol Failure?" 307–45, offers a new, more valid interpretation than is found in earlier texts and corrects the version presented by Rashīd al-Dīn, which I depended upon too greatly in my *Khubilai Khan*.

32. Smith, "'Ayn Jālūt," 332–35, believes that their failures were due, in large part, to their continued use of steppe tactics in a terrain unsuitable for them. For example, Syria did not have sufficient water and grass for the Mongol horses.

33. B. Grekov and A. Iakoubovski, *La Horde d'Or* (trans. by François Thuret), 74–82; Charles J. Halperin, *Russia and the Golden Horde*, 27–29; Bertold Spuler, *Die Goldene Horde: Die Mongolen in Russland, 1223–1502*, 38–45.

34. Boyle, *Cambridge History of Iran*, 356–60.

35. Rossabi, *Khubilai Khan*, 70–95.

36. David Morgan, "The Mongols and the Eastern Mediterranean," 203; Richard, "Mongols and Franks," 51; see Runciman, *History of the Crusades*, 362–67, for more on the perceptions of the Outremer communities. For more on European attitudes toward the Mongols, see Peter Jackson, "The Crusade Against the Mongols."

37. C. Brunel, "David d'Ashby, auteur méconnu des *Faits des Tartares*," 39–46; Jean Richard, *La Papauté et les missions d'orient au moyen âge (xiii–xiv siècles)*, 90–103.

38. de Rachewiltz, *Papal Envoys*, 151.

39. Robert Chazan, *Daggers of Faith: Thirteenth-Century Christian Missionizing and Jewish Response*, 2.

40. For accounts of Chinese travelers to Central Asia during that time, see Emil Bretschneider, *Mediaeval Researches from Eastern Asiatic Sources*.

41. For sources on the Önggüds, see Igor de Rachewiltz, "The Secret History of the Mongols," 16:59, n. 182.

42. Igor de Rachewiltz, "Turks in China Under the Mongols: A Preliminary Investigation of Turco-Mongol Relations in the 13th and 14th Centuries," in Morris Rossabi, ed., *China Among Equals*, 289–92.

43. Budge, *Monks*, 39; see also J. M. Fiey, *Chrétiens syriaques sous les Mongols*, 1:9–176, and, for European travelers to China, see Henry Yule, *Cathay and the Way Thither* (rev. by Henri Cordier).

44. A good bibliography on Nestorianism is by Matti Moosa in Mircea Eliade, ed., *The Encyclopedia of Religion*, 10:372.

45. Alphonse Mingana, *The Early Spread of Christianity in Central Asia and the Far East*, 9–10.
46. de Rachewiltz, *Papal Envoys*, 136; the quote is from Budge, *Monks*, 32.
47. Budge, *Monks*, 37.
48. Budge, *Monks*, 126.
49. A. C. Moule, *Christians in China Before the Year 1550*, and Paul Pelliot, *Recherches sur les chrétiens d'Asie centrale et d'Extrême-Orient*, offer useful introductions to Nestorian practices.
50. Budge, *Monks*, 127.
51. Pelliot, *Recherches*, 249, describes the "two marriages" as typical of the Nestorians who derived from the Middle East. Sauma's contemporary Bar Hebraeus (1225/26–1286), son of a Jewish physician but himself a convert to the Jacobite Christian order and eventually a bishop in that Church, apparently met both Sauma and his traveling companion, Bar Markos, and erroneously identified them as Uyghurs. Bar Hebraeus's history was so influential that many works refer to Sauma as an Uyghur rather than an Önggüd. See E. A. Wallis Budge, *The Chronography of Gregory Ab'ûl Faraj: the Son of Aaron, the Hebrew Physician Commonly Known as Bar Hebraeus*, 1:492.
52. For the sources on which this section is based, see Chapter 1 of my *Khubilai Khan*.
53. On Sorghaghtani, see Morris Rossabi, "Khubilai Khan and the Women in His Family," in W. Bauer, ed., *Studia Sino-Mongolica: Festschrift für Herbert Franke*, 158–62.
54. John A. Boyle, trans., *The Successors of Genghis Khan*, 212.
55. Owen Lattimore, "A Ruined Nestorian City in Inner Mongolia," in Owen Lattimore, *Studies in Frontier History*, 221–40; see also H. D. Martin, "Preliminary Report on Nestorian Remains North of Kuei-hua, Sui-yuan," 232–49; and Ch'en Yüan, "On the Damaged Tablets Discovered by Mr. D. Martin in Inner Mongolia," 250–56.
56. Budge, *Monks*, 132.

Chapter 2. A Pilgrimage to the West

1. Charles J. Halperin, "Russia in the Mongol Empire in Historical Perspective," 250; for additional details on this struggle, see Bertold Spuler, *Die Goldene Horde: Die Mongolen in Russland, 1223–1502*, 41–49, and B. Grekov and A. Iakoubovski, *La Horde d'Or* (trans. by François Thuret), 76–82.
2. For one view of this conflict, see John A. Boyle, trans., *The Successors of Genghis Khan*, 248–65.
3. Morris Rossabi, "The 'Decline' of the Central Asian Caravan Trade," 354–55. For the importance of religious pilgrimages in another religion, Islam, see Dale Eickelman and James Piscatori, eds., *Muslim Travellers*, 5–21.
4. Luke 18:21.
5. Henry Yule, *Cathay and the Way Thither*, 3:164.
6. Niels Steensgaard, *Carracks, Caravans, and Companies: The Structural Crisis in the European-Asian Trade in the Early 17th Century*, 17–21.

7. E. A. Wallis Budge, trans., *The Chronography of Gregory Ab'ûl Faraj, the Son of Aaron, the Hebrew Physician Commonly Known as Bar Hebraeus*, 1:492.

8. James A. Montgomery, trans., *The History of Yaballaha III*, 21; E. Gismondi, *Amri et Slibae de patriarchis Nestorianium commentaria*, 1:3–4.

9. A. C. Moule and Paul Pelliot, *Marco Polo: The Description of the World*, 1:79.

10. Paul Pelliot, *Recherches sur les chrétiens d'Asie centrale et d'Extrême Orient*, 256–58, refutes this interpretation.

11. Louis Ligeti, *Monuments en écriture 'Phags-pa: pièces de chancellerie en transcription chinoise*, 109–16, for examples of these *p'ai-tzu.*

12. On these postal stations, see Peter Olbricht, *Das Postwesen in China unter der Mongolenherrschaft im 13. und 14. Jahrhundert*, and Haneda Tōru, *Genchō ekiden zakko.*

13. Michael Loewe, *Records of Han Administration*, 1:48.

14. Moule and Pelliot, *Marco Polo*, 1:248.

15. See, for example, Louis Hambis, "Notes sur l'histoire de Corée a l'époque mongole," 151–218, and Inaba Shoju, trans., "The Lineage of the Sa skya pa: A Chapter of the Red Annals," 109–10.

16. Pelliot, *Recherches*, 260.

17. Ai Buqa's son Körgüz, the "Prince George" of Marco Polo's account, eventually married Khubilai's granddaughter Hu-ta-te-mi-shih and, after her death, Khubilai's great-granddaughter Ai-ya-mi-shih and was to be converted to Catholicism by the Franciscan missionary John of Monte Corvino, who ultimately became archbishop of Tai-tu. See Christopher Dawson, ed., *Mission to Asia*, 225–27.

18. J. B. Chabot, "Histoire du Patriarche Mar Jabalaha III et du moine Rabban Çauma," 586.

19. Moule and Pelliot, *Marco Polo*, 1:150–51. For more on the Tanguts or Hsi Hsia, see Ruth Dunnell, "Who Are the Tanguts?" 78–89, and her *Tanguts and the Tangut State of Ta Hsia*; and E. I. Kychanov, *Ocherk Istorii Tangutskogo Gosudarstva.*

20. E. A. Wallis Budge, trans., *The Monks of Kûblâi Khân, Emperor of China*, 138.

21. Henry Yule, trans., *The Book of Ser Marco Polo*, 1:197.

22. See Jean Pierre Abel-Rémusat, *Histoire de la ville de Khotan*, for some translations of early texts concerning Khotan. For its significance on the trade routes to the West, see Morris Rossabi, "Trade Routes in Inner Asia," prepared for Denis Sinor, ed., *Cambridge History of Inner Asia*, and, for its later role, see Morris Rossabi, "Ming China's Relations with Hami and Central Asia, 1404–1513: A Reexamination of Traditional Chinese Foreign Policy."

23. James Legge, trans., *A Record of Buddhistic Kingdoms*, 17–18.

24. Roy A. Miller, *Accounts of Western Nations in the History of the Northern Chou Dynasty*, 11.

25. See Emil Bretschneider, *Mediaeval Researches from Eastern Asiatic Sources*, 47–49, 246–50, for additional notes on Khotan.

26. Moule and Pelliot, *Marco Polo*, 1:147.

27. Yet it is not as laden with fanciful stories as other travel or geographic accounts. See, for example, Guy Le Strange, trans., *The Geographi-*

cal Part of the Nuzhat-al-Qulub Composed by Hamd-Allah Mustawfi of Qazwin in 740 (1340), who writes: "in the Khotan province . . . there is here a valley . . . and in that valley the high road is clearly marked out . . . Should anyone who passes by that high road wander away from the straight line, his breath is caught by the vapours arising from the ground here round about, and he perishes therefrom," 280.

28. Morris Rossabi, *Khubilai Khan: His Life and Times*, 106–10, offers additional details.

29. Moule and Pelliot, *Marco Polo*, 1:143.

30. On Nestorianism in the town, see Paul Pelliot, *Notes on Marco Polo*, 1:209; and M. Aurel Stein, *Ancient Khotan*, 1:71–72.

31. There is no significant work on the importance of this struggle for Eurasian history.

32. Chabot, "Histoire du Patriarche," 592.

33. Albert von Le Coq, *Buried Treasures of Chinese Turkestan* (trans. by Anna Barwell), 155. See also Yule, *Book of Ser Marco Polo*, 1:197.

34. Ann K. S. Lambton, *Landlord and Peasant in Persia*, 92.

35. Lambton, *Landlord*, 77, offers a concise description of conditions for the peasantry.

36. David Morgan, *Medieval Persia, 1040–1797*, 65.

37. Le Strange, *Geographical Part*, 189; Guy Le Strange, *The Lands of the Eastern Caliphate*, 388–90; Bernard Lewis, P. M. Holt, and Ann K. S. Lambton, eds., *The Cambridge History of Islam*, 1:145–47.

38. John A. Boyle, trans., *The History of the World Conqueror*, 2:501.

39. John A. Boyle, ed., *The Cambridge History of Iran*. Volume 5, 338.

40. W. Barthold, *An Historical Geography of Iran* (trans. by Svat Soucek), 102–3.

41. H. A. R. Gibb, trans., *Ibn Battuta: Travels in Asia and Africa, 1325–1354*, 177. A recent colorful account of Ibn Baṭṭūṭa's travels is Ross E. Dunn, *The Adventures of Ibn Battuta*.

42. Le Strange, *Lands*, 389.

43. Aydin Sayili, *The Observatory in Islam*, 193–95. A photograph of the remains of the observatory is in Morgan, *The Mongols*, 153.

44. Chabot, "Histoire du Patriarche," 596; Gismondi, *Amri et Slibae*, 3–4.

45. See Gaston Wiet, *Baghdad: Metropolis of the Abbasid Caliphate* (trans. by Seymour Feiler) for Baghdad at its height; on its decline in the late thirteenth century, see Janet Abu-Lughod, *Before European Hegemony: The World System, A.D. 1250–1350*, 195–96. See also Keith Weissman, "Mongol Rule in Baghdad, 1258–1301," for more on this city.

46. Jean Maurice Fiey, *Chrétiens syriaques sous les Mongols*, 90, 95; I have not had access to Jean Maurice Fiey, *Mossoul chrétienne*.

47. Moule and Pelliot, *Marco Polo*, 1:100.

48. Fiey, *Chrétiens*, 35.

49. Laurence E. Browne, *The Eclipse of Christianity in Asia*, 155–56.

50. Jean Maurice Fiey, *Communautés syriaques en Iran et Irak des origines à 1552*, 7:413, writes that Markos was eventually buried here.

51. Budge, *Monks*, 143–44.

52. Chabot, "Histoire du Patriarche," 598–99.

53. David Morgan, "The Mongols and the Eastern Mediterranean," 204; on this anti-Islamic incident see Budge, *Bar Hebraeus*, 1:447.

54. Barthold, *Historical Geography*, 217–19; see also Bertold Spuler, "La situation de l'Iran a l'époque de Marco Polo," in *Oriente Poliano*, 126.

55. Ross E. Dunn, *The Adventures of Ibn Battuta*, 100.

56. Le Strange, *Lands*, 160.

57. H. A. R. Gibb, trans., *Ibn Battuta: Travels in Asia and Africa, 1325–1354*, 101. See also Karl Jahn, *Täbris*.

58. Moule and Pelliot, *Marco Polo*, 1:104.

59. Le Strange, *Geographical Part*, 80. The presence of foreigners, from around the world, in Tabrīz led, for example, to the production of silk textiles with "a mixture of traditional Middle Eastern elements and Chinese motifs" (Anne E. Wardwell, *"Panni Tartaricis*: Eastern Islamic Silks Woven with Gold and Silver, 13th and 14th Centuries," 110), which were designed for export to Italy, Spain, and other regions in Europe. Some of these textiles are beautifully illustrated in the Wardwell article.

60. Luciano Petech, "Les marchands italiens dans l'empire mongol," 560.

61. Dawson, *Mission*, 229.

62. See Fiey, *Communautés syriaques*, 281, for the large number of Christian churches in this whole region.

63. J. Spencer Trimingham, *Christianity Among the Arabs in Pre-Islamic Times*, 164–70.

64. Chabot, "Histoire du Patriarche," 600.

65. Sirarpie Der Nersessian, *The Armenians*, 37.

66. Sirarpie Der Nersessian, *Armenia and the Byzantine Empire*, 8–10.

67. Der Nersessian, *The Armenians*, 40.

68. On the cordiality of Armeno-Mongol relations, see John A. Boyle, "The Journey of Het'um, King of Little Armenia, to the Court of the Great Khan Möngke," 175–89.

69. Der Nersessian, *The Armenians*, 110. (On these buildings, see M. F. Brosset, *Les ruines d'Ani*.)

70. Budge, *Monks*, 147.

71. William Emhardt and George Lamsa, *The Oldest Christian People*, 58–60. See also Aubrey Vine, *The Nestorian Churches*, 16–30.

72. Chabot, "Histoire du Patriarche," 601.

73. Chabot, "Histoire du Patriarche," 601.

74. Budge, *Monks*, 147.

75. Chabot, "Histoire du Patriarche," 605. See N. V. Pigulevskaia, *Istoriia Mar Iabalakhi i Rabban Saumy*, 6–7, on the significance of his election.

76. Chabot, "Histoire du Patriarche," 606.

77. Budge, *Monks*, 154.

78. Budge, *Monks*, 155.

79. David Morgan, *Medieval Persia*, p. 68, writes that Abakha "expired at midnight after a drinking bout in his tent, gibbering about a non-existent black bird, possibly the Mongol equivalent of a pink elephant." For relations with the Mamlūks, see Reuven Amitai-Preiss, "In the Aftermath of 'Ayn Jālūt: The Beginnings of the Mamlūk-Īlkhānid Cold War."

80. On Aḥmad's reign, see Bertold Spuler, *Die Mongolen in Iran*, 69–71, and the interesting view in Budge, *Bar Hebraeus*, 1:467–71.
81. Boyle, *Cambridge History of Iran*, 368.
82. Budge, *Bar Hebraeus*, 1:472–73. For the embassy to the Mamlūks, see Adel Allouche, "Tegüder's Ultimatum to Qalāwūn," 1–21. Allouche argues that Aḥmad's embassies to the Mamlūks were not at all friendly.
83. Chabot, "Histoire du Patriarche," 76.
84. Budge, *Monks*, 159.
85. Chabot, "Histoire du Patriarche," 77.
86. Budge, *Monks*, 161.
87. Boyle, *Cambridge History of Iran*, 365.
88. Spuler, *Die Mongolen*, 71–72; Arghun perhaps disingenuously is reported to have said that "I will not take part in the killing of him [Aḥmad]," although he would allow others to execute his uncle. Budge, *Bar Hebraeus*, 1:472.
89. Budge, *Monks*, 162.
90. Chabot, "Histoire du Patriarche," 79.

Chapter 3. The Mongols, the Muslims, and the Europeans

1. On the Outremer communities, see Jean Richard, *The Latin Kingdom of Jerusalem* (trans. by Janet Shirley).
2. John A. Boyle, "The Journey of Het'um I, King of Little Armenia, to the Court of the Great Khan Möngke," 178–81; see also Sirarpie Der Nersessian, "The Armenian Chronicle of the Constable Smpad or of the 'Royal Historians,'" 141–68. For some minimal contacts between Khubilai and the Ilkhans, see Thomas Allsen, "Notes on Chinese Titles in Mongol Iran."
3. Igor de Rachewiltz, *Papal Envoys to the Great Khans*, 151.
4. E. Tisserant, "Une lettre de l'Ilkhan Abaga adressée en 1268 au pape Clement IV," 547–56; see also Antoine Mostaert and Francis W. Cleaves, "Trois documents mongols des Archives secrètes vaticanes," 419–506. Clement was an ally of Charles of Anjou. See Geoffrey Barraclough, *The Medieval Papacy*, 118–21.
5. Frederic C. Lane, *Venice: A Maritime Republic*, 73–77. In 1261 Genoa had helped the Byzantines oust Venice from Constantinople after a five decades' long occupation and thus to undermine the Black Sea monopoly enjoyed by the Venetians. Genoa took charge of the Central Asian or Old Silk Road commerce and became a critical intermediary in the trade in slaves between the Golden Horde and the Mamlūks.
6. Steven Runciman, *A History of the Crusades*. Volume 3, 337–39. Runciman offers a detailed narrative of relations among the European states during those years.
7. Michael Prestwich, *Edward I*, 562–63.
8. Robert Chazan, *Daggers of Faith: Thirteenth-Century Missionizing and the Jewish Response*, 45. At the same time Philip the Fair also forcibly sought to convert the Jews in France. See William C. Jordan, *The French Monarchy and the Jews from Philip Augustus to the Last Capetians*, 180.

9. Simon Lloyd, *English Society and the Crusades, 1216–1307*, 25–31; from 1216 to 1307 Christians from the Outremer communities and, after 1291, the communities' remnants, sent fifty-one letters eliciting help, and the Armenians and the Mongols also wrote to the monarchs, thus adding to the total. See also C. Kohler and C. V. Langlois, "Lettres inédites concernant les Croisades (1275–1307)," 46–63. The Outremer communities, as well as other Christian regions, themselves dominated Muslim populations within their domains. See the various essays in James Powell, ed., *Muslims Under Latin Rule*.

10. Christopher Tyerman, *England and the Crusades, 1095–1588*, 124–28.

11. Prestwich, *Edward I*, 75–76.

12. John A. Boyle, ed., *The Cambridge History of Iran*. Volume 5, 356–60. Barakh, the Mongol Khan of Central Asia, had repeatedly initiated territorial disputes with the Ilkhanids. With no immediate threat from the Mamlūks, Abakha had no choice but to attend to the challenge posed by Barakh and to put aside his struggle with the Muslims to his west. After some delays and inconclusive engagements, the troops of the two Khans met in July of 1270, and Abakha's forces earned a smashing victory, which ensured relative tranquillity along these frontiers for about a century.

13. Prestwich, *Edward I*, 82.

14. Horace K. Mann, ed., *The Lives of the Popes in the Middle Ages*, 17:39–40.

15. Prestwich, *Edward I*, 327. For some of his problems in Wales, see R. R. Davies, *Domination and Conquest: The Experience of Ireland, Scotland, and Wales, 1100–1300*, and David Walker, *Medieval Wales*. Philip II of France and Rudolf of Hapsburg, in addition, did not make an appearance in Lyons. For a popular but reliable work on the Crusades, see René Grousset, *Histoire des Croisades et du Royaume franc de Jérusalem*.

16. A. A. Vasiliev, *History of the Byzantine Empire, 324–1453*, 584–90.

17. Mann, *Lives of the Popes*, 17:40–42. The religious leaders of Europe (even after the accession in 1277 of Pope Nicholas III, who was somewhat more sympathetic to a political agreement with the Mongols) and the Ilkhans of Persia began to communicate at cross-purposes. They did not share objectives nor perhaps did they understand each other's intentions.

18. Robert Fawtier, *The Capetian Kings of France: Monarchy and Nation (987–1328)* (trans. by Lionel Butler and R. J. Adam), 33–34.

19. E. A. Wallis Budge, trans. *The Chronography of Gregory Ab'ûl Faraj: The Son of Aaron, the Hebrew Physician Commonly Known as Bar Hebraeus*, 1:457. Capitalizing on the brief vacancy in the Sultanate of the Mamlūks was precluded. Right before his death, in fact, Baybars had dealt a devastating blow to the Mongols in Asia Minor. A Mongol army stationed in Abulustan to maintain jurisdiction over the Saljuq Turks was defeated and routed by Baybars in April of 1277. Learning of this disastrous defeat, Abakha immediately set forth for Asia Minor, intending to exact at least some minimal revenge. See Mann, *Lives of the Popes*, 17:41–42.

20. Budge, *Bar Hebraeus*, 1:465.

21. To ensure sanction for an invasion of the Byzantine Empire, Charles needed to undermine the union between the Catholic and Ortho-

dox churches that had been negotiated at the Council of Lyons. The death of Pope Nicholas III in August of 1280 allowed him to impose his own candidate, a Frenchman who adopted the name Martin IV, on the Papacy by February of the following year. In October of 1281, Martin IV excommunicated Michael, thus severing the union between the two churches and giving Charles a free hand in the East. Meanwhile, in July of 1281 Charles negotiated with Venice the Treaty of Orvieto, which called for a joint campaign against the Byzantines. Charles's troops were defeated by the Byzantines in a preliminary clash in Berat (in modern Albania), but he was not deterred. He was intent on seizing and occupying the Byzantine Empire. See Donald M. Nicol, *Byzantium and Venice*, 195–206, for more details on these events.

22. Lloyd, *English Society*, 32; marriages among the crowned heads of Europe and their progeny were quite common. Edward's aunt Margaret had married St. Louis, so the French King Philip III was Edward's first cousin. Edward himself was the son-in-law of Alphonso X, King of Castile, and at one time he proposed a marriage between his daughter and the son of Rudolf of Hapsburg. A marital alliance with the Ilkhans would simply have followed this pattern and would probably have facilitated military and political cooperation.

23. Lloyd, *English Society*, 25.

24. Tyerman, *England and the Crusades*, 231.

25. Mann, *Lives of the Popes*, 16:443–46.

26. de Rachewiltz, *Papal Envoys*, 156–57.

27. Mann, *Lives of the Popes*, 17:42–43.

28. E. Allison Peers, trans., *Blanquerna: A Thirteenth-Century Romance of Ramon Lull*, 325; See also Devin DeWeese, "The Influence of the Mongols on the Religious Consciousness of Thirteenth-Century Europe," 60–62.

29. Denis Sinor, "Interpreters in Medieval Inner Asia," 318–19.

Chapter 4. An Embassy to the West

1. E. A. Wallis Budge, trans., *The Chronography of Gregory Ab'ûl Faraj: The Son of Aaron, the Hebrew Physician Commonly Known as Bar Hebraeus*, 1:475–76.

2. E. A. Wallis Budge, trans., *The Monks of Kûblâi Khân, Emperor of China*, 165.

3. Budge, *Monks*, 166.

4. This omission is in striking contrast to many of the other accounts by emissaries and travelers during this era. See, for example, Jean Richard, *La Papauté et les missions d'orient au moyen âge (xiii–xiv siècles)*, and Ross E. Dunn, *The Adventures of Ibn Battuta*.

5. Luciano Petech, "Les marchands italiens dans l'empire mongol," 561; for another European at the Mongol court in East Asia, see the charming book by Leonardo Olschki, *Guillaume Boucher: A French Artist at the Court of the Khans*.

6. See Jean Sauvaget, "Caravansérails syriens du moyen-âge," 98–121. The quote is from Arminius Vambery, *History of Bokhara from the Earliest Period down to the Present*, 137. For other facilities that promoted travel in

this period, see Morris Rossabi, "The 'Decline' of the Central Asian Caravan Trade," 353–54.

7. Budge, *Monks*, 167.

8. George Hourani, *Arab Seafaring in the Indian Ocean in Ancient and Early Medieval Times*, 113.

9. John Beckwith, *The Art of Constantinople: An Introduction to Byzantine Art*, 29–30, 134.

10. David Talbot Rice, *Byzantine Art*, 56.

11. Angeliki Laiou, *Constantinople and the Latins: The Foreign Policy of Andronicus II, 1282–1328*, 7. A. A. Vasiliev in his *History of the Byzantine Empire, 324–1453*, 583, argues that the scholarly Andronicus should have been a professor, not a ruler, a judgment confirmed by his later inept foreign policy. See Kenneth Setton, "The Papacy and the Levant (1204–1571)," 114:149.

12. Bruce Lippard, "The Mongols and Byzantium, 1243–1341," 192.

13. Budge, *Monks*, 168.

14. Lord Kinross, *Hagia Sophia*, 38.

15. Leonardo Olschki, *Marco Polo's Asia*, 219.

16. Olschki, *Marco Polo's Asia*, 224.

17. A. C. Moule, *Christians in China Before the Year 1550*, 141. Also note Moule's statistics (161–63) on the relatively few Christian families in one of the larger such Christian communities in China.

18. Budge, *Monks*, 169–70. The renowned Muslim traveler Ibn Baṭṭūṭa also visited the Hagia Sophia about forty years later but "did not go inside because he would have had to prostrate himself before the cross" (Dunn, *Ibn Battuta*, 171).

19. J. B. Chabot, "Histoire du Patriarche Mar Jabalaha III et du moine Rabban Çauma," 86; according to Kinross, *Hagia Sophia*, 21, Constantine "was buried in the mausoleum he had built for the Twelve Apostles—and for his successors—on the fourth hill of his city . . ." Thus, Rabban Sauma could not have seen his tomb in Hagia Sophia. The Nestorian cleric must have seen Hagia Sophia at its best, because Michael Palaeologus had restored it just twenty years before his arrival in Constantinople. See Deno John Geanakoplos, *Emperor Michael Palaeologus and the West, 1258–1282: A Study in Byzantine-Latin Relations*, 124.

20. Budge, *Monks*, 169.

21. For the travels of William and John, see Christopher Dawson, ed., *Mission to Asia*; for the suggestion that Polo dealt principally with the Mongol elite, see Richard Humble, *Marco Polo*, 222.

22. See Dunn, *Ibn Battuta*.

23. Chabot, "Histoire du Patriarche," 86. The Venetians carted away any such relics from Constantinople during their rule of the city from 1204 to 1261.

24. Olschki, *Marco Polo's Asia*, 153; A. C. Moule and Paul Pelliot, *Marco Polo: The Description of the World*, 1:432.

25. J. Spencer Trimingham, *Christianity Among the Arabs in Pre-Islamic Times*, 235–42.

26. Budge, *Monks*, 170.

27. Budge, *Monks*, 171. Several Popes in the late thirteenth and early

fourteenth centuries sought to persuade European monarchs and the Italian city-states to join in a Crusade to support the Kingdom of Naples against the Kings of Aragon, who supported Sicily. See Norman Housley, *The Italian Crusades*, 1–5.

28. Budge, *Monks*, 171.

29. Horace K. Mann, ed., *The Lives of the Popes in the Middle Ages*, 16:369–79.

30. See, for example, the demands made by the Ming court upon envoys from Central Asia (as described in K. M. Maitra, *A Persian Embassy to China*, 60–61).

31. Budge, *Monks*, 172.

32. Robert Brentano, *Two Churches: England and Italy in the Thirteenth Century*, 282, describes a number of sites that were turned over to the newly founded Dominican order. On the present condition of Santa Sabina, see *Michelin: Rome*, 194.

33. Mann, *Lives of the Popes*, 17:5.

34. Budge, *Monks*, 173. Jean Richard, "La mission en Europe de Rabban Çauma et l'union des églises," 162–64, writes that the conversation between Rabban Sauma and the Cardinals was hampered because of poor translations.

35. Matti Moosa, "Nestorian Church," in Mircea Eliade, ed., *The Encyclopedia of Religion*, 10:369; E. Tisserant, "Nestorienne (L'église)," in Alfred Vacant and Eugene Mangenot, eds., *Dictionnaire de théologie catholique*, 11:207–18.

36. Budge, *Monks*, 173–74.

37. Budge, *Monks*, 174.

38. For a handy survey of Nestorian beliefs and for Asian views of St. Thomas, see A. C. Moule, *Christians in China Before the Year 1550*, 22–26; for a brief survey of some recent discoveries of Nestorian monuments and of some useful sources on Nestorianism in China and Central Asia, see Kahar Barat, "Old Uyghur Christianity and the Bible," 12–25.

39. Budge, *Monks*, 177.

40. Budge, *Monks*, 177.

41. Budge, *Monks*, 178.

42. Loretta Santini, *Rome and Vatican*, 89.

43. Bartolomeo Nogara, *Les Trésors d'Art du Vatican*, 39.

44. Santini, *Rome and Vatican*, 92.

45. Chabot, "Histoire du Patriarche," 97.

46. Budge, *Monks*, 178–79.

47. On the contemporaneous and later struggles between the French monarchs and the Papacy, see Robert Fawtier, *The Capetian Kings of France: Monarchy and Nation (987–1328)*, 37–38; Charles T. Wood, ed., *Philip the Fair and Boniface VIII: State vs. Papacy;* and Charles T. Wood, *The French Appanages and the Capetian Monarchy*, 81.

48. Cecilia Pericoli Ridolfini, *St. Paul's Outside the Walls: Rome*, 7.

49. Ridolfini, *St. Paul's*, 11.

50. Ridolfini, *St. Paul's*, 16. See also Robert Brentano, *Rome Before Avignon*, 67.

51. Acts 7:54–60; 8:1–3.

52. George Ferguson, *Signs and Symbols in Christian Art,* 143.

53. Ferguson, *Signs,* 137–38.

54. For the present condition of San Pietro in Vincoli, see *Michelin: Rome,* 132.

55. Budge, *Monks,* 179.

56. Budge, *Monks,* 180; also see Brentano, *Rome Before Avignon,* 66–68.

57. *Michelin: Rome,* 135.

58. Budge, *Monks,* 180. For the theft of sacred relics in medieval times, see the intriguing work of Patrick J. Geary, *Furta Sacra: Thefts of Relics in the Central Middle Ages.* Rabban Sauma's account does not mention that the facade of the church had mosaics that were associated with the Virgin Mary and reputedly had miraculous powers. See Brentano, *Rome Before Avignon,* 87.

59. David Abulafia, *Italy, Sicily, and the Mediterranean, 1100–1400,* 227.

60. David Waley, *The Italian City-Republics,* 21–22.

61. Benjamin Kedar, *Merchants in Crisis: Genoese and Venetian Men of Affairs and the Fourteenth-Century Depression,* 6.

62. Lauro Martines, *Power and Imagination: City States in Renaissance Italy,* 131.

63. On Genoese relations with the increasingly weak Byzantine Empire during the reign of Emperor Andronicus II (1282–1328), see Michel Balard, *La Romanie Genoise (xii–début au xv siècle),* 1:55–69.

64. Ferguson, *Signs,* 128–29.

65. On the cathedral, see Giuseppe Banchero, *Il Duomi di Genova; Chiese di Genova,* 63–82; Carlo Ceschi, *Chiese di Genova,* 153–244, which has excellent black-and-white photographs; and Bartolomeo Pesce, *La Cattedrale di Genova,* 19–35.

66. Budge, *Monks,* 181.

67. Chabot, "Histoire du Patriarche," 105.

Chapter 5. Paris, Bordeaux, Rome, and Return

1. Robert Fawtier, *The Capetian Kings of France: Monarchy and Nation (987–1328),* 32–35.

2. E. A. Wallis Budge, trans., *The Monks of Kûblâi Khân, Emperor of China,* 183.

3. Michael Prestwich, *Edward I,* 324–25.

4. Prestwich, *Edward I,* 324.

5. See again Charles T. Wood for these conflicts, particularly his *Philip the Fair and Boniface VIII: State vs. Papacy.*

6. Budge, *Monks,* 183.

7. Gordon Leff, *Paris and Oxford Universities in the Thirteenth and Fourteenth Centuries,* 9.

8. Hastings Rashdall, *The Universities of Europe in the Middle Ages* (new ed. by F. M. Powicke and A. B. Emden), 3:325–31.

9. Joseph Strayer, ed., *Dictionary of the Middle Ages,* 9:405.

10. Leff, *Paris and Oxford Universities,* 48.

11. Leff, *Paris and Oxford Universities,* 9.

12. J. B. Chabot, "Histoire du Patriarche Mar Jabalaha III et du moine Rabban Çauma," 107; see also Roger Bourderon, et al., *Histoire de St.-Denis*.

13. Alain Erlande-Brandeburg, *The Abbey Church of Saint-Denis*, 17.

14. Many of the most significant of these tombs, particularly those from the T'ang dynasty, have still not been excavated, but those few that have whet the appetite for the remainder.

15. Erlande-Brandeburg, *Abbey Church of Saint-Denis*, plates 24–25.

16. Budge, *Monks*, 184.

17. For one explanation of Polo's omissions, see John W. Haeger, "Marco Polo in China: Problems with Internal Evidence," 22–30.

18. Louis Grodecki, *Sainte-Chapelle*, 5–6.

19. Budge, *Monks*, 185.

20. Grodecki, *Sainte-Chapelle*, 14–18.

21. Budge, *Monks*, 185.

22. Budge, *Monks*, 186.

23. Maurice Powicke, *The Oxford History of England: The Thirteenth Century, 1216–1307*, 252; Simon Lloyd, *English Society and the Crusades, 1216–1307*, 232; Christopher Tyerman, *England and the Crusades, 1095–1588*, 235, quotes Edward as saying to Rabban Sauma: "I have the sign of the Cross on my body." For more on Edward's dealings with the Ilkhans, see Laurence Lockhart, "The Relations between Edward I and Edward II of England and the Mongol Īl-Khāns of Persia," 26–29.

24. Lloyd, *English Society*, 232–34.

25. Budge, *Monks*, 184.

26. Prestwich, *Edward I*, 84, 157–59.

27. Budge, *Monks*, 186.

28. Budge, *Monks*, 187.

29. Chabot, "Histoire du Patriarche," 111.

30. Horace K. Mann, ed., *The Lives of the Popes in the Middle Ages*, 17:6–7.

31. Mann, *Lives of the Popes*, 17:9–11.

32. Chabot, "Histoire du Patriarche," 113.

33. Budge, *Monks*, 113.

34. Budge, *Monks*, 191.

35. On the present site, see *Michelin: Rome*, 133–35.

36. Budge, *Monks*, 192.

37. Budge, *Monks*, 191.

38. Budge, *Monks*, 194.

39. Budge, *Monks*, 195–96. Mann, *Lives of the Popes*, 17:47–48, finds no evidence of a Papal letter granting authority over Eastern Christians to Mar Yaballaha.

40. F. Delorme and A. L. Tautu, eds., *Acta romanurum pontificum ab Innocentio V ad Benedictum XI, 1276–1304*, 3:5:t. 2, 124–25. His shrewdness on this occasion is at odds with the oft-stated assertion that "Nicholas lacked the qualities that make a successful ruler of men" (Mann, *Lives of the Popes*, 17:10).

41. Delorme and Tautu, *Acta*, 127.

42. Delorme and Tautu, *Acta*, 128.

43. Delorme and Tautu, *Acta*, 128–29.

44. It may be, though, as one modern scholar of Christianity asserts, that by this time there was a blurring of the doctrinal differences between the Nestorians and the Western Church. See Christopher Dawson, ed., *Mission to Asia*, xxix.

45. Delorme and Tautu, *Acta*, 135–36.

46. Delorme and Tautu, *Acta*, 133.

47. See M. H. Laurent, "Rabban Sauma, Ambassadeur de l'il-khan Argoun, et la cathédrale de Veroli," 331–65.

48. Budge, *Monks*, 197; N. V. Pigulevskaia, *Istoriia Mar Iabalakhi i Rabban Saumy*, 18–23, on the translation.

49. Budge, *Monks*, 198–99. For Mongol recipes, see Paul Buell, "Pleasing the Palate of the Qan: Changing Foodways of the Imperial Mongols."

50. John A. Boyle, ed., *The Cambridge History of Iran*. Volume 5, 371–72.

51. Antoine Mostaert and Francis W. Cleaves, *Les Lettres de 1289 et 1305 des Ikhan Arʁn et Öljeitü a Philippe le Bel*, 18. Buscarel added his own letter in which he "inform[ed] Philip that Arghun, having heard that it would be difficult for him to transport the required number of horses across the sea, was willing to place at his disposal 20,000–30,000 animals as a gift or at a reasonable price." See John A. Boyle, *The Mongol World Empire, 1206–1370*, 13:560. See also Roland Bonaparte, *Documents sur l'époque mongole des xiii et xiv siècles*, plate 14, for the original of these letters.

52. Boyle, *Cambridge History of Iran*, 372.

53. Steven Runciman, *A History of the Crusades*. Volume 3, 401–02. In 1290 Arghun sent still another embassy, led by a Mongol named Chaghan, to the Pope. The religious leader of the Western world, who had just learned of the conquest of Acre by the Mamlūks in 1291, now appeared ready to call for a Crusade and sought, via Chaghan, to enlist Arghun in a joint attack against the Muslims. It was too late, however, for Arghun had died before Chaghan's return. See Boyle, *Mongol World Empire*, 13:561.

54. Mann, *Lives of the Popes*, 16:448.

55. Jean Richard, *The Latin Kingdom of Jerusalem*, 2:430. As Joseph Needham noted in *Science and Civilisation in China*, 1:225, "it was in this final period of unsettlement, before . . . the liquidation of the Levantine crusader strongholds, that the last effort at a Christian-Mongol alliance was made . . ."

56. Budge, *Monks*, 203; Pigulevskaia, *Istoriia Mar Iabalakhi*, 9.

57. Budge, *Monks*, 205.

58. Budge, *Monks*, 206.

59. Budge, *Monks*, 206.

60. See James Hamilton, "Le texte turc en caractères syriaques du grand sceau cruciforme de Mār Yahballāhā III," 155–70.

61. Runciman, *History of the Crusades*, 402.

Selected Bibliography

Abel-Rémusat, Jean Pierre. *Histoire de la ville de Khotan*. Paris: Deboublet, 1820.

Abulafia, David. *Italy, Sicily, and the Mediterranean, 1100–1400*. London: Variorum Reprints, 1987.

Abu-Lughod, Janet. *Before European Hegemony: The World System, A.D. 1250–1350*. New York: Oxford University Press, 1989.

Allouche, Adel. "Tegüder's Ultimatum to Qalāwūn." *International Journal of Middle Eastern Studies* 22, 4 (1990): 1–21.

Allsen, Thomas. "Notes on Chinese Titles in Mongol Iran." *Mongolian Studies* 14 (1991): 27–39.

Amitai-Preiss, Reuven. "In the Aftermath of ʿAyn Jālūt: The Beginnings of the Mamlūk-Īlkhānid Cold War." *Al-Masāq* 3 (1990): 1–21.

Balard, Michel. *La Romanie Genoise (xii–début au xv siècle)*. 2 vols. Rome: École Française de Rome, 1978.

Banchero, Giuseppe. *Il Duomi di Genova*. Genova: Dai Fratelli Febrand Q. Giovanni, 1855.

Barat, Kahar. "Old Uyghur Christianity and the Bible." *American-Asian Review* 5, 2 (Summer 1987): 12–25.

Barraclough, Geoffrey. *The Medieval Papacy*. London: Thames and Hudson, 1968.

Barthold, W. *An Historical Geography of Iran*. Trans. by Svat Soucek. Princeton: Princeton University Press, 1984.

Beckwith, John. *The Art of Constantinople: An Introduction to Byzantine Art*. London: Phaidon Press, 1967.

Bedrossian, Robert. "The Turco-Mongol Invasions and the Lords of Armenia in the 13th–14th Centuries." Columbia University Ph.D. dissertation, 1979.

Bonaparte, Roland. *Documents sur l'époque mongole des xiii et xiv siècles*. Paris, 1895.

Bourderon, Roger, et al. *Histoire de St.-Denis*. Paris: Privat, 1988.

Boyle, John A. *The History of the World Conqueror*. 2 vols. Manchester: Manchester University Press, 1958.

———. "The Death of the Last ʿAbbāsid Caliph: A Contemporary Muslim Account." *Journal of Semitic Studies* 6, 2 (Autumn 1961): 145–61.

———. "The Journey of Hetʾum, King of Little Armenia, to the Court of the Great Khan Möngke." *Central Asiatic Journal* 9, 3 (1964): 175–89.

———. *The Mongol World Empire, 1206–1370*. London: Variorum Reprints, 1977.

———, ed. *The Cambridge History of Iran*. Volume 5: *The Saljuq and Mongol Periods*. Cambridge: Cambridge University Press, 1968.

———, trans. *The Successors of Genghis Khan*. New York: Columbia University Press, 1971.

Brentano, Robert. *Rome Before Avignon*. New York: Basic Books, 1974.

———. *Two Churches: England and Italy in the Thirteenth Century*. Reprint. Berkeley: University of California Press, 1988.

Bretschneider, Emil. *Mediaeval Researches from Eastern Asiatic Sources*. 2 vols. Reprint. New York: Barnes & Noble, 1967.

Brosset, M. F. *Les ruines d'Ani*. St. Petersburg, 1861.

Browne, Laurence E. *The Eclipse of Christianity in Asia*. New York: Howard Fertig, 1967.

Brunel, C. "David d'Ashby, auteur méconnu des *Faits des Tartares*." *Romania* 84 (1958): 39–46.

Budge, E. A. Wallis, trans. *The Monks of Kûblâi Khân, Emperor of China*. London: Religious Tract Society, 1928.

———. *The Chronography of Gregory Ab'ûl Faraj: the Son of Aaron, the Hebrew Physician Commonly Known as Bar Hebraeus*. 2 vols. London: Oxford University Press, 1932.

Buell, Paul. "Pleasing the Palate of the Qan: Changing Foodways of the Imperial Mongols." *Mongolian Studies* 13 (1990): 57–81.

Campbell, Mary. *The Witness and the Other World: Exotic European Travel Writing, 400–1600*. Ithaca: Cornell University Press, 1988.

Ceschi, Carlo. *Chiese di Genova*. Genova: Stringa Editore, 1966.

Chabot, J. B. "Histoire du Patriarche Mar Jabalaha III et du moine Rabban Çauma." *Revue de l'orient latin* 1 (1893): 567–610; 2, 1 (1894): 73–142; 2, 2 (1894): 235–304.

Chazan, Robert. *Daggers of Faith: Thirteenth-Century Christian Missionizing and Jewish Response*. Berkeley: University of California Press, 1989.

Ch'en Yüan. "On the Damaged Tablets Discovered by Mr. D. Martin in Inner Mongolia." *Monumenta Serica* 3 (1937–38): 250–56.

Chiese di Genova. Genova: Sagip Editrice, 1986.

Davies, R. R. *Domination and Conquest: The Experience of Ireland, Scotland, and Wales, 1100–1300*. Cambridge: Cambridge University Press, 1990.

Dawson, Christopher, ed. *Mission to Asia*. New York: Harper & Row, 1966.

Delorme, F., and A. L. Tautu, eds. *Acta romanurum pontificum ab Innocentio V ad Benedictum XI, 1276–1304*, 3:5:t. 2: 124–36. Rome: Codicem Fontes, 1954.

Der Nersessian, Sirarpie. *Armenia and the Byzantine Empire*. Cambridge, Mass.: Harvard University Press, 1947.

———. "The Armenian Chronicle of the Constable Smpad or of the 'Royal Historians.'" *Dumbarton Oaks Papers* 13 (1959): 141–68.

———. *The Armenians*. London: Thames and Hudson, 1969.

DeWeese, Devin. "The Influence of the Mongols on the Religious Consciousness of Thirteenth-Century Europe." *Mongolian Studies* 5 (1978–79): 407–33.

Dunn, Ross E. *The Adventures of Ibn Battuta.* Berkeley: University of California Press, 1986.

Dunnell, Ruth. "Who Are the Tanguts?" *Journal of Asian History* 18, 1 (1984): 78–89.

————. *Tanguts and the Tangut State of Ta Hsia.* Princeton University Ph.D. dissertation, 1983.

Eickelman, Dale, and James Piscatori, eds. *Muslim Travellers.* Berkeley: University of California Press, 1990.

Eliade, Mircea, ed. *The Encyclopedia of Religion.* 16 vols. New York: Macmillan, 1987.

Emhardt, William, and George Lamsa. *The Oldest Christian People.* New York: Macmillan, 1926.

Erlande-Brandeburg, Alain. *The Abbey Church of Saint-Denis.* Paris: Editions de la Tourolle, 1984.

Fawtier, Robert. *The Capetian Kings of France: Monarchy and Nation (987–1328).* Trans. by Lionel Butler and R. J. Adam. London: Macmillan, 1960.

Ferguson, George. *Signs and Symbols in Christian Art.* New York: Oxford University Press, 1954.

Fiey, Jean Maurice. *Mossoul chrétienne.* Beirut, 1959.

————. *Chrétiens syriaques sous les Mongols.* Louvain: Corpus Scriptorum Christianorum Orientalium, 1975.

————. *Communautés syriaques en Iran et Irak des origines à 1552.* London: Variorum Reprints, 1979.

Fletcher, Joseph. "The Mongols: Ecological and Social Perspectives." *Harvard Journal of Asiatic Studies* 46, 1 (June 1986): 11–50.

Franke, Herbert. "Additional Notes on Non-Chinese Terms in the Yuan Imperial Dietary Compendium *Yin-shan Cheng-yao.*" *Zentralasiatische Studien* 4 (1970): 7–16.

Geanakoplos, Deno John. *Emperor Michael Palaeologus and the West, 1258–1282: A Study in Byzantine-Latin Relations.* Cambridge, Mass.: Harvard University Press, 1959.

Geary, Patrick J. *Furta Sacra: Thefts of Relics in the Central Middle Ages.* 2nd ed. Princeton: Princeton University Press, 1990.

Gibb, H. A. R., trans. *Ibn Battuta: Travels in Asia and Africa, 1325–1354.* Reprint. New York: Augustus M. Kelley, 1969.

Gismondi, E. *Amri et Slibae de patriarchis Nestorianium commentaria.* 2 vols. Rome, 1896–1899.

Grekov, B., and Iakoubovski, A. *La Horde d'Or.* Trans. by François Thuret. Paris: Payot, 1939.

Grodecki, Louis. *Sainte-Chapelle.* 3rd ed. Paris: Caisse nationale des monuments historiques et des sites, 1979.

Grousset, René. *Histoire des Croisades et du Royaume franc de Jérusalem.* 3 vols. Paris: Librairie Plon, 1934–1936.

Gumilev, L. N. *Searches for an Imaginary Kingdom: The Legend of the Kingdom of Prester John.* Trans. by R. E. F. Smith. Cambridge: Cambridge University Press, 1987.

Guzman, Gregory G. "Simon of Saint-Quentin and the Dominican Mission of the Mongol Baiju: A Reappraisal." *Speculum* 46, 2 (April 1971): 232–49.

———. "Simon of Saint-Quentin as Historian of the Mongols and the Seljuk Turks." *Medievalia et Humanistica* n.s. 3 (1972): 155–78.

———. "The Encyclopedist Vincent of Beauvais and His Mongol Extracts from John of Plano Carpini and Simon of Saint-Quentin." *Speculum* 49, 2 (April 1974): 287–307.

Haeger, John W. "Marco Polo in China: Problems with Internal Evidence." *Bulletin of Sung and Yuan Studies* 14 (1978): 22–30.

Halperin, Charles J. "Russia in the Mongol Empire in Historical Perspective." *Harvard Journal of Asiatic Studies* 43, 1 (June 1983): 239–61.

———. *Russia and the Golden Horde.* Bloomington: Indiana University Press, 1985.

Hambis, Louis. "Notes sur l'histoire de Corée a l'époque mongole." *T'oung Pao* 45 (1957): 151–218.

Hamilton, James. "Le texte turc en caractères syriaques du grand sceau cruciforme de Mār Yahballāhā III." *Journal asiatique* 260 (1972): 155–70.

Haneda Tōru. *Genchō ekiden zakko*. Tokyo, 1930.

Hirth, Friedrich, and William W. Rockhill, trans. *Chau Ju-kua: His Work on the Chinese and Arab Trade in the Twelfth and Thirteenth Centuries Entitled Chu-fan-chi*. St. Petersburg: Printing Office of the Imperial Academy of Sciences, 1911.

Hourani, George. *Arab Seafaring in the Indian Ocean in Ancient and Early Medieval Times*. Princeton: Princeton University Press, 1951.

Housley, Norman. *The Italian Crusades*. Oxford: Clarendon Press, 1982.

Humble, Richard. *Marco Polo*. New York: G. P. Putnam's Sons, 1975.

Inaba Shoju, trans. "The Lineage of the Sa skya pa: A Chapter of the Red Annals." *Memoirs of the Research Department of the Toyo Bunko* 22 (1963): 107–23.

Jackson, Peter. "The Crusade Against the Mongols." *Journal of Ecclesiastical History* 42 (1991): 1–18.

Jackson, Peter, and David Morgan. *The Mission of Friar William of Rubruck*. London: Hakluyt Society, 1990.

Jahn, Karl. *Täbris, Ein Mittelalterliches Kulturzentrum zwischen Ost und West*. Graz: Herman Böhlaus, 1968.

Joinville, Jean Sire de. *Histoire de Saint Louis, Roi de France*. Paris: Impremerie de Goetschy, 1822.

———. *Histoire de Saint Louis*. Paris: Librairie de la Société de l'histoire de France, 1868.

Jordan, William C. *The French Monarchy and the Jews from Philip Augustus to the Last Capetians*. Philadelphia: University of Pennsylvania Press, 1989.

Kedar, Benjamin. *Merchants in Crisis: Genoese and Venetian Men of Affairs and the Fourteenth-Century Depression.* New Haven: Yale University Press, 1976.

Kinross, Lord. *Hagia Sophia.* New York: Newsweek Book Division, 1972.

Kohler, C., and C. V. Langlois. "Lettres inédites concernant les Croisades (1275–1307)." *Bibliothèque de l'école des Chartes* 52 (1891): 46–63.

Kychanov, E. J. *Ocherk Istorii Tangutskogo Gosudarstva.* Moscow: Nauka, 1968.

Lach, Donald F. *Asia in the Making of Europe.* Volume 1: *The Century of Discovery,* Book 1. Chicago: University of Chicago Press, 1965.

Laiou, Angeliki. *Constantinople and the Latins: The Foreign Policy of Andronicus II, 1282–1328.* Cambridge, Mass.: Harvard University Press, 1972.

Lambton, Ann K. S. *Landlord and Peasant in Persia.* London: Oxford University Press, 1953.

Lane, Frederic C. *Venice: A Maritime Republic.* Baltimore: Johns Hopkins University Press, 1973.

Lao Yan-shuan. "Notes on Non-Chinese Terms in the Yuan Imperial Dietary Compendium *Yin-shan Cheng-yao.*" *Bulletin of the Institute of History and Philology, Academia Sinica* 39 (October 1969): 399–416.

Lapidus, Ira. *Muslim Cities in the Later Middle Ages.* Cambridge, Mass.: Harvard University Press, 1967.

Lary, George. *The Medieval Alexander.* Ed. by D. J. A. Ross. Cambridge: Cambridge University Press, 1956.

Lattimore, Owen. *Studies in Frontier History.* London: Oxford University Press, 1962.

Laurent, M. H. "Rabban Sauma, Ambassadeur de l'il-khan Argoun, et la cathédrale de Veroli." *Mélanges d'Archéologie et d'histoire publ. par l'école française de Rome* 70 (1958): 331–65.

Le Coq, Albert von. *Buried Treasures of Chinese Turkestan.* Trans. by Anna Barwell. London: Allen & Unwin, 1928.

Leff, Gordon. *Paris and Oxford Universities in the Thirteenth and Fourteenth Centuries*. New York: John Wiley and Sons, 1968.

Legge, James, trans. *A Record of Buddhistic Kingdoms*. Oxford: Clarendon Press, 1886.

Le Strange, Guy, trans. *The Geographical Part of the Nuzhat-al-Qulub Composed by Hamd-Allah Mustawfi of Qazwin in 740 (1340)*. Leyden:E. J. Brill, 1919.

———. *The Lands of the Eastern Caliphate*. Reprint. New York: Barnes & Noble, 1966.

Lewis, Bernard, P. M. Holt, and Ann K. S. Lambton, eds. *The Cambridge History of Islam*. 2 vols. Cambridge: Cambridge University Press, 1970.

Ligeti, Louis. *Monuments en écriture 'Phags-pa: pièces de chancellerie en transcription chinoise*. Budapest: Akademiai Kiado, 1972.

Lippard, Bruce. "The Mongols and Byzantium, 1243–1341." Indiana University Ph.D. dissertation, 1984.

Lloyd, Simon. *English Society and the Crusades, 1216–1307*. Oxford: Clarendon Press, 1988.

Lockhart, Laurence. "The Relations Between Edward I and Edward II of England and the Mongol Īl-Khāns of Persia." *Iran* 6 (1968): 23–31.

Loewe, Michael. *Records of Han Administration*. 2 vols. Cambridge: Cambridge University Press, 1967.

Maitra, K. M. *A Persian Embassy to China*. New York: Paragon Books Reprint Corporation, 1970.

Mann, Horace K., ed. *The Lives of the Popes in the Middle Ages*. Volumes 16 and 17. London: Kegan Paul, Trench, Trubner, 1931–32.

Martin, H. D. "Preliminary Report on Nestorian Remains North of Kuei-hua, Sui-yuan." *Monumenta Serica* 3 (1937–38): 232–49.

Martines, Lauro. *Power and Imagination: City States in Renaissance Italy*. New York: Alfred A. Knopf, 1979.

McLean, Norman. "An Eastern Embassy to Europe in the Years 1287–88." *English Historical Review* 14 (1899): 299–312.

Michelin: Rome. London: Michelin Tyre, 1985.

Miller, Roy A. *Accounts of Western Nations in the History of the Northern Chou Dynasty*. Berkeley: University of California Press, 1959.

Mingana, Alphonse. *The Early Spread of Christianity in Central Asia and the Far East*. Manchester: The University Press, 1925.

Mirsky, Jeannette, ed. *The Great Chinese Travelers*. Chicago: University of Chicago Press, 1964.

Montgomery, James A., trans. *The History of Yaballaha III, Nestorian Patriarch and of His Vicar Bar Sauma*. New York: Columbia University Press, 1927.

Morgan, David. *The Mongols*. London: Basil Blackwell, 1986.

————. *Medieval Persia, 1040–1797*. London: Longman, 1989.

————. "The Mongols and the Eastern Mediterranean." *Mediterranean Historical Review* 4, 1 (June 1989): 198–211.

Mostaert, Antoine, and Francis W. Cleaves. *Les lettres de 1289 et 1305 des ilkhan Aryun et Öljeitü a Philippe le Bel*. Cambridge, Mass.: Harvard University Press, 1962.

————. "Trois documents mongols des Archives secrètes vaticanes." *Harvard Journal of Asiatic Studies* 15 (1952): 419–506.

Moule, A. C. *Christians in China Before the Year 1550*. London: Society for Promoting Christian Knowledge, 1930.

Moule, A. C., and Paul Pelliot. *Marco Polo: The Description of the World*. 2 vols. London: George Routledge & Sons, 1938.

Needham, Joseph. *Science and Civilisation in China*. Volume 1. Cambridge: Cambridge University Press, 1961.

Nicol, Donald M. *Byzantium and Venice*. Cambridge: Cambridge University Press, 1988.

Nogara, Bartolomeo. *Les Trésors d'Art du Vatican*. Bergamo: Istituto Italiano d'arti Grafiche, 1950.

Ohsson, Constantin Mouradgea d'. *Histoire des Mongols, depuis Tchinguiz-khan jusqu'à Timour-Bey ou Tamerlan*. 4 vols. The Hague and Amsterdam: Les Frères Van Cleef, 1834–35.

Olbricht, Peter. *Das Postwesen in China unter der Mongolenherrschaft im 13. und 14. Jahrhundert*. Wiesbaden: Otto Harrassowitz, 1954.

Olschki, Leonardo. *Marco Polo's Precursors*. Baltimore: Johns Hopkins University Press, 1943.

———. *Guillaume Boucher: A French Artist at the Court of the Khans*. Baltimore: Johns Hopkins University Press, 1946.

———. *Marco Polo's Asia*. Berkeley: University of California Press, 1960.

Oriente Poliano. Rome: Istituto Italiano per il Medio ed Estremo Oriente, 1957.

Peers, E. Allison, trans. *Blanquerna: A Thirteenth-Century Romance of Ramon Lull*. London: Jarrolds Publishers, 1926.

Pelliot, Paul. *Notes on Marco Polo*. 2 vols. Paris: Adrien-Maisonneuve, 1959–1963.

———. *Les Mongols et la Papauté*. Paris: Librairie August Picard, 1923.

———. *Recherches sur les chrétiens d'Asie centrale et d'Extrême Orient*. Ed. by Jean Dauvillier and Louis Hambis. Paris: Imprimerie nationale, 1973.

Pesce, Bartolomeo. *La Cattedrale di Genova*. Genova: Edizione Sigla Effi, 1955.

Petech, Luciano. "Les marchands italiens dans l'empire mongol." *Journal asiatique* 250, 4 (1962): 549–74.

Pigulevskaia, N. V. *Istoriia Mar Iabalakhi i Rabban Saumy*. Moscow: Izdatelstvo Vostochnoi Literaturi, 1958.

Powell, James, ed. *Muslims Under Latin Rule*. Princeton: Princeton University Press, 1990.

Powicke, Maurice. *The Oxford History of England: The Thirteenth Century, 1216–1307*. Oxford: Clarendon Press, 1953.

Prestwich, Michael. *Edward I*. London: Methuen, 1988.

Queller, Donald. "Thirteenth-Century Diplomatic Envoys: *Nuncii* and *Procuratores*." *Speculum* 35, 2 (April 1960): 196–213.

Rachewiltz, Igor de. *Papal Envoys to the Great Khans*. London: Faber & Faber, 1971.

———. "The Secret History of the Mongols." *Papers on Far Eastern History* 4 (September 1971): 115–63; 5 (March 1972): 149–75;

10 (September 1974): 55–82; 13 (March 1976): 41–75; 16 (September 1977): 27–65; 18 (September 1978): 43–80; 21 (March 1980): 17–57; 23 (March 1981): 111–46; 26 (September 1982): 39–84.

Rashdall, Hastings. *The Universities of Europe in the Middle Ages*. New ed. by F. M. Powicke and A. B. Emden. 3 vols. Oxford: Oxford University Press, 1936.

Rice, David Talbot. *Byzantine Art*. London: Penguin Books, 1954.

Richard, Jean. "La mission en Europe de Rabban Çauma et l'union des églises." *Convegno di science morali storiche e filologiche: Accademia nazionale dei Lincei*, pp. 162–67. Rome: Accademia Nazionale dei Lincei, 1957.

———. "The Mongols and the Franks." *Journal of Asian History* 3, 1 (1969): 45–57.

———. *La Papauté et les missions d'orient au moyen âge (xiii–xiv siècles)*. Rome: École française de Rome, Palais Farnese, 1977.

———. *The Latin Kingdom of Jerusalem*. Trans. by Janet Shirley. Amsterdam: North Holland Publishing, 1979.

Richards, D. S., ed. *Islam and the Trade of Asia*. Philadelphia: University of Pennsylvania Press, 1967.

Ridolfini, Cecilia Pericoli. *St. Paul's Outside the Walls: Rome*. Bologna: Grafica Editoriale, 1967.

Rockhill, William W., trans. *The Journey of William of Rubruck to the Eastern Parts of the World*. London: Hakluyt Society, 1900.

Rossabi, Morris. "Ming China's Relations with Hami and Central Asia, 1404–1513: A Reexamination of Traditional Chinese Foreign Policy." Columbia University Ph.D. dissertation, 1970.

———. "Khubilai Khan and the Women in His Family." In *Studia Sino-Mongolica: Festschrift für Herbert Franke*, ed. by Wolfgang Bauer, pp. 153–80. Wiesbaden: Franz Steiner Verlag, 1979.

———. *Khubilai Khan: His Life and Times*. Berkeley: University of California Press, 1988.

———. "The 'Decline' of the Central Asian Caravan Trade." In *The Rise of Merchant Empires*, ed. by James D. Tracy, pp. 351–70. Cambridge: Cambridge University Press, 1990.

————. "Trade Routes in Inner Asia." Unpublished paper prepared for Denis Sinor, ed., *Cambridge History of Inner Asia.*

————, ed. *China Among Equals: The Middle Kingdom and Its Neighbors, 10th–14th Centuries.* Berkeley: University of California Press, 1983.

Rowling, Marjorie. *Everyday Life of Medieval Travellers.* London: B. T. Batsford, 1971.

Runciman, Steven. *A History of the Crusades.* Volume 3: *The Kingdom of Acre.* Cambridge: Cambridge University Press, 1954.

Santini, Loretta. *Rome and Vatican.* Rome: Plurigraf Narni-Terni, 1975.

Sauvaget, Jean. "Caravansérails syriens du moyen-âge." *Ars Islamica* 4 (1937): 98–121.

Sayili, Aydin. *The Observatory in Islam.* Ankara: Publications of the Turkish Historical Society, no. 38, 1960.

Schafer, Edward H. *The Golden Peaches of Samarkand.* Berkeley: University of California Press, 1963.

Setton, Kenneth. "The Papacy and the Levant (1204–1571)." *Memoirs of the American Philosophical Society* 114 (1976).

Sinor, Denis. "Un voyageur du treizième siècle: le Dominicain Julien de Hongrie." *Bulletin of the School of Oriental and African Studies, London University* 14, 3 (1952): 589–602.

————. "The Mongols and Western Europe." In *A History of the Crusades.* Volume 3: *The Fourteenth and Fifteenth Centuries,* ed. by Harry W. Hazard, pp. 513–44. Madison: University of Wisconsin Press, 1975.

————. "Interpreters in Medieval Inner Asia." *Asian and African Studies* 16, 3 (November 1982): 293–320.

————. "Diplomatic Practices in Medieval Inner Asia." In *The Islamic World, from Classical to Modern Times: Essays in Honor of Bernard Lewis,* ed. by C. E. Bosworth, Charles Issawi, Roger Savory, and A. L. Udovitch, pp. 337–55. Princeton: Darwin Press, 1989.

Slessarev, Vsevolod. *Prester John: The Letters and the Legend.* Minneapolis: University of Minnesota Press, 1959.

Smith, John Masson. "'Ayn Jālūt: Mamlūk Success or Mongol Failure?" *Harvard Journal of Asiatic Studies* 44, 2 (December 1984): 307–45.

Spence, Jonathan. *The Question of Hu.* New York: Alfred A. Knopf, 1988.

Spuler, Bertold. *Die Goldene Horde: Die Mongolen in Russland, 1223– 1502.* Wiesbaden: Otto Harrassowitz, 1965.

―――. *Die Mongolen in Iran: Politik, Verwaltung, und Kultur der Ilchanzeit, 1220–1350.* Berlin: Akademie-Verlag, 1968.

Steensgaard, Niels. *Carracks, Caravans, and Companies: The Structural Crisis in the European-Asian Trade in the Early 17th Century.* Copenhagen: Scandinavian Institute of Asian Studies Monograph Series 17, 1973.

Stein, M. Aurel. *Ancient Khotan.* 2 vols. Oxford: Clarendon Press, 1907.

Strayer, Joseph, ed. *Dictionary of the Middle Ages.* 13 vols. New York: Charles Scribner's Sons, 1982–1989.

Tisserant, E. "Une lettre de l'Ilkhan Abaga adressée en 1268 au pape Clement IV." *Muséon* 59 (1946): 547–56.

Trimingham, J. Spencer. *Christianity Among the Arabs in Pre-Islamic Times.* London: Longman, 1979.

Tyerman, Christopher. *England and the Crusades, 1095–1588.* Chicago: University of Chicago Press, 1988.

Vacant, Alfred, and Éugene Mangenot, eds. *Dictionnaire de théologie catholique.* 15 vols. Paris: Librairie Letouzey et Ané, 1908–1950.

Vambery, Arminius. *History of Bokhara from the Earliest Period down to the Present.* London: H. S. Kinn, 1873.

Vasiliev, A. A. *History of the Byzantine Empire, 324–1453.* Madison: University of Wisconsin Press, 1952.

Vine, Aubrey. *The Nestorian Churches.* London: Independent Press, 1937.

Voegelin, Eric. "The Mongol Orders of Submission to European Powers, 1245–1255." *Byzantion* 15 (1940–41): 378–413.

Waley, Daniel. *The Italian City-Republics.* 3rd ed. London: Longman, 1988.

Walker, David. *Medieval Wales.* Cambridge: Cambridge University Press, 1990.

Wardwell, Anne E. *"Panni Tartaricis*: Eastern Islamic Silks Woven with Gold and Silver, 13th and 14th Centuries." *Islamic Art* 3 (1988–89): 95–173.

Watanabe, Hiroshi. *Marco Polo Bibliography, 1477–1983.* Tokyo: Toyo Bunko, 1986.

Weissman, Keith. "Mongol Rule in Baghdad, 1258–1301." University of Chicago Ph.D. dissertation, 1990.

Wiet, Gaston. *Baghdad: Metropolis of the Abbasid Caliphate.* Trans. by Seymour Feiler. Norman: University of Oklahoma Press, 1971.

Wood, Charles T. *The French Appanages and the Capetian Monarchy.* Cambridge, Mass.: Harvard University Press, 1966.

————, ed. *Philip the Fair and Boniface VIII: State vs. Papacy.* 2nd ed. New York: Holt, Rinehart & Winston, 1971.

Wyngaert, Anastasius van den. *Sinica Franciscana.* 5 vols. Quaracchi-Firenze: Collegio di S. Bonaventura, 1929–1954.

Yule, Henry, trans. *The Book of Ser Marco Polo, the Venetian Concerning the Kingdoms and Marvels of the East.* 2 vols. 3rd ed., rev. by Henri Cordier. London: John Murray, 1903.

————. *Cathay and the Way Thither.* Rev. ed. by Henri Cordier. Reprint, 4 vols. in 2. Taipei: Ch'eng-wen Publishing, 1966.

INDEX

Abakha (Ilkhan), 60, 66–67, 69–
  70, 75, 76–77, 84, 85, 108,
  167
  embassies to West, 92
  proposed collaboration with
    West, 89–93
'Abbāsid Caliph, 14
'Abbāsid caliphate, 5, 14, 18, 64,
  67, 70
'Abbāsid dynasty, 17
'Abd al-Rahmān, 78
Abghan, King of Edessa, 126–27
Acre, 4, 89, 175
Addai (Thaddaeus), 122
Aḥmad (Ilkhan), 77–82, 93–94, 97
Ai Buqa, 50, 51
'Alā al-Dīn 'Atā-Malik Juvainī, 77
'Ali al-Riḍā, 62
Alphonso II, King of Aragon, 143
Ananias, 130, 131
Andrew of Longjumeau, 13–
  14, 15
Andronicus II, Byzantine Em-
  peror, 106–9, 115
Angevins, 118
Ani, 70–71
Ani Cathedral, 71
Arabia, 3, 56
Arabian Nights, 61
Aragon, Aragonese, 118, 134, 139,
  142–43, 153

Arbil, 65, 66
Architecture, 71, 112
  church, 132, 147
Arghun, 77, 78, 79–82, 83, 97, 98
  death of, 174, 175
  embassy to West, 99–101, 115,
    119, 142, 153, 156, 159, 163
  letter of Pope Nicholas to, 164–
    67, 169
  and proposed alliance with West,
    173–75
  and Rabban Sauma's return
    from West, 170–73
Arigh Böke, 20, 37–38
Aristotle, 146
Armenia, 70–71
Ascelinus (friar), 14
Ashot the Great, 70
Asia, 115
  Europe and, 3–22, 179
Astronomy, 63
'Ayn Jālūt, battle at, 18, 19, 37
Ayyubid dynasty, 7, 14, 18
Āẓarbāyjān, 19, 62, 63, 67, 75, 77,
  79, 83

Baghdad, 14, 17, 62, 64–65, 66–
  67, 68, 74, 76–77, 111, 121,
  177
Bagratid dynasty, 70
Baidu, 177

Bar Hebraeus, 43, 44
Bar Sauma (Rabban Sauma), 1–3,
  12, 76, 168–69
  characteristics of, 99–100
  death of, 177–78
  description of Nestorianism,
  121–25
  diary, 1, 54–55, 114
  early life of, 22–36
  influence of, 179–80
  languages, 33, 100
  Nestorianism, 29–36
  Visitor-General in China, 72–75,
  76, 121, 164
Bar Sauma (Rabban Sauma) mission to West, 2, 23, 38, 39–58,
  83, 99–180
  finances, 42–44, 51
  logistics of, 42–44, 47–48
  report on, 101–3, 171
  spiritual goal of, 23, 40–41, 42,
  43–44, 133
Bar Sauma (Rabban Sauma) narrative account, 1–2, 23, 52–53,
  54–55, 57, 61–62, 64, 74, 75,
  78, 79, 80, 82, 100, 101, 113–
  14, 115, 124, 126–27, 132,
  133, 150, 155, 160, 162, 171
  editor-translator, 2, 12, 24, 29,
  51, 54, 74, 102, 105–6, 113,
  114, 133, 150, 171, 177
Baradeus, Jacob (Ya'qub Bar-
  Addai), 69
Baraqa, 93
Basilica of San Giovanni in Laterano (St. John Lateran, Rome),
  132–33, 161
Basilica of San Pietro (St. Peter's,
  Rome), 125–28
Basilica of Santa Maria Maggiore
  (St. Mary Major, Rome), 133,
  163
Batu (Mongol leader), 5–6
Bay of Naples, 117–18
Baybars, 87, 93
Béla IV, King of Hungary, 5
Benoit XI, Pope, 178

Berke (ruler of Golden Horde),
  18–19
Bernini, Giovanni, 126
Beth Garmai, 65
Beth Zabdai, 65
Black Sea, 102, 104, 105
Blanquerna (Lull), 97–98
Boniface VIII, Pope, 144, 178
Boucher, Guillaume, 16
Bramante, Donato, 126
Brigandage, 4, 56, 57–58, 72, 141
Buddhism, Buddhists, 9, 15, 17,
  19, 53, 54, 60, 155, 179
Buscarel de Gisolf, 173
Byzantine Emperor, 91, 94
Byzantine Empire, 25, 84, 85, 91,
  92, 94–95, 101, 136, 138
  Bar Sauma trip to, 102, 106–17
  relationship with Ilkhanate,
  108–9, 115
  relics from, 152

Cambio, Arnolfo di, 126, 128–29
Capetian Kings, 147
Caravanserais, 104–5
Cathedral of Hagia Sophia (Con-
  stantinople), 71
Cathedral of San Andrea (St. An-
  drew, Veroli), 169–70
Cathedral of San Lorenzo (St.
  Laurence, Genoa), 136–37
Catholic Church, 91, 94, 101, 178
  Philip IV and, 143–44
  proposed union with Orthodox,
  108
  supremacy of, 168
Catholicism, 123–24
Central Asia, 4, 5, 9, 23, 42, 119
  Nestorianism in, 25, 26, 178
  political struggles in, 56, 57, 76
  postal stations/garrisons in,
  48–49
  roads in, 49, 140
Chaghadai Khan, Khanate, 9, 19,
  21, 33, 38, 39, 83, 89
Charles Martel, 118
Charles of Anjou, 85–89, 91, 92,

94–95, 96, 108, 117, 139, 142, 143, 153
and Sicilian Vespers, 118
Charles of Valois, 139, 142
Charles II (Charles of Salerno), 118, 143
Cherchen River, 51
China, Chinese, 3, 8, 20, 22, 23, 49, 56, 61, 115, 122
and Europe, 3–5
Khubilai Khan's government in, 39
Ministry of Rites, 120
Nestorianism in, 25, 26
scholarship in, 146–47
trade with West, 3–4
Chinese Emperors
burial of, 149
Chinggis (Genghis) Khan, 6, 7–8, 9, 24, 31, 33
Chinggisid line, 31–33
Christian Empire in the East, 95
Christianity, 24, 36, 70, 116, 123, 179
differences from Nestorianism, 124, 150
Eastern branch of, 158
heretical sects, 25–26
holy sites of, 43
Holy Week ceremonies, 160–63
hostility to, in Persia, 173, 176
in Ilkhanate, 60, 97, 98
in Middle East, 4, 5
Mongols and, 14, 15, 22, 44–46, 97, 98
Papal authority in, 165–66
spread of, 121–22
in Tabrīz, 69
Church of Saint-Denis (Paris), 147–49
Church of St. Gregory of Gagik (Ani), 71
Church of Saints Sergius and Bacchus, 116
Church of San Paolo Fuori le Mura (St. Paul's Outside the Walls, Rome), 128–31

Church of San Pietro in Vincoli (St. Peter in Chains, Rome), 131
Church of Santa Croce (Holy Cross, Rome), 162
Church of Santa Sabina (Rome), 120
Church of the Holy Apostles (Ani), 71
Church of the Nicean fathers (Constantinople), 112–13
Church of the Redeemer (Ani), 71
Clement IV, Pope, 84, 87
College of Cardinals, 119–25, 156, 157, 158
Confucius, 146–47
Constantine, Emperor, 112, 116, 126, 132
Constantinople, 84, 104, 105, 106, 108, 109–13, 114–15, 117, 127
Council of Ephesus, 24
Council of Lyons, 94, 108, 124
Crusader states, 20, 21, 87, 89, 91
Crusades, 4, 5, 6, 85–89, 91, 92, 94
Fourth Crusade, 84
proposed, to recover Holy Land, 3, 7, 95–96, 99, 119, 123, 134, 139, 142, 144, 152, 153–56, 159, 166, 172, 173–75, 178
St. Louis, 14, 15
Cyprus, 14

Damascus, 17, 18, 173
Dark Ages, 4
Dasht-i Kavīr Desert, 62
David of Ashby, 21–22, 91
Denha, Mar (Patriarch), 62–64, 65, 66–67, 69–70, 71–75, 76, 80
death of, 74
Dominicans, 69, 120

East Asia, 2, 3, 4, 5
East-West contact

East-West contact (*cont'd*)
emissaries, 7, 12–16, 20–22, 41
travel in, 22–23
East-West trade, 3–4, 19, 54, 55, 57, 70–71
Ecumenical Councils, 91
Thirteenth, 6–7, 12–14
Edessa, 122
Edward I, King of England, 85–89, 91, 92, 95–96, 123, 142–43, 173–75
Bar Sauma's meeting with, 153–56, 166, 167
Egypt, 7, 14, 18
Eurasia, 3, 5
Europe, 2
and Asia, 3–22, 178–79, 180
disunity in, 21, 83–94, 123, 133
and proposed coalition to recapture Holy Land, 94–98
Ezekiel (prophet), 65

Fa-hsien, 53
Fang Mountains, 34, 35
Firdausi, 61
France, 3, 85, 87, 92, 139, 140–41
Franciscans, 69, 97, 167
Frederick II, Holy Roman Emperor, 6–7
Fusṭāṭ, 4

Gascony, 85, 142, 153
Geikhatu, 175–77
Genoa, Genoese, 22, 69, 84, 95, 135
Bar Sauma in, 134–38, 156–58
Geopolitics, 180
Ghazan (Ilkhan), 68, 171, 174, 177
Ghazan Khan, 58, 60
Giwargis, Mar, 30
Gobert de Helleville, 153, 169, 173
Gobi Desert, 51
Golden Horde, 9, 12, 18–19, 21, 37, 40, 67, 80, 83, 108
raid on lands of Arghun, 174
split with Ilkhans, 71
Great Church of Köke, 64

Great Khan (Khan of Khans), 7, 9, 15, 16, 20, 65, 75, 98
Great Khanate, 20
succession struggles, 31–33, 37–38, 39
Great Palace (Constantinople), 106–7
Gregory X, Pope, 91–92
Güyüg (Great Khan), 7, 12, 14–15, 31

Hagia Sophia, 109–12
Han dynasty, 3, 53
Hang-chou, 112
Harāt, 26
Hārūn al-Rashīd, 61, 62
Henry III, King of England, 85
Het'um, 20
Ḥimṣ, battle of, 76, 93, 95
History of the Mongols (Ystoria Mongolarum) (John of Plano Carpini), 7, 12–13
Hohenstaufens, 87
Holy Land, 4, 7, 41, 91, 92, 100
controlled by Mamlūks, 71, 85, 99
Muslim occupation of, 14, 139
proposed alliance to recapture, 94, 96, 142, 144, 153, 154, 155–56, 166–67, 174–75, 178
relics from, 152
Holy Roman Emperors, 6, 22, 127–28, 143, 157
Holy Roman Empire, 7
Holy sites, 72, 100, 101, 114, 115, 116, 125
Constantinople, 109–13
France, 144, 147–52
Gascony, 155
Genoa, 136–37, 138
Rome, 125–34, 138
Honorius III, Pope, 120
Honorius IV, Pope, 96, 97, 119, 123, 157
House of Anjou, 117
Hsi Hsia (Tangut) Empire, 51
Hugo Gantelmes, 168

Hülegü, 17–22, 37, 40, 60, 63, 64, 77, 84, 91, 92, 97, 108
Hungary, 5–6, 21

Ibn Baṭṭūṭa, 62, 68, 115
Ilkhanate, 9, 19–20, 75–76, 80
    attempts to unite with Europe to defeat Muslims, 20–22, 84–85, 89–98, 99, 152, 159, 166–67, 173–75, 178
    and divided Europe, 83–94
    Genoese trade with, 134
    holy sites, relics, 72
    political turbulence, 174
    Rabban Sauma and Markos at, 58–74, 75–76
    Rabban Sauma emissary from, 2–3, 99–138, 142, 153, 155
    relationship with Byzantine Emperors, 108–9, 115
    students in, 147
Ilkhans, 9, 37, 56, 77–82
    conversion to Islam, 174, 177, 178
    split with Golden Horde, 70–71
    succession struggles, 77
India, 3, 51, 122
Innocent IV, pope, 6–7, 12
Islam, 4, 12, 26, 75, 77, 83, 96, 155, 179
    conversion of Ilkhans to, 174, 177, 178
Islamic caliphate, 4
Islamic dynasties, 17, 21
Italian city-states, 84–85, 92, 134
    government of, 135
Italy, 3, 85
    Bar Sauma in, 117–38

Jacobites, 25, 69, 155
James the Great, St., 133
Japan, 39
Jazīrat ibn-'Umar, 104
Jerome of Ascoli, 157–58
Jerusalem, 4, 7, 40, 44, 46, 50, 63, 70, 72, 99
    controlled by Mamlūks, 71

hopes for liberation of, 121, 123
    proposed alliance to recover, 142, 153, 166
    see also Holy Land
Jews, 22, 58, 87, 173
John Chrysostom, 112, 116
John of Monte Corvino, 69
John of Plano Carpini, 2, 7, 9, 12–13, 14, 16, 115
John of Tusculum, 157
John the Baptist, 112, 137
John XXI, Pope, 92
Judaism, 173, 176
Julian (friar), 5–6
Justinian, Emperor, 69, 109, 112

K'ai-p'ing (later Shang-tu, Xanadu), 39
Kashgar, 55–56
Ked Bukha, 17–18
Khaidu, 38–39, 55, 56, 57, 73, 83
Khan(s), 8, 9–12, 14
Khara Khitay, 5
Khara Khorum, 7, 16, 20, 26
Khotan, 52–54
Khotan Darya (river), 53
Khubilai (Kublai) Khan, 1, 9, 15, 20, 23, 37–40, 50, 57, 63, 66, 69–70, 78–79, 97
    conflict with Khaidu, 55, 56, 73
    death of, 178
    and Ilkhanate, 84
    and Rabban Sauma journey to West, 43–46
Khurāsān, 57, 58, 61, 62, 174
Korea, Koreans, 5, 39
Körgüz, 61
Ko-sheng, 49–50
Kun Buqa, 50, 51
K'un-lun Mountains, 51, 53
Kurds, 99

Lake Urmiya, 67, 79
Laurence, St., 136
Lazarus, 112
Le Coq, Albert von, 57

Lesser Armenia (Cilicia), 17, 19–
20, 70–71, 84
Letters patent, 46, 56, 66, 69, 76,
78, 79, 101, 164
Literacy, 24, 44
Louis IX (St. Louis), King of
France, 7, 14–15, 16, 85, 87–
89, 92, 139, 147, 152, 166
Luke, St., 112
Lull, Ramon, 97–98
Lyons, 6, 91

Mamlūk dynasty, 18
Mamlūk Sultanate, 108
Mamlūks, 7, 18, 19, 20, 21, 37,
40, 71
and Ilkhanate, 76, 77–78, 79, 83
proposed Ilkhanate/West collaboration against, 84–85, 87,
89–98, 99, 107, 113–14, 119,
122–23, 133–34, 136, 142,
144, 152, 155–56, 158, 159,
166, 167, 172, 173–75, 178
Manchuria, 48
Manṣūriyya, 61
Mar Mari (monastery), 64
Marāgha, 67, 71, 80, 173, 176, 177
observatory at, 63, 147
Mari (disciple of Addai), 122
Maria (daughter of Michael
Palaeologus), 108
Markos/Mar Yaballah, 34–36, 38,
157, 163, 164, 171
as Catholicus, 74–82
death of, 178
and death of Rabban Sauma,
177–78
journey to West, 39–58
letters of Pope Nicholas to, 167–
68, 169
appointed Metropolitan, 72–75
and Rabban Sauma's return
from West, 172–73, 176–77
and Rabban Sauma's trip to
West, 100–1, 120–21, 122–23,
153, 159
Martin IV, Pope, 94, 96
Marv, 26

Mary, mother of Jesus, 25, 133,
150, 164
Mary Magdalene, 112
Matthew, St., 133
Mediterranean Sea, 4, 102, 105
Mediterranean trade, 84, 85
Merchant caravans, 42, 57
Merchants, 3, 53–54, 57, 100, 104,
105, 168
ethnic, linguistic diversity of, 54
Genoese, 134–35
Nestorian, 27
in Tabrīz, 68–69
Venetian, 89
Mesopotamia, 104, 122
Metropolitans (Nestorian), 27, 29,
72–73
Michael of Tar'īl, Mar, 65–66,
74, 75
Michael Palaeologus, Byzantine
Emperor, 91, 106, 108
Middle East, 2, 5, 14, 83, 178–79
Mongol pacification of, 17–22
Nestorians in, 25, 26
trade with China, 3–4
warfare, brigandage, 72
Middle Kingdom, 3, 69
Miran, 52
Missionaries, 3, 22, 23–24, 26–27,
69, 97–98, 168
Monastery of St. Michael, 112–
13
Möngke, Great Khan, 15–16, 17,
31–33, 37, 38, 39
Möngke Temür, 93
Mongol court, 50, 66, 106
and Bar Sauma journey to West,
43–44, 46, 70
Mongol Empire, Mongols, 9, 16,
31, 61, 62, 74, 83, 117
capital city, 67–68
and Christian Europe, 178–79,
180
conquests, expansionism, 4–7, 8,
17–22, 58–60, 104
crisis in world of, 37–40
emissaries to, from West, 7, 12–
16, 21–22

governance, administration, 24, 43, 58–60
lack of unity, 18–19, 33, 44, 46, 55
links with Genoa, 134
marital alliances, 50
military tactics and strategy, 6, 13, 19, 118
and Nestorianism, 26, 27
Outremer and, 85
political structure of, 7–9
power struggles, 44, 46
practices of, 13, 16–17
proposed collaboration with, against Muslims, 7, 12–16, 17, 20–22, 89–98, 119, 134, 142, 158, 167, 173–75, 179
Rabban Sauma emissary from, 120–21, 122, 123
religious policy, 9–10, 60
succession struggles, 31, 77
Mongol era
East and West in, 3–22
Mongolia, 8, 9, 20, 23, 26, 115
Monophysite interpretation, 69
Mosul, 65, 78, 104
Mount Etna, 117
Muslims, 15–16, 18, 19–20, 65, 99, 114
in control of Holy Land, 139
Crusades against, 5, 7
and Ilkhanate, 58, 60, 62, 65, 66, 77, 78, 80
opposition to Christians and Jews, 173
proposed East-West alliance against, 12, 14–15, 20–22, 40, 84–85, 89–98, 144, 155–56

Naples, 1, 92, 95, 116, 117–18, 134, 139
Naṣīr al-Dīn Ṭūsī, 61, 63
Navigation, 105
Nestorian Church, 50, 155, 167–68
implied papal authority over, 164, 165–66
organization of, 27

Nestorianism, Nestorians, 12, 16, 17, 19, 23–29, 66, 111, 170, 173
decline of, 178
hierarchy in, 72
holy sites, 64
liturgy, 159–60
persecution of, 99, 171, 173, 178
of Rabban Sauma, 29–36
Rabban Sauma's description of, 121–25
relationship with Ilkhanate, 76, 78–79
rituals, 27
in Ṭūs, 62–63
and Western Christianity, 150
Nicholas III, Pope, 97
Nicholas IV, Pope, 143, 157–69
Ning-hsia, 51–52, 78
Nishapur, 26
Nomukhan, 55
North Africa, 19, 179
North China, 4, 9, 20, 37
Notre-Dame (Paris), 149–50, 154

Oases, 47–48, 53, 55, 104–5
Ögödei, 9, 31, 38
house of, 33
Önggüd (people), 23–24, 34, 35, 50–51, 100
Orthodox Church, 91, 94, 108, 155
differences from Catholic, 124, 150
Outremer, 4, 21, 84–85, 87, 92, 167
security of, threats to, 71, 83, 89, 99, 158, 175, 178

Papacy, 20, 92, 95, 144, 145
Papal authority, 6–7, 128, 144
over Nestorian Church, 164, 165–66
Papal emissaries, 9, 12–16, 21–22, 41
Paris, 139–53
university, 144–47

Patriarch (Catholicus), 27, 29
  Mar Denha, 63–64, 66–67, 69–70, 71–72
  Markos, 74–82
Paul, St., 130, 131–32
Pax Mongolica, 3, 22, 55, 73
Persia, 17, 20, 22, 23, 26, 57, 83, 179
  Christianity in, 122
  hostility to Judaism and Christianity in, 173, 176, 178
  Ilkhanate in, 9
  Mongols' conquests in, 5
  Muslims in, 18
  political tensions in, 60–61
  Rabban Sauma in, 1, 2, 100, 156
  Rabban Sauma's return to, 163–64, 169–80
  Rabban Sauma's trip to, 42–58, 114, 119
  religious conflict in, 65
Persian Gulf, 3
Peter, St., 131, 132
Peter of Molina, 168
Peter III of Aragon, 95
Philip the Apostle, 133
Philip III (called "the Bold"), King of France, 85, 92, 139
Philip IV (the Fair), King of France, 139, 141–45, 150–53, 154, 166, 167, 169, 173–75
Pietro of Lucalongo, 69
Pirates, 4, 103, 105
Poland, 6, 21
Polo, Marco, 2, 17, 24, 34, 41, 44, 46, 49, 51, 52–53, 54, 55–56, 65, 68, 69, 112, 115
  credulity of, 116
  omissions by, 150
Pope(s), 120, 123, 125, 126, 127–28, 133, 134, 153, 156
  see also Papacy; Papal authority
Postal stations/garrisons, 48–49
Prester John, 5, 14, 24
Proselytizing, 12, 15, 22, 87, 168–69
  by Nestorians, 26–27
  see also Missionaries

Protection costs, 4, 42, 102
Provence, 143

Qalawun, 93

Rashīd al-Dīn, 18
Red Sea, 3
Relics, 29, 72, 100, 101, 116, 122, 125, 176
  Constantinople, 112–13
  Genoa, 136–37
  Paris, 151–52
  Rabban Sauma's request for gift of, 164
  Rome, 130–31, 132, 133, 162
Religion(s), 9–12, 19, 60–61
  see also under specific type, e.g., Christianity
Religious sites
  see Holy sites
Religious toleration, 9–12, 27, 60
Roman Empire, 3, 25, 163
Rome, 6, 40–41, 117
  Rabban Sauma in, 119–34, 138, 157, 158–69
Rudolf of Hapsburg, 157
Russia, 4–5, 9

Sabadinus, 104
Sa'd al-Dawla, 173
Sainte-Chapelle (Paris), 149, 150–52
Salāh al-Dīn (Saladin), 7
Saljuq Turks, 70, 93
Saracens, 5
Scotland, 87, 96
Seleucia-Ctesiphon, 27, 64, 122
Shāh-nāma (Firdausi), 61
Shamanism, 9, 24
Shams al-Dīn Juvainī, 61, 77, 78
Shiban, 23, 24
Shī'is, 62
Shih-tzu ssu, 34
Sicilian Vespers, 95, 108, 109, 118
Sicily, 87, 92, 94–95, 117, 134, 139
Silk Road, 3, 27, 52, 55, 57, 119
Simon (Metropolitan of China), 72–73

Simon Magus, 132
Sixtus II, Pope, 136
Sorghaghtani Beki, 31
South China, 9, 20, 39
Southern Silk Road, 52
Southern Sung China, 37, 38, 111
Stephen, St., 130
Sung dynasty, 4, 5
Sylvester, Pope, 116
Syria, 3, 7, 14, 17, 18, 20, 69, 83, 93, 97
   Mamlūks in, 89, 99
   Mongols' attempts to conquer, 174

Tabrīz, 13–14, 67–69, 99
Tai-tu, 1, 23, 30, 34, 39, 41, 46, 49, 75, 99, 156
Taklamakan Desert, 52–53, 55
Talas, 56
T'ang dynasty, 3–4, 26, 53, 56
Tarim Basin, 51
Taxes, 19, 58, 83
Tegüder
   see Aḥmad
Theodora, Empress, 69
Thomas, St., 122
Thomas of Anfossi, 102
Tigris River, 64–65
Tolui, 31, 33, 39
Trade, traders, 27, 54, 95, 108–9
   East-West, 3–4, 19, 54, 55, 57, 70–71
   Genoese, 134–35
   Mediterranean, 84, 85
   in Tabrīz, 68–69
   see also Merchants
Trade caravans, 68
   see also Merchant caravans
Trade routes, 5, 104–5
Travel, travelers, 54, 55, 57–58
   in Europe, 140–41
Treaty of Oloron-Sainte-Marie, 143, 153

Trebizond, 104, 105
Trinity
   concepts of, 12, 25, 123–24, 167
Tunis, 87
Turkistan, 55
Turkmen, 108
Turks, 99, 122
Ṭūs, 61–62

Ughetto (interpreter), 102
Ultimogeniture, 31
Umayyad dynasty, 56
Urban IV, Pope, 22
Urmiya, 79
Uyghur Turks, 24

Vassalli, James, 92
Vassalli, John, 92
Vatican, 22, 96, 118, 119, 125, 138, 140, 143
Vatican Archives, 164–65, 170
Veglione (Vilione), Pietro, 68–69
Venice, Venetians, 22, 84, 95, 106, 112, 136, 138

Wales, 87, 92, 96, 153
West
   embassy to, 99–138
   Ilkhans' collaboration with, 84–85, 89–98, 99
West Asia, 4
William of Rubruck, 2, 15–17, 26, 54, 115
Women (Mongol), 12, 16, 26

Yaballaha III, Mar
   see Markos/Mar Yaballaha
Yeh-li-mi-shih, 50
Yeh-lü Ta-shih, 5
Yellow River, 49, 51
Yisun Sümeyin Tor, 34
Yüan dynasty, 9, 48
Yüeh-lieh, 50

About the Author

Born in Alexandria, Egypt, in 1941, Morris Rossabi is an expert on Chinese and Central Asian history, and on the Mongols in particular. His previous books include *Khubilai Khan: His Life and Times*, as well as other titles dealing with the history of China. He is Visiting Professor of East Asian and Central Asian History at Columbia University and Professor of History at Queens College of the City University of New York, and was formerly the director of the School of Chinese Studies at the China Institute. He conducts research in nine languages, travels extensively, and lives in New York City.